Books by Fran Stewart

The Biscuit McKee Mystery Series:

> *Orange as Marmalade*
> *Yellow as Legal Pads*
> *Green as a Garden Hose*
> *Blue as Blue Jeans*
> *Indigo as an Iris*
> *Violet as an Amethyst*
> *Gray as Ashes*
> *Red as a Rooster*
> *Black as Soot*
> *Pink as a Peony*
> *White as Ice*

A Slaying Song Tonight

The ScotShop Mysteries:

A Wee Murder in My Shop
A Wee Dose of Death
A Wee Homicide in the Hotel

Poetry:

> *Resolution*

For Children:

> *As Orange As Marmalade/*
>   *Tan naranja como Mermelada*
>   *(a bilingual book)*

Non-Fiction:

> *From The Tip of My Pen: a workbook for writers*
> *BeesKnees #1: A Beekeeping Memoir (#1 of 6 volumes)*
> *BeesKnees #2: A Beekeeping Memoir (#2 of 6 volumes)*
> *BeesKnees #3: A Beekeeping Memoir (#3 of 6 volumes)*
> *BeesKnees #4: A Beekeeping Memoir (#4 of 6 volumes)*
> *BeesKnees #5: A Beekeeping Memoir (#5 of 6 volumes)*
> *BeesKnees #6: A Beekeeping Memoir (#6 of 6 volumes)*
> *Clear as Mud*
> *Clearly Me*
> Coming Soon - *Crystal Clear*

Clearly Me

Fran Stewart

Clearly Me

Fran Stewart

© 2021 Fran Stewart

All rights reserved. No part of this book may be used or reproduced in any manner whatsoever without written permission from the author, except by a reviewer who may quote brief passages in a review.

ISBN: (Softcover) 978-1-951368-23-4

This book was printed in the United States of America.

Published by

My Own Ship Press
PO Box 490153
Lawrenceville GA 30049
myownship@icloud.com

franstewart.com

Dedicated to:

Diana
Erica
Eli
Veronica
Darlene
Savannah
Aiden
Marcia
and Peggy

(This is the order in which I met you.)

Fran Stewart

Intro

When I decided to publish all my Facebook author page entries, it never occurred to me that it would turn out to be a major endeavor. After all, I'd already written them, so what could be the problem with just putting them together into a book?

I'm sure that, with those plans, I gave God a great big chuckle that day. She's probably still laughing about it.

Before you complain about how *Clear as Mud*, the first volume in these memoirs, was priced at $39.99, let me explain a little bit about the publishing industry. I completely understand that the COVID-19 crisis has left a lot of industries reeling, and the publishing industry is no exception. Still, even before the pandemic, publishers seemed determined to guarantee that the creative process behind the book (the author) always got the tiniest slice of the pie.

To give you just one example, every time someone buys one new copy of one of my *ScotShop Mysteries*, the royalty payment I receive is 23 cents. This is for a book that's priced at $7.99. If you buy a book that's used, then the author gets nothing.

I'm not complaining. I've sold tens of thousands of my books, but the big income doesn't come until people are buying hundreds of thousands or—wouldn't this be lovely?—millions of an author's books. Most of the people who sell that many books have hired a publicist, to the tune of anywhere from $5,000 to $20,000. Obviously, I didn't do that.

But, back to the $39.99 price tag for Clear as Mud. It's a big book (8.5 x 11) for a reason. If it had been the size of my other books (the Biscuit McKee mysteries & the BeesKnees books), it would have been more than a thousand pages long. It's full-color printing because of all the photos—and that costs a good deal more than black & white printing. If I'd priced it any less than $39.99, I would have LOST money every time somebody bought one. Clearly Me (2019) is pretty much the same size as Clear as Mud, so it's the same price. And the next volume, Crystal Clear (2020), will be there as well. I truly hope you've found them worth it.

So, I've had to see these three books as part of the legacy I'm leaving my children and grandchildren (and great-grandchildren and so on). If you <u>bought</u> *Clear as Mud*, I'm astonished and gratified indeed. I'm also humbled that you have obviously wanted to share my life as I've revealed it in these pages.

I wish you the very best—good friends, good health, and good laughs.

    --Fran
        from my house beside a creek
        on the other side of Hog Mountain GA
        November 2020

January 2019

Beneath the Skin

Tuesday January 1, 2019 — One of the loveliest, most loving women I ever knew was 18 years older than I when I met her on the day I took my son to his kindergarten class for the first time. Shirley Murray taught because she loved teaching. As I grew to know her over the years (she taught my daughter's kindergarten class as well) she encouraged me to begin journaling as a way to begin healing my life.

Some time ago, I found this poem by Jeannette Encinias. It's full of lovely thoughts to share at the beginning of this New Year. No matter where you are on your journey, I hope you will remember that "you have decades of learning and leaving and loving sewn into the corners of your eyes."

Happy New Year.

Beneath the Sweater and the Skin
~ Jeannette Encinias

How many years of beauty do I have left?
she asks me.
How many more do you want?
Here. Here is 34. Here is 50.

When you are 80 years old
and your beauty rises in ways
your cells cannot even imagine now
and your wild bones grow luminous and
ripe, having carried the weight
of a passionate life.

When your hair is aflame
with winter
and you have decades of
learning and leaving and loving
sewn into
the corners of your eyes
and your children come home
to find their own history
in your face.

When you know what it feels like to fail
ferociously
and have gained the
capacity
to rise and rise and rise again.

When you can make your tea
on a quiet and ridiculously lonely afternoon
and still have a song in your heart
Queen owl wings beating
beneath the cotton of your sweater.

Because your beauty began there
beneath the sweater and the skin,
remember?

This is when I will take you
into my arms and coo
YOU BRAVE AND GLORIOUS THING
you've come so far.
I see you.
Your beauty is breathtaking.

If I ever get old and frail, would somebody please read this to me?

~ ~ ~

Walking into 2019

Wednesday 01/02/2019—My dear friend Darlene Carter read this to me when we did our MasterMind session a couple of days ago. She and I both plan to print it out and keep it close at hand throughout the coming year.

MasterMind, in this case, is not the game, but a spiritual process developed by Marianne Williamson. Darlene and I have been sharing this adventure for the past eighteen years, and it never ceases to amaze us with the way it leads us to new insights and ah-ha moments.

By the way, thank you to the people who checked in with me via phone calls or messages during the past week and a half when I dropped off the edge of the Facebook world. I appreciate your concern, and I'm delighted not only that you noticed I was gone, but that you reached out in your concern. I'm so much better now.

I'm walking into 2019 with a clear heart and mind. If you owe me, don't worry about it. If you wronged me, it's all good, lesson learned. If you're angry with me, you won - I've let it go. If we aren't speaking, it's cool - I truly wish you well. If you feel I've wronged you, I apologize - it wasn't intentional. I'm grateful for every experience that I received. Life is too short for pent up anger, holding of grudges and extra stress or pain! Here's to 2019!!! Remember forgiving someone is for you so don't block your blessings. Make 2019 a year of positivity and a season of forgiveness.

~ ~ ~

Ta-Da List

Thursday 01/03/2019 — I think this is a great idea. Ta-Da! instead of To-Do. Enthusiasm, excitement, expectancy (to quote Marianne Williamson).

What do you think? Is it worth trying for a day or two? A week or two? Maybe for the rest of our lives?

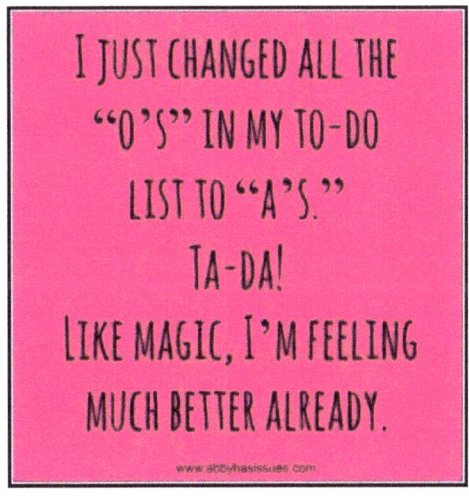

Fran Stewart

~ ~ ~

Wonder of a book (12/28/18)

Friday 01/04/2019 — Emily Dickinson wrote that "there is no frigate like a book." Nowadays when fewer and fewer people have any idea what a frigate is (a light, fast boat that is rowed or sailed), people depend on other ways of expressing that thought.

Carl Sagan, as you can see here, spoke of the book as "the greatest human invention, binding together people who never knew each other."

I find, time and again, when my readers reach out to me through messages or emails, that these connections between people can go very deep, and I truly appreciate those links, particularly today.

> WHAT AN ASTONISHING THING A BOOK IS.
> IT'S A FLAT OBJECT MADE FROM A TREE WITH FLEXIBLE PARTS ON WHICH ARE IMPRINTED LOTS OF FUNNY DARK SQUIGGLES.
> BUT ONE GLANCE AT IT AND YOU'RE INSIDE THE MIND OF ANOTHER PERSON, MAYBE SOMEONE DEAD FOR THOUSANDS OF YEARS. ACROSS THE MILLENNIA, AN AUTHOR IS SPEAKING CLEARLY AND SILENTLY INSIDE YOUR HEAD, DIRECTLY TO YOU.
> WRITING IS PERHAPS THE GREATEST OF HUMAN INVENTIONS, BINDING TOGETHER PEOPLE WHO NEVER KNEW EACH OTHER, CITIZENS OF DISTANT EPOCHS.
> BOOKS BREAK THE SHACKLES OF TIME.
> A BOOK IS PROOF THAT HUMANS ARE CAPABLE OF WORKING MAGIC.
> — CARL SAGAN

(illustration by Chris Riddell)

~ ~ ~

Goats Eating Christmas Trees

Saturday 01/05/2019 — I found a great news item from the Canadian Broadcast System. It was too good not to share. If you want to read it, do a search for *Christmas trees goats CBC*. I hope it brightens your day.

I had so much fun visiting various goat farms several times when I was researching *Indigo as an Iris*, and I am to this day intrigued by goats. It was particularly fun to gaze into their rectangular pupils.

Incidentally, your chickens will also appreciate a Christmas tree to eat, scratch at, and snuggle into. But please, no ornament hooks, tinsel, or that horrible spray fake snow.

Photo Credit: CBC News

~ ~ ~

Why Ships Sink

Monday 01/07/2019 — Good old Archimedes. "Any body completely or partially submerged in a fluid at rest is acted upon by an upward (buoyant) force the magnitude of which is equal to the weight of the fluid displaced by the body."

I do wonder whether the "fluid" is supposed to be at rest or the "body" is supposed to be at rest, but other than that one grammatical inconsistency, it's a pretty good statement, wouldn't you say?

Of course, I like this other saying, too — the one in today's picture. In a lot of ways, it says the same thing as Archimedes.

Have a buoyant day.

~ ~ ~

Ella Vader

Tuesday 01/08/2019 — I love the way the English language lends itself to plays on words.

Last week I met with a book club that had chosen to read *Green as a Garden Hose*, my third Biscuit McKee Mystery, for their January choice. We got to talking about puns and wordplay, and I had great fun pointing out that one of the less-savory characters in that book was named Kelvin. Someone in the book described him as "an absolute Zero of a man."

Not everybody got it. Not everybody will get it. But the ones who do may at least get a smile out of it — or maybe even a big whoop of laughter.

As I said, I love the English language.

For extra credit, you can find out where I got the names of the two law firms that appear in the Biscuit McKee series:

Bushy, Bagot, & Green

and

Scroop, Grey, & Cambridge

Pasture Bedtime

Wednesday 01/09/2019 — While we're talking about puns . . .

~ ~ ~

Arrows

Thursday 01/10/2019 — This collection of arrows and squiggly figures stumped me for a bit when I found it stuffed between old notes in a file folder of my parents' diaries. What it was doing there, I have no idea. How it got there is a mystery. Where it came from is one of those facts lost to the modern mind.

Still, I liked its message (once I figured it out), so I thought I'd share it with you.

Clearly Me

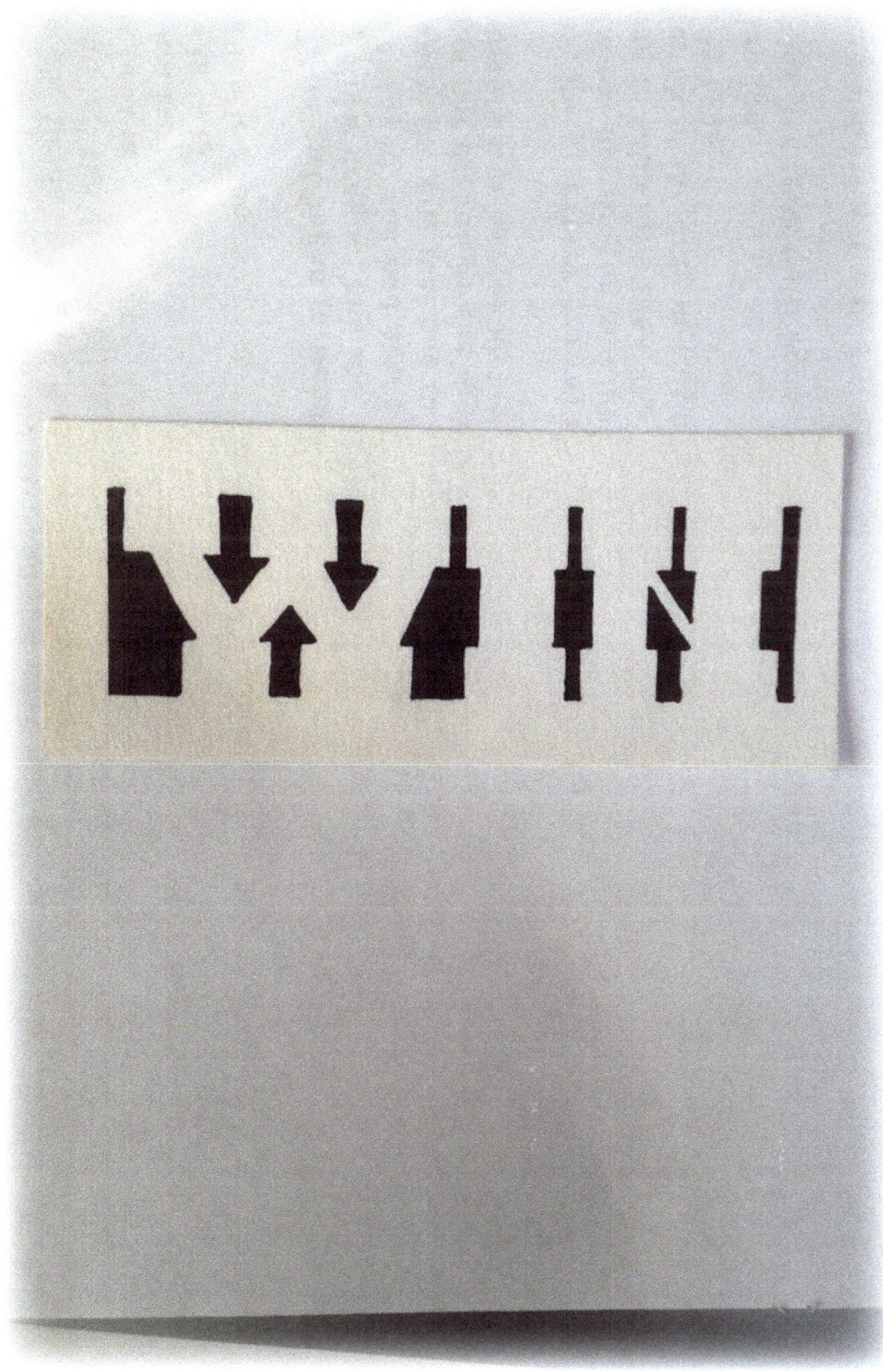

Auburn library questions

Friday 01/11/2019 — I love libraries. About a month ago I took this photo of a display at the Auburn GA public library when I went there to participate in a writing group that evolved from some memoirs classes I taught there last fall.

The librarians had put up the simple question — "Can you guess the book these first lines came from?"

Since the question was in the teen section, and since I haven't read very many YA books, I couldn't identify a single one of them. What about you?

~ ~ ~

Snow Joy

Saturday 01/12/2019 — It's been eight years since this area of Georgia had a big enough snowstorm so the grandkids could go sledding on an air mattress.

What else could they have used? Nobody sells sleds or snow shovels around here. There are times I miss Vermont. The thought of being able to strap on cross country skis beside the back deck and head out across a snowy expanse sounds exhilarating, doesn't it?

Then there are the more frequent times I recall that I was never any good at skiing. In fact, I fell more than I glided.

There are the times I remember the crisp invigorating air of a sub-zero day.

Then there are the other times when I remember my frost-bitten fingers that one time we were stupid enough to go out camping when it was forty-below.

Here in the Atlanta area spring starts in February — in fact, yesterday I saw crocuses beginning to push up through the dead leaves.

I'm not sure of this, but maybe snowstorms are more fun in memory than they were in real life?

~ ~ ~

visible song (1/11/19)

Monday 01/14/2019 — In every book I've written, if the story is set during a cold spell, I mention at some point or other something about puffs of breath visible in front of people's noses.

But in all my years I've never even thought of (much less seen) the puffs of air coming from a bird's beak. This photo - that came from (I think) National Geographic - captures the visible song so beautifully, I wanted to share it with you. I wish I could give you an exact source. The photographer deserves full credit.

[**2020 Note**: I was sad to find that this picture had been photoshopped. Now I'm sorry I gave it any space whatsoever in these posts.]

~ ~ ~

Etch-a-sketch

Tuesday 01/15/2019 — Remember etch-a-sketch? Do they even have those things nowadays?

Probably not.

The one thing I remember most about my etch-a-sketch was how much I enjoyed the erasing. It was such fun to see all those lines disappearing. Hmm… (???) Maybe that's why I turned out to be such a fervent editor.

~ ~ ~

Recalculating

Wednesday 01/16/2019 — I have a Garmin GPS whose maps haven't been updated.for two years because when I was moving things around and boxing things up to prepare for the major house-remodeling I did two years ago, I misplaced the cord and it has one of those one-of-a-kind connections on one end, so I can't plug any other cord into the GPS. All these new roads that keep cropping up? — I can't tell where they are.

Time and again I drive along a perfectly visible road, and my GPS shows me schlepping across a field. "Off-road," it warns me. "Recalculating."

GRRRRR!

Of course, it's my own fault for having misplaced the cord in the first place. (Double-grrrr)

~ ~ ~

Go the Extra Mile (1/15/19)

Thursday 01/17/2019 — This sign was in the middle school library where I volunteer once a week.

The interesting thing is — I'm constantly finding people in my life who go the extra mile, so I try to keep up with them!

How about you? Do you know people who take the time to do that extra nice thing for you? If you can't think of anybody, open your eyes!

~ ~ ~

Fuzzy in the Cat Tree

Friday 01/18/2019 — There's something going on. Is it unique to me, or is there some sort of cosmic plan afoot?

Every year I can remember—every year before this one, that is—for the first few weeks after New Year's Day, whenever I've written a check or dated a card or letter, my first impulse is to write the previous year. And then I have to change the 1995 to 1996, or 2002 to 2003, or 2016 to 2017. This year, though, I haven't written 2018 even once.

Is there something special about 2019?

Meanwhile, Fuzzy Britches sits in her cat tree overlooking my letter-writing, approving the movements of the universe. That's what cats do.

~ ~ ~

Total Lunar Eclipse

Saturday 01/19/2019 — I'm sure you've already heard about this or read about it. I found a site, though, that would give me the exact times when the various sections of the lunar eclipse began and ended in my area.

If you go to timeanddate.com, choose Sun & Moon from the menu across the top of the screen, and then pick Eclipses from the drop-down menu, you should get the times for your zip code.

It also has a video that shows just how the moon travels through earth's shadow.

I love it when people take the time to put together information like this. My thanks to them!

Fran Stewart

~ ~ ~

If We Had No Winter

Monday 01/21/2019 — I first met Anne Bradstreet when I was in college, taking a course about early American literature. I was struck by the clarity of her voice.

I love making connections across the centuries.

I do wonder if some day in the far distant future, someone will say, "I discovered Fran Stewart recently, and was struck by the way she created characters that came alive for me."

Wouldn't that be wonderful?

p.s. The lunar eclipse last night was magnificent. A clear, cloudless night. Visible through my skylights, too, so I didn't have to brave the cold from 10:30 till 2:00.

I kept watch from inside, setting aside my book (and a couple of cats) every nine minutes—the snooze alarm on my phone—to check the progress, then going outside when the red glow began to appear. At a little past midnight, the Full Blood Moon filled me with such awe, I came close to tears.

> IF WE HAD NO WINTER THE SPRING WOULD NOT BE SO PLEASANT.
>
> ~Anne Bradstreet, 1672

~ ~ ~

Cats on Ancient Manuscripts

Tuesday 01/22/2019 — Speaking of making connections across the centuries, the British Library website, which I accessed through another site called Medieval Manuscripts Blog, has an entire article showing how cats used to mess up ancient manuscripts with muddy or inky paw prints.

The most my cats do (since they're indoor cats and don't get their feet muddy) is walk /.oimnytvc][.,oinb across my keyboard. When I'm writing longhand, I usually have the writing pad balanced on top of a purring cat's back, so all I get is some shaky-looking writing from the subterranean rumblings.

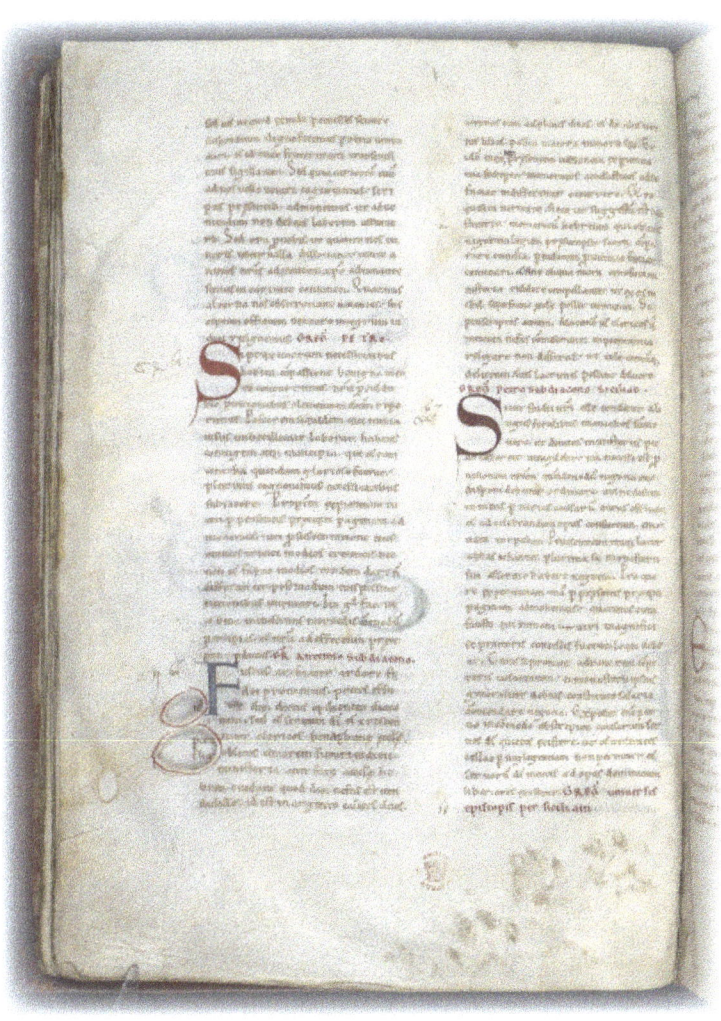

~ ~ ~

"Listen"

Wednesday 01/23/2019 — How often have you stood absolutely still, seeing or sensing something you want almost desperately? Something seemingly bigger than yourself says, "Leave it." So you wait.

Then, in a life-transforming instant, you know somehow you have permission to step forward into that new exciting realm. "Take it," says your inner voice, and you do.

I did that years ago when I had always wanted to write a mystery, but kept telling myself I couldn't ("Leave it!") until that magical day when I knew it was time to begin ("Take it!"), and the result was *Orange as*

Fran Stewart

Marmalade, my first book.

Just like my grand-dog Limerick with the spaghetti.

Who or what has been holding you back, telling you that you can't do what you're longing to do?

Is it time to listen to that other voice?

~ ~ ~

Reading

Thursday 01/24/2019 — I read one of those ubiquitous statistics the other day that said 26% of adult Americans claim not to have read a book during the last twelve months.

Why on earth would anyone even consider admitting something as shameful as that?

Okay, okay, I'm showing my extremely biased attitude. But, really! How can someone not want to read a book? Fiction, non-fiction, mystery, fantasy, romance, sci-fi, historical, biography, memoirs, suspense, how-to, self-help, paranormal . . . Surely there's at least one book out there that can entice a person, any person, to want to read more.

All it takes is one. I'm convinced of it. The question, though, is how to hook them on that first book. If you can figure out the answer to that, please let me know.

~ ~ ~

Paper Bags and Kevlar

Friday 01/25/2019 — What does a paper bag have in common with Kevlar?

I'm glad you asked.

They were both invented by women. The dishwasher, Monopoly, disposable diapers, circular saws, and marine signal flares — all were invented by women.

Look around you. What needs to be improved? What could be better accomplished in a different way? Maybe the next invention, the next discovery is right there at your fingertips. In the meantime, though, you can enjoy all these other conveniences and be thankful to the women who thought about them. Like, the next time you're driving in a rainstorm, you can thank Mary Anderson for having invented windshield wipers.

~ ~ ~

The Bigger the Cheerio

Saturday 01/26/2019 — A great way to end this week.

For all the talk I do (to myself mostly) about cutting down on sugar, there is something about a glazed Krispie Kreme doughnut that will get me every time.

And homemade fudge. Don't get me started on fudge.

Enjoy your weekend. I'll be back Monday morning.

~ ~ ~

Why Tock Tick

Monday 01/28/2019 — I love to find out where things come from.

Especially intriguing little articles on the internet. Especially from the BBC.

So, after seeing this image of the cuckoo clock and the intriguing article around it, I Googled "tock tick bbc" to find the following article by Mark Forsyth, who wrote a book called *The Elements of Eloquence*.

He's talking about some rules of our language that we're not aware of us. None of us. Well, some of us, perhaps, but certainly not I.

Fascinating!

Fran Stewart

Why 'tock-tick' does not sound right to your ears

Ever wondered why we say tick-tock, not tock-tick, or ding-dong, not dong-ding; King Kong, not Kong King? Turns out it is one of the unwritten rules of English that native speakers know without knowing.

The rule, explains a BBC article, is: "If there are three words then the order has to go I, A, O. If there are two words then the first is I and the second is either A or O. Mishmash, chit-chat, dilly-dally, shilly-shally, tip top, hip-hop, flip-flop, tic tac, sing song, ding dong, King Kong, ping pong."

There's another unwritten rule at work in the name Little Red Riding Hood, says the article.

"Adjectives in English absolutely have to be in this order: opinion-size-age-shape-colour-origin-material-purpose noun. So you can have a lovely little old rectangular green French silver whittling knife. But if you mess with that word order in the slightest you'll sound like a maniac."

That explains why we say "little green men" not "green little men," but "Big Bad Wolf" sounds like a gross violation of the "opinion (bad)-size (big)-noun (wolf)" order. It won't, though, if you recall the first rule about the I-A-O order.

That rule seems inviolable: "All four of a horse's feet make exactly the same sound. But we always, always say clip-clop, never clop-clip."

This rule even has a technical name, if you care to know it—the rule of ablaut reduplication—but then life is simpler knowing that we know the rule without knowing it.

For more: BBC

PLAY IT BY EAR: If a word sequence sounds wrong, it is probably wrong

~ ~ ~

Be Decisive

Tuesday 01/29/2019 — It won't be long now. Yesterday I began setting up the beta tests for my online class about how to write your memoirs — the stories of your life. Stay tuned. I'll let you know how this unfolds.

In the meantime, I have a 4-session class going on at my local library, and I'll be teaching a 6-session class at BULLI, the Brenau University Lifetime Learning Institute, beginning the last Thursday in March. Once I decided to put my focus on guiding people to write their memoirs, I took myself out of the squirrel category and into — well, into something else that is new and exciting.

Life is good.

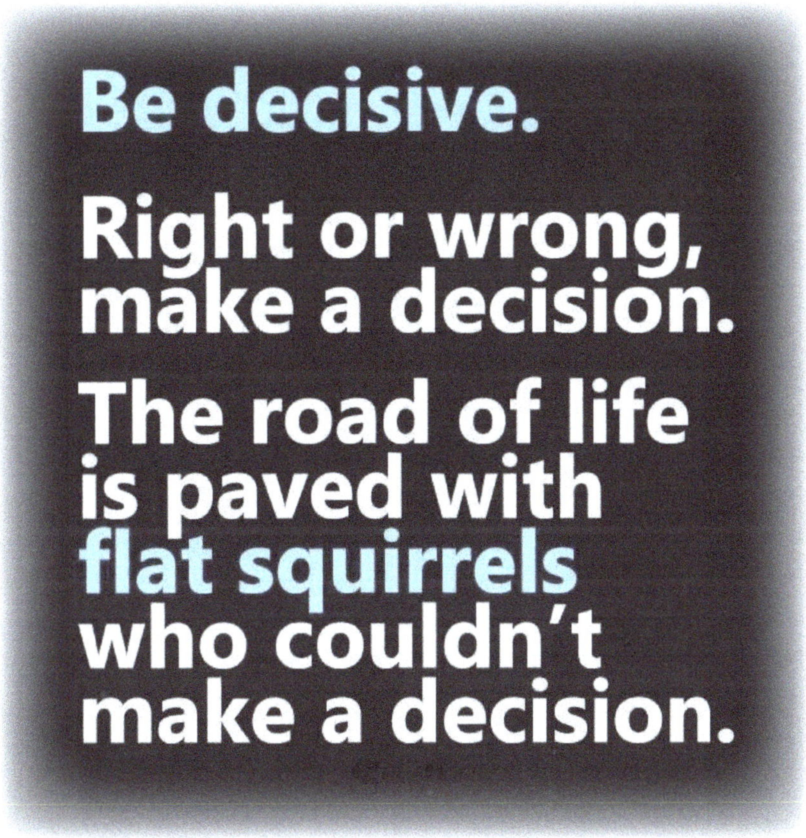

> **Be decisive.**
>
> **Right or wrong, make a decision.**
>
> **The road of life is paved with flat squirrels who couldn't make a decision.**

~ ~ ~

Comfort Zone

Wednesday 01/30/2019 — I'm definitely stretching outside my comfort zone with these online memoir classes I'm planning to teach.

First, I'm experimenting like crazy with the online conference program called Zoom. All those options, all those buttons! Wish me luck, please.

I've put together a PowerPoint to explain one of lessons I teach about perspective. I know, I know — any 5th-grader can put together a truly impressive-looking PowerPoint — but for me it's new territory.

Then there are the decisions — more PowerPoints? what sort of limit to class size? what days? what times?

And so on. As I said, wish me luck, please.

~ ~ ~

Two Kinds of People

Thursday 01/31/2019 — So, which kind of person are you?

And, did you think this was as funny as I did?

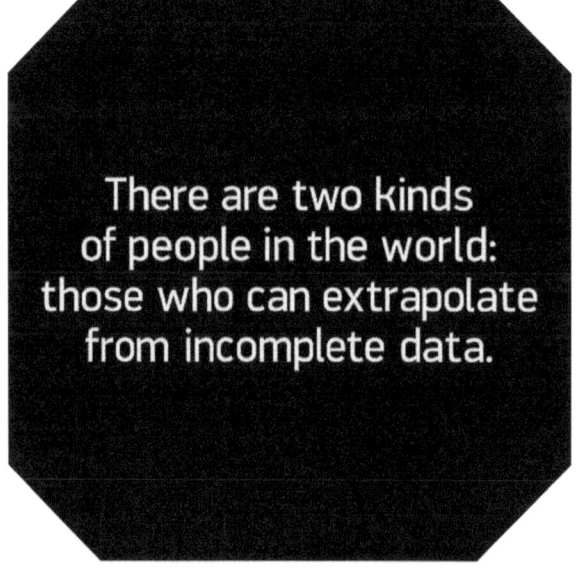

February 2019

The Pledge to the Flag

Friday 02/01/2019 — Last month a woman named Pam Dewey spoke to our Atlanta Branch of the NLAPW (National League of American Pen Women). She has a website called "Meet Myth America" on which she researches and dispels the myths we've all gotten so used to that we don't even question them.

And there are a lot of them.

This particular one, about the origins of the Pledge of Allegiance was particularly disturbing.

Please understand—I'm not intending to start a political discussion here. I was simply intrigued by the depth of her research, and completely surprised by what she came up with.

Had you ever heard any of this?

Two Things Define You

Saturday 02/02/2019 — I've finally decided that a tendency toward patience must be an inbred sort of quality. Not that it can't be learned. Not that it can't be encouraged. Ditto with attitude.

In teaching memoirs classes over the last year, I've heard stories of incredible loss, tempered with a deep appreciation for the "everything" as people struggle, stumble, or sometimes even bounce back after car wrecks, house fires, family deaths, personal health losses. I am consistently inspired by the resiliency of the human spirit.

But patience and a good attitude help a great deal.

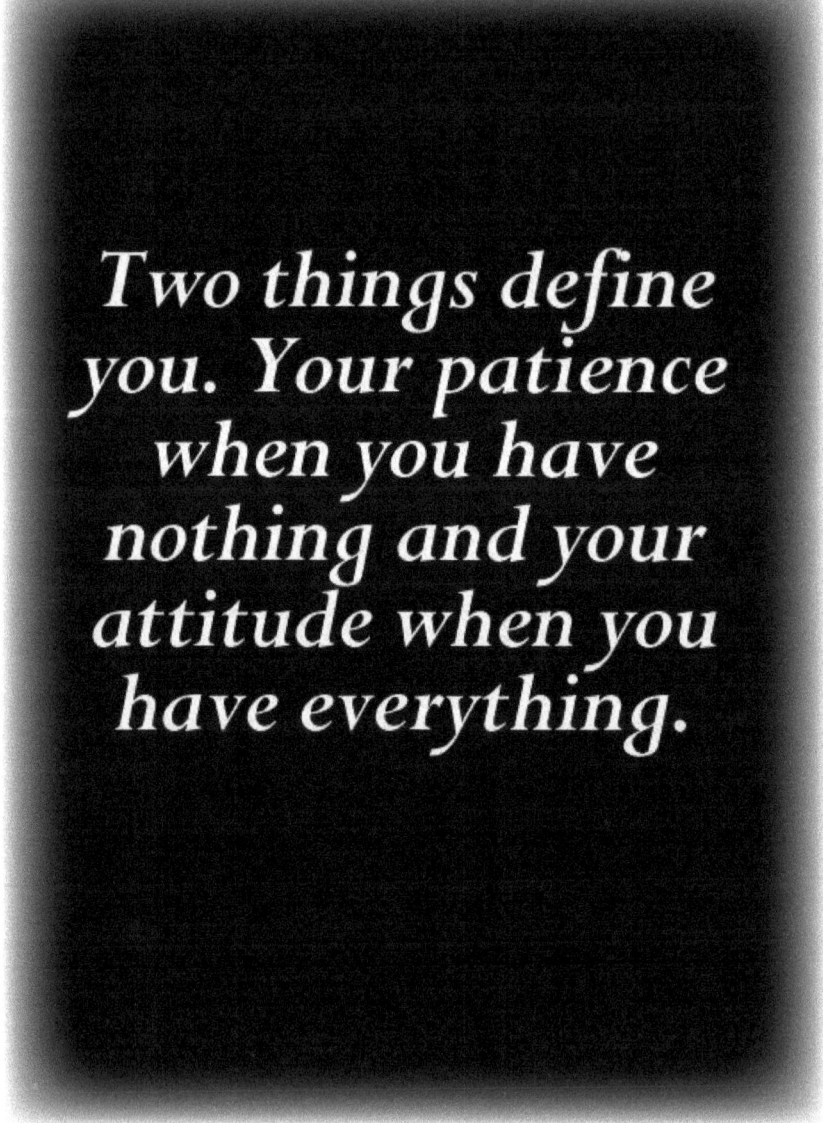

~ ~ ~

Callie

Monday 02/04/2019 — Callie: Rest in Peace

~ ~ ~

Walkie Talkie

Tuesday 02/05/2019 — First – thank you to everyone who commented or called about my loss of Callie. I truly appreciate your heartfelt sharing of my grief. I firmly believe Callie is running through fields of clover (or the infinite equivalent thereof) on the other side of the rainbow bridge. Fuzzy Britches still seems a little lost, wandering around, looking behind things and under blankets (a favorite hiding place of Callie), but this morning she seemed a little brighter.

Life goes on, and it's time to smile.

> If the person who named Walkie Talkies named everything
>
> Stamps = Lickie Stickie
> Defibrillators = Hearty Starty
> Bumble bees = Fuzzy Buzzy
> Pregnancy test = Maybe Baby
> Fork = Stabby Grabby
> Socks = Feetie Heatie
> Hippo = Floatie Bloatie
> Nightmare = Screamy Dreamy

~ ~ ~

And a box of shells…

Wednesday 02/06/2019 — Ah! I love the English language, with multiple meanings for so many of its words. Today's picture is a perfect example. I'm obviously well-protected, because I have all these elements ready at hand.

I'm worried about crime, so I asked a friend from Texas what I needed to defend my home. He said a 9mm, a couple clips, and a box of shells. I put it together pretty quickly. Still not sure how it's suppose to work, though...

~ ~ ~

Dancing beside Art

Thursday 02/07/2019 — Every February, the Atlanta Branch of the NLAPW presents a program we call "Painted Sounds," in which members show a work they've created – a work of art, a composition, or a written piece.

We bring three copies of our creation (photo, printout, or CD) and afterwards other members can choose one piece they'd like to reinterpret in their own medium. Then, in April, we bring back our original pieces as well as our interpretation of the other member's work. Several years ago, for instance, I read a poem about the life lesson I learned the night my mother died. That April Ann Alexander, one of our Art members not only showed us the painting she had done to reflect her feelings about my poem, but she also gave me

Fran Stewart

that painting. To this day it graces my wall with sheer joy as she shows me walking from the darkness of my mother's life into a glorious dawning day.

Hence the name: Painted Sounds, for Ann took the sound of my words and transformed them into visual art.

Here's another example of that same process. This child, dancing before a painting, is a perfect example of taking one form of art and transforming it into another. It's such a joyous image, I just had to share it with you.

~ ~ ~

Eli to Mexico Beach

Friday 02/08/2019 — It feels good to have raised two kids who give back to their communities – and to other people's communities as well. This is my son right after he finished shopping for Hurricane Relief Supplies for Mexico Beach and Port St. Joe. He ran a Go Fund Me effort so friends all over the US could contribute.

He came by my house to pick up a bunch more things – blankets, jackets, a chain saw, cleaning supplies, soups… – and he'll be delivering the whole vanload tomorrow. His sister leaves this afternoon with her own vehicle full of items, and they're going to meet up there and help local residents with cleanup chores.

I'm darn proud of the two of them.

Creative hotels

Saturday 02/09/2019 — How to turn one of those "It's Tuesday, so this must be Brussels" trips into an adventure: stay in a hotel that uses ingenuity. I thoroughly enjoyed scrolling through this story and thought you might find it as delightful as I did. Just do a search for *50 times hotels surprised everyone*.

Enjoy!

Van Gogh's Family Tree

Monday 02/11/2019 — My friend Karen Krotz tagged me on this one, and I couldn't wait to share it with you.

These puns wouldn't work in the U.K., where Van "GO" is pronounced Van "GOFF."

Just one more example of the many ways American English is so different than British English.

Fun, huh?

I couldn't help but notice, by the way, that only five of these relate to females, when in truth all of them (except the magician and the RV person) would be equally applicable to both men and women. Just one more example of the ways in which most people still assume automatically that "human beings" means men.

FAMILY TREE OF VINCENT VAN GOGH

His dizzy aunt	Verti Gogh
The brother who ate prunes	Gotta Gogh
The brother who worked at a convenience store	Stop N Gogh
The grandfather from Yugoslavia	U Gogh
His magician uncle	Where-diddy Gogh
His Mexican cousin	A Mee Gogh
The Mexican cousin's American half-brother	Gring Gogh
The nephew who drove a stage coach	Wells-far Gogh
The constipated uncle	Can't Gogh
The ballroom dancing aunt	Tang Gogh
The bird lover uncle	Flamin Gogh
An aunt who taught positive thinking	Way-to-Gogh
The little bouncy nephew	Poe Gogh
A sister who loved disco	Go Gogh
The brother with low back pain	Lum Bay Gogh
And his niece who travels the country in an RV	Winnie Bay Gogh

I saw you smiling . . .. there ya Gogh

Use Libraries

Tuesday 02/12/2019 — I'm always amazed when I walk into a library. The wealth of information, the variety of topics, the delight of the tactile and visual sense of holding a book in my hands—a book I might not have discovered if it hadn't been sitting there on the shelf waiting for me.

I'm reading *My Beloved Country* by Sonia Sotomayor. It's her autobiography, in which she opens when her family discovered that she had diabetes. With an alcoholic father and an emotionally detached mother, Sonia had to learn to give herself her daily insulin shot.

Last night I read the chapter in which she talks of watching Perry Mason on TV when she was a child. She decided she wanted to be a judge.

When I watched Perry Mason as a kid, I decided I could have written a better script.

She's an associate justice on the Supreme Court. I'm a writer. Thank you, Perry Mason.

And, thank you, libraries.

~ ~ ~

I'll Clean Tomorrow

Wednesday 02/13/2019 — This is sort of how I've felt lately, only instead of a nap, I've been working on the class outlines for the online memoirs classes I'll be starting (one on Saturday 2/23 and the other 3/20), and instead of a movie, I've been rearranging my overrun kitchen counters. Of course, a book is always a good distraction, so I'm leaving that as a good excuse for not vacuuming and dusting. After all, pollen season will soon be here in Georgia, and the weather will be mild enough to have all the windows open, so all the tables (and couches and chairs and floors and pictures) will be covered with yellow, so why bother dusting until summer comes?

Grand Avenue by Mike Thompson for February 02, 2019

~ ~ ~

Knitting

Thursday 02/14/2019 — I spend a lot of evenings knitting while I listen to a book on my CD player. Over the years I've knitted with a lot of types of material – one holiday I even knitted a prayer shawl out of tinsel.

Knitting is like writing in a lot of ways. You take a never-ending variety of yarns (words/phrases/idioms/attributions) and knit them into a unique pattern (story/poem/book).

I must admit, though, I've never knitted (or written) anything out of pasta.

Although this one sort of looks like pasta …

~ ~ ~

Opportunity

Friday 02/15/2019 — Spirit and Opportunity. I love those names of the two Mars probes launched by NASA in 2003 and landed in 2004. Each planet-roving vehicle was expected to last 90 days after touchdown. That was 15 years ago. The people who designed, built, launched, and watched over them have finally come to the end of the road.

Spirit was declared dead in June of 2011.

Last Wednesday, the same pronouncement was made for Opportunity, often called "Oppy" by its fans.

But not all is lost. Another probe, Curiosity, was launched in 2012, and it's still working, roaming around the Red Planet.

If you'd like to read the story by Nicole Mortillaro, one of my favorite science writers, search for *CBC Mars Opportunity Rover Dead*.

You are the Artist

Saturday 02/16/2019 — Good grief! Hold onto your paintbrush and color your own canvas!

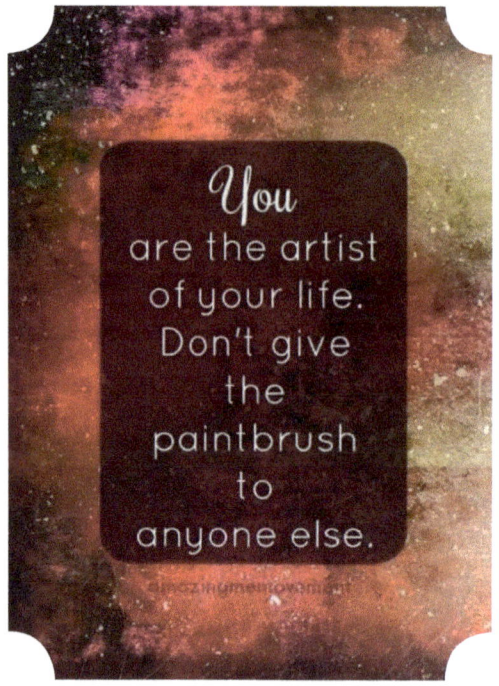

~ ~ ~

Euston Station Bodies

Monday 02/18/2019 — All the times I passed through Euston Station and its nearby park when I visited London – and I never guessed that I was walking above 40,000 graves, some of them more than 24 feet below the surface.

I found an article from Canadian News (CBC.ca) that showcases the archeological dig that is exhuming the human remains, finding some startling effects such as the man who was buried with a wooden stake across his chest, and some that are truly poignant, such as the child whose body was buried with her doll.

Do a search to find it. When you do, I hope you enjoy reading it as much as I did.

~ ~ ~

How do you want to be remembered?

Tuesday 02/19/2019 — Speaking of dead bodies, as we were yesterday, I figured this thought was particularly apt.

I want to be remembered as someone who used her brain and her heart together, as someone who inspired others, as someone who did the best she could no matter the circumstances, as someone who was compassionate, as someone who laughed every day of her life and shared the joy with others.

How do you want to be remembered?

Planted

Wednesday 02/20/2019 — Yesterday, as I was teaching one of my memoirs classes, we talked a lot about a sense of perspective. I happen to think this thought for the day shows exactly what we discussed.

We all have dark times, but can you imagine the shift in thinking when we take the broader view?

Buried or planted?

Lost or exploring?

Confused or open to possibilities?

I'd say that sort of shift is life affirming. Let's go for it today.

Eli and Veronica at the White Tent

Thursday 02/21/2019 — Since several people have sent me messages asking for a follow-up on my son Eli and daughter Veronica's hurricane relief effort, here's a photo they took of themselves in the white tent in front of some of the material they had just delivered earlier this month.

I know it looks like the White Tent is jam packed, but it doesn't take long for that much material to be distributed. Anyone who is in need who comes to the White Tent can take whatever he or she needs—at no charge. This is all volunteer and all contributions are deeply appreciated.

By the way, I found out recently that one of the things they need is can openers (not the electric kind, since many people are still without electricity).

~ ~ ~

Treeprint & Fingerprint

Friday 02/22/2019 — I've always felt a particular kinship to trees. The more I learn about them, the more I find myself admiring the many ways they communicate, the many ways they contribute to the value of life on earth, the many lessons they have to teach us.

It made sense, then, to see this comparison of the rings of a tree with the rings of a fingerprint.

What sort of special connection do you feel to some non-human part of this world?

Tree stump and human fingerprint-

~ ~ ~

I opened a book

Saturday 02/23/2019 — Yesterday I had an R.A.D. experience. Don't worry – I'll explain what that is.

A week or so ago one of the members in my book club posted a quotation that said. "A person who reads lives a thousand lives. A person who never reads lives only once."

My reply to her was this:

> And how much richer we are for our thought-provoking discussions. I often read a
> book and wish I had someone right here beside me to talk about the ideas I just read.
> I've never had that—not in my college dorm, not in my marriage, and certainly not
> as I live alone. So, I double—triple—appreciate all of you in our book club.

One of the members then replied to my comment:

> Maybe you need to come visit me on the farm every now and then and we'll have a **RAD** day, Read All Day. We can curl up on the couches and talk to each other about what we're reading!

That's what we did yesterday. Of course, it wasn't all reading. In fact, we spent the first couple of hours talking, looking at all the renovations she and her husband are making on their new (to them) house, and of course, eating lunch. It was too rainy to check out her horses—other than to look at them through the kitchen windows—but we planned another day for a long walk through the back meadow and the woods.

Then . . . we did curl up on couches with our separate books. Every time one of us chuckled or gasped or said "Huh???" we'd stop for a moment and talk about what was going on. It helped that each of us had already read the book the other was reading, so we didn't have to supply background material.

Our **RAD** was a complete delight.

I hope YOU have a friend to talk to about the books you read.

I Opened a Book

"I opened a book and in I strode.
Now nobody can find me.
I've left my chair, my house, my road,
My town and my world behind me.
I'm wearing the cloak, I've slipped on the ring,
I've swallowed the magic potion.
I've fought with a dragon, dined with a king
And dived in a bottomless ocean.
I opened a book and made some friends.
I shared their tears and laughter
And followed their road with its bumps and bends
To the happily ever after.
I finished my book and out I came.
The cloak can no longer hide me.
My chair and my house are just the same,
But I have a book inside me."

— Julia Donaldson

Dear Men

Sunday 02/24/2019— Dear Men,

Imagine you have a daughter …

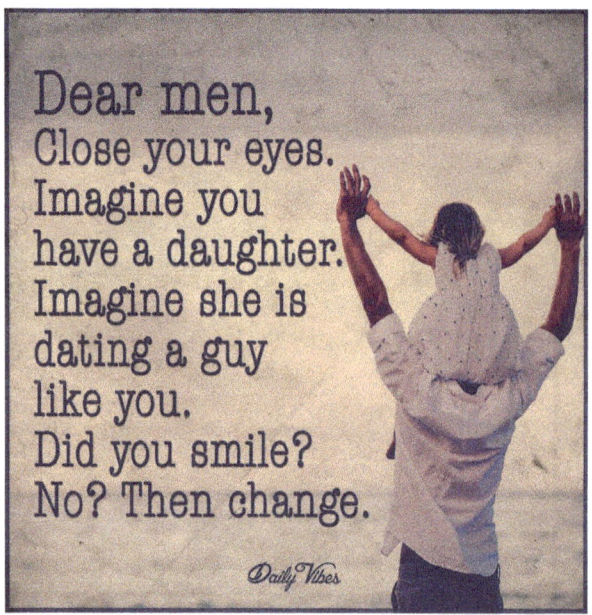

~ ~ ~

Don't Even Ask

Monday 02/25/2019 — I think this just about says it all.

> [**2020 Note:** In getting this manuscript ready for publication in book form, I've had to go searching through years' worth of my photos to paste the pictures into a Word document. Usually that hasn't been much of a problem (other than the time-consumption), but here I've come up against the fact that I didn't put a title on this post, nor did I describe the photo involved, so I have NO idea what was "saying it all."
>
> Not a problem, I thought. I'll just scroll down (and down and down and down and down) through the FB posts to February of 2019 and see what photo I'd used.
>
> Did you ever try to scroll back more than a year and a half?
>
> Doesn't work. FB stopped moving when I reach August of 2019.
>
> So, please don't ask what I was writing about in this post. I have no idea.]

~ ~ ~

Things You Loved Most

Tuesday 02/26/2019 — I'd like to add something to this lovely thought.

I've begun more and more to look at the people I love or admire the most and I ask myself "What is the lesson I can learn from this person?"

From one person I've learned a deep appreciation of the smallest elements of the natural world; from another I have learned empathy for a friend who struggles with addictions; a different friend has taught me that confidence can be developed; another teaches me the value of laughter.

I don't want to wait until these people have left my life before I learn the lessons they can teach.

~ ~ ~

A Child Who Reads

Wednesday 02/27/2019 — I'm always faintly puzzled by people who say they don't like to read. I'd like to believe it's just that they haven't yet found the right book to spark their interest.

But, how can one not find the right book when so many are available on such a wide variety of topics?

How can one live without the breadth and depth of knowledge to be found in books?

How can one get through a day without reading?

Fran Stewart

Okay, okay. I know how. Watch enough TV, tune into enough YouTube videos, coast through enough social media sites focusing only on the pictures, and it might be easy to think, "Ah yes, look at all the knowledge I've gained. Now I know how to live, how to vote, and what to pay attention to."

Sorry, folks. I'll take books over that routine any day.

~ ~ ~

How to Read More

Thursday 02/28/2019 — Happy final day of February. While we're talking about the importance of reading, I thought these instructions were particularly apt.

I wish I'd been doing #6 all my life. I just completed Supreme Court Justice Sonia Sotomayor's autobiography *My Beloved World*, and *Where the Crawdads Sing* by Delia Owens—my book club's selection for our March meeting.

I like to have two books going at once—usually one fiction and one non-fiction. An upstairs book and a downstairs book. Until the CD player in my car broke, I used to have a third book to listen to while driving. Now I listen to NPR or I turn off the radio and enjoy the silence.

Do you keep a reading log? What have you recently finished reading? What are you reading now?

HOW TO READ MORE

1. THROW YOUR PHONE IN THE OCEAN
   (OR KEEP IT IN AIRPLANE MODE)

2. CARRY A BOOK AT ALL TIMES

3. HAVE ANOTHER BOOK READY BEFORE YOU FINISH THE ONE YOU'RE READING
   (MAKE A STACK OF BOOKS TO-READ OR LOAD UP YOUR E-READER)

4. IF YOU AREN'T ENJOYING A BOOK STOP READING IT IMMEDIATELY
   (FLINGING IT ACROSS THE ROOM HELPS PROVIDE CLOSURE)

5. SCHEDULE ONE HOUR A DAY FOR READING ON YOUR CALENDAR LIKE YOU WOULD AN IMPORTANT MEETING
   (TRY COMMUTES, LUNCH BREAKS, OR GETTING INTO BED AN HOUR EARLY)

6. KEEP A READING LOG AND SHARE IT
   (PEOPLE WILL SEND YOU EVEN MORE GOOD BOOKS TO READ)

AUSTINKLEON.COM

March 2019

Helping Someone

Friday 03/01/2019 — While I agree wholeheartedly with today's saying, I'd also like to note that if you help someone, you WILL get something in return. You'll get a warm fuzzy feeling of accomplishment. And it's okay to expect that. It's one of the many values of kindness.

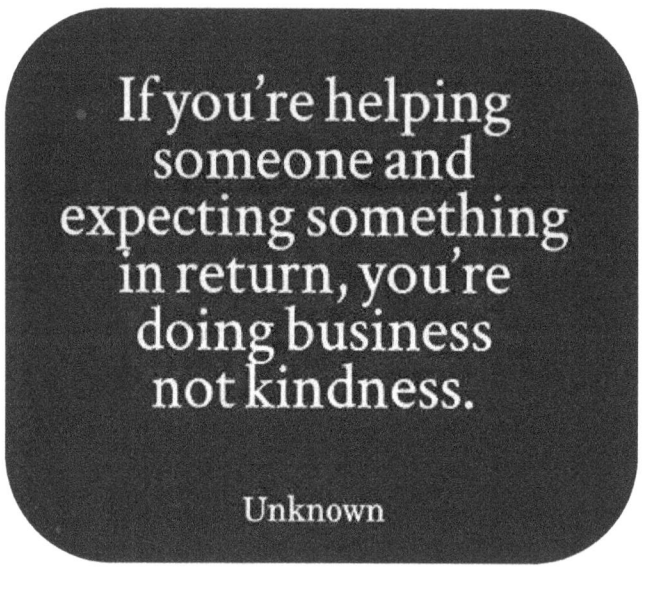

~ ~ ~

Dancing Shadows

Saturday 03/02/2019 — This is how I felt this morning when I awoke. I'll let you guess whether I mean the person on the left or the shadow on the left.

~ ~ ~

March Forth

Monday 03/04/2019 — I love this day – or rather, this date. It's the only time during the year that our calendars give us marvelous directions.

March Forth! Just see what you can accomplish and what you can be.

~ ~ ~

Best Way to Move Forward

Tuesday 03/05/2019 — It's funny how often we're the ones holding ourselves back. In fact, I'd go so far as to say it's ALWAYS ourselves who do the holding.

It's easy to blame our reticence on someone else. "I'd be able to do [fill in the blank] if only so-and-so would (or wouldn't) [fill in the blank]."

Believe it or not, years ago in another lifetime I used to sell cosmetics for one of those multilevel companies. I did a pretty good job of selling, but when it came to getting a "team" together (so I could get a cut of everything they sold), I couldn't seem to make it happen.

I wasted a lot of time and energy blaming other people, everyone from the team members themselves to the man in my life who grumped every time I had a meeting to attend – but the truth of the matter was that I'm simply lousy at that kind of leadership, and I was never motivated by all the froo-froo stuff the company kept setting up as incentives. A mink coat? You've got to be kidding.

It wasn't their fault. I was the roadblock.

Fran Stewart

I didn't know how to get myself out of the way, so I finally just quit.

Thank goodness.

Now, with the memoirs classes I'm teaching, there's no drive to produce more, sell more, accomplish more. Watching my students is a lot like puttering in a garden. I can rake away the fallen leaves from last autumn to give the spring shoots a little more space to emerge into. I can watch the petals unfold as people discover their potential. I can beam when someone finally gets the best way to express that magical moment in her life.

Nothing's holding me back. Nothing's holding them back.

It's miraculous.

Moses Lost in the Desert (11/23/18)

Wednesday 03/06/2019 — I've had a Garmin GPS for about ten years. It was my son's, and then when he went to Thailand for a year to work for his Master SCUBA Diving Certification, he loaned it to me. By the time he got back, he just gave it to me. I really hadn't been trying to manipulate the situation, but I guess I might have overdone it emailing him to tell me how the GPS has saved me from getting horribly lost on the way home in the dark from this library or that book event or another art show.

I bought the lifetime map updates. All I had to do was plug the thing into my computer with the little cord (included in the package) and let it run for hours while it updated every road change in the USA.

Then, three years ago, while planning for a major house-remodeling job, I packed the little cord away somewhere.

Three years, and I still can't find the blinkin' thing.

Can't find a place to buy a replacement cord either.

Phooey.

So now, while I'm driving down a road that's perfectly plain for me to see, my GPS thinks I'm in the middle of a field. And just think about what it does when a city changes a formerly one-way street to a two-way. Poor GPS just about busts a gut trying to get me to turn around.

To Be Happy

Thursday 03/07/2019 — How true this is. Last Tuesday at a memoirs class I'm teaching I hooked my foot around the leg of a chair and dragged it behind me as I walked around the classroom. "I'm not hanging onto any garbage from the past," I proclaimed.

I'm sorry to report that there have been numerous times during my life when I've toted emotional garbage as heavy and entangling as that chair.

Felt good finally to let it go.

Now, the trick is not to collect any more of it!

~ ~ ~

Ground Coffee

Friday 03/08/2019 — Happy Friday. It's time for a laugh.

Enjoy your day!

~ ~ ~

Don't forget

Saturday 03/09/2019 — With the change to daylight savings time coming up tonight, I've been thinking a lot recently about the effect of sunlight on my life. Thank goodness for the skylights I have. As I sit writing this, the dawn light (albeit the cloudy dawn light) illuminates my computer, making electric lights superfluous.

I don't know about you, but I never enjoy the shift to DST – in part because I think it's one of the more stupid decisions our government made. I remember a debate when I was in 7th grade as to the value of DST. The boy arguing in favor of it had an evening paper route. He said his father was against DST. "Dad's a milkman," the boy said.

Nowadays there aren't any milkmen, and I don't know of any kids who have paper routes. At least not in the Atlanta area. Newspapers here are delivered by anonymous drivers who throw the papers out the car window as they zip past. At least I have a great paper-deliverer couple. They always make a point of getting my paper onto my driveway – never in the gutter.

Usually I plan for the change to DST by setting my alarm 5 minutes earlier each day for a couple of weeks before the change. That way, when the Sunday morning hits, my body doesn't feel like it's 4:30 when the clock says 5:30.

But this year, I flat forgot to do that. At least I didn't schedule anything I have to drive to tomorrow or Monday.

~ ~ ~

Don't Worry

Monday 03/11/2019 — Don't worry — I'm not considering taking up skateboarding. And my daughter's talked me out of trying skydiving, simply because she didn't want me throwing up in the little bitty, highly cramped airplane. Did I tell you I have motion sickness? And claustrophobia?

Dancing. I can handle that.

Walking and picking up trash as I go along.

And then there's always laughter to keep one vibrant.

Wanna join me?

~ ~ ~

Here's to Strong Women

Tuesday 03/12/2019 — Celebrate yourself today, and all the strong women who have gone before you and prepared the way. Let's celebrate the strong women who surround us, and the strong women whose way we will pave.

Limerick's Pillow

Wednesday 03/13/2019 — I was all set to post one of those inspiring sayings this morning, but then my daughter sent me this picture of Limmie's new pillow. One of my ongoing resolutions is to laugh a lot every day. I couldn't resist laughing at this, nor could I resist sharing it. Hope it brings you a chuckle as well.

More Selective

Thursday 03/14/2019 — I am so very blessed to have a number of dear friends. They are the quarters in my life. I also treasure the pennies, though, the people I glimpse throughout my life, the ones who form a background to my days.

The most amazing thing happens sometimes. This is alchemy at its best, when someone who once was a penny in my life gradually becomes a quarter. You know who you are!

Thus, I am rich indeed.

~ ~ ~

Too Lazy

Friday 03/15/2019 — This is for my friends in the North Country. Take a break from the snow today, build yourself a snow lounger, and curl up (inside) with a cup of hot tea.

Fran Stewart

~ ~ ~

Not Amused

Saturday 03/16/2019 — Do you ever think about how often we humans anthropomorphize the world around us? We go outside at sunrise to hear the riotous morning sounds coming from nearby trees and bushes, and we call it the dawn chorus, as if we're listening to a choir put there for our enjoyment. Any ornithologist, though, will tell us that those birds are proclaiming their territorial boundaries or advertising for a mate. We think "Hallelujah Chorus," while they're saying, "Back off, buddy," or "Here I am."

By the same token, who of us can look at this photo and see anything other than a disgruntled vehicle?

Of course, we humans can take it to extremes. A case in point: the Victorians who swathed their table legs in excess fabric lest someone see a bare leg and think lascivious thoughts.

What do I do to counteract this tendency to see everything from a human point of view? I'm glad you asked.

I walk outside in the morning, hear the dawn chorus, and—even though I know what's going on in my yard, I still think "Hallelujah!"

This car is not amused

Books Are

Monday 03/18/2019 — I've been thinking a lot lately about the role of books in my life. Not only that I've written them and, as a result, have met a number of amazing people whom I never would have met otherwise, but also the books I've read over the years.

They've filled all of these niches, from mirrors reflecting who I am, to steppingstones that have allowed me to cross seemingly insurmountable barriers, to the quiet corners I yearn for on a regular basis. They have warmed me against the cold drafts not only of the outside weather, but the inside weather as well. And there are those who have anchored me when the world around me seemed storm-tossed.

One of the things I love about the book club I attend regularly is that so many new vistas open around me as the various members introduce me to books I might never have found otherwise. When we meet tomorrow, I'll find a whole new world to occupy.

What have you read recently that helped or illumined you, that warmed you or reflected you, that anchored you or that let you fly?

GRANT SNIDER (AFTER RUDINE SIMS BISHOP)

Ship at the airport

Tuesday 03/19/2019 — As I write this, a dozen or so starlings are raiding my bird feeders. I keep hoping they'll give up. I keep charging over to the front door, opening it and slamming it—which does send them flapping across the cul-de-sac—but then they come right back the moment I move away from the door.

I'm tired of feeding them, but if I stop putting out seed, the smaller birds—the birds I actually like—will suffer.

So I keep chasing them away, searching for the same solution-ship at my front-yard-airport. Where'd the harbor go?

I need a sign that says, "Starlings go away!"

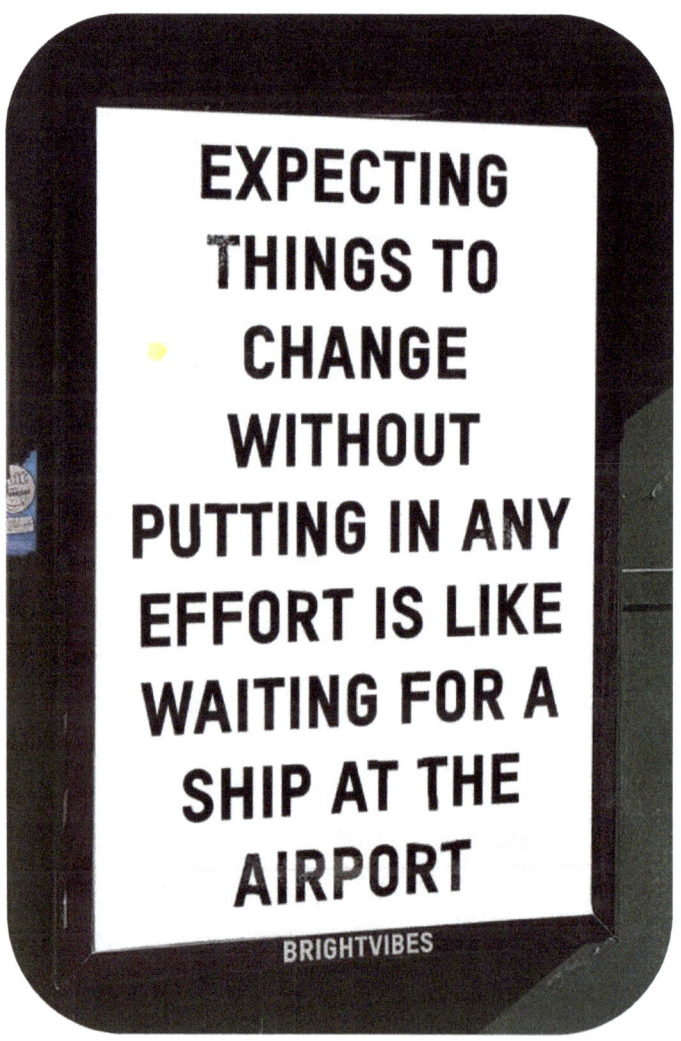

~ ~ ~

Joy in the Snow

Wednesday 03/20/2019 — So, I tried yesterday to find something good about those starlings – to find some sort of joy in them, since I obviously wasn't going to get rid of them.

They truly are lovely, with their iridescent feathers gleaming. They're agile as can be and smart as the dickens. I have these squirrel-proof birdfeeders (I can hear you saying, "Yeah, right") that slide closed when the weight of a squirrel or of a heavy bird lands on the pegs at the base of the seed ports.

Do you know what the starlings do? They land. The port closes. They give a little jump, just enough for the port to open. As it does so, they snatch a seed. Jump open snatch. Jump open snatch. It's like watching a circus.

And, I must admit, it makes me laugh. I still have more than a dozen robber-birds, but I'm chuckling all the way to the front door as I try to scare them away.

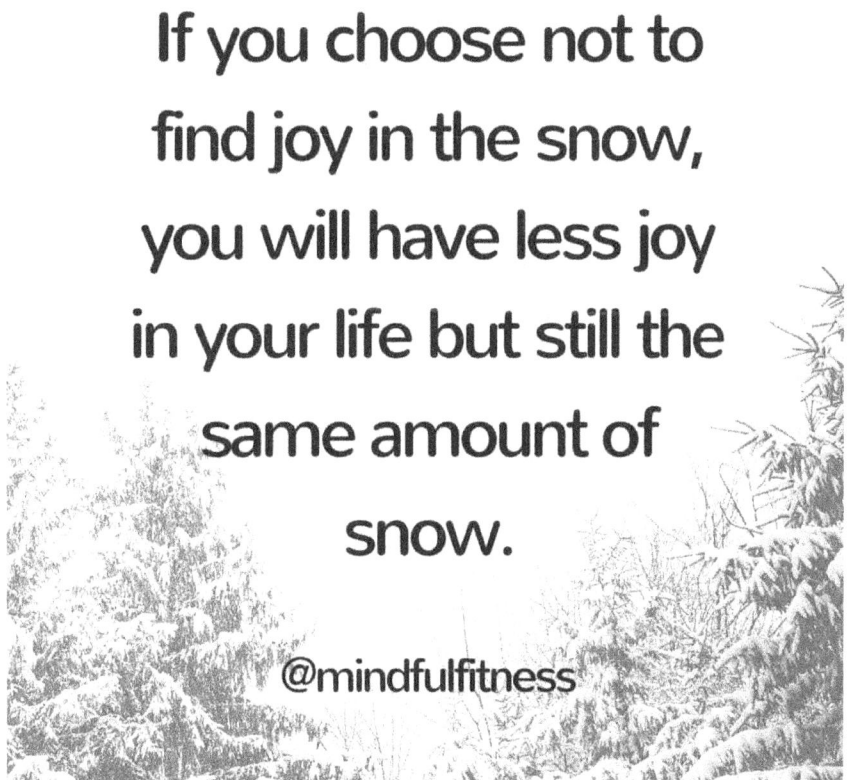

Equinox

Thursday 03/21/2019 — I love the times of the Equinox, when the day and night are balanced. I'm reminded of *Thurisaz*, the Nordic Gateway Rune, which is a symbol for that time of transition, when one reflects on both the inner and the outer life. It is a time when one sees the threads that make up the time before now, ready to stretch into the time to come. Now is not the moment to make an earth-shaking decision. Now is the time to contemplate and to see oneself in balance.

Once that is done, we step through the gateway into the upcoming season, whether it's the season of the year or the next season of our life.

~ ~ ~

Don't Have Time

Friday 03/22/2019 — Setting priorities is a favorite "think-about-it" of mine. Four years ago, when I came within a whisper of dying, I did a whole lot of such thinking. What was truly important to me? What needed to be done? What didn't? What mattered to me? What was simply not that important?

If you've ever had a brush with death, you'll probably know what I mean. If you haven't had one, why wait for that almost-killed-me moment before making the changes that will create a more meaningful life?

Only you can make time for what truly matters. Only I could make that time in my own life.

I'm so glad I did.

~ ~ ~

Storing Bodies

Saturday 03/23/2019 — I used to have a 10 cubic foot refrigerator. It was so short I had to bend over to get out the milk. Finally, my son helped me put it up on a stand so I could get to the things on the bottom shelf without crawling on my knees.

Since I don't do much cooking, I didn't need even ten cubic feet. I could have made do with half that amount of space.

My point is, I have a pretty good visual for just how small 7 cubic feet would be. Just big enough for one person. Yes.

The next time you want to store a body – go to Lowe's.

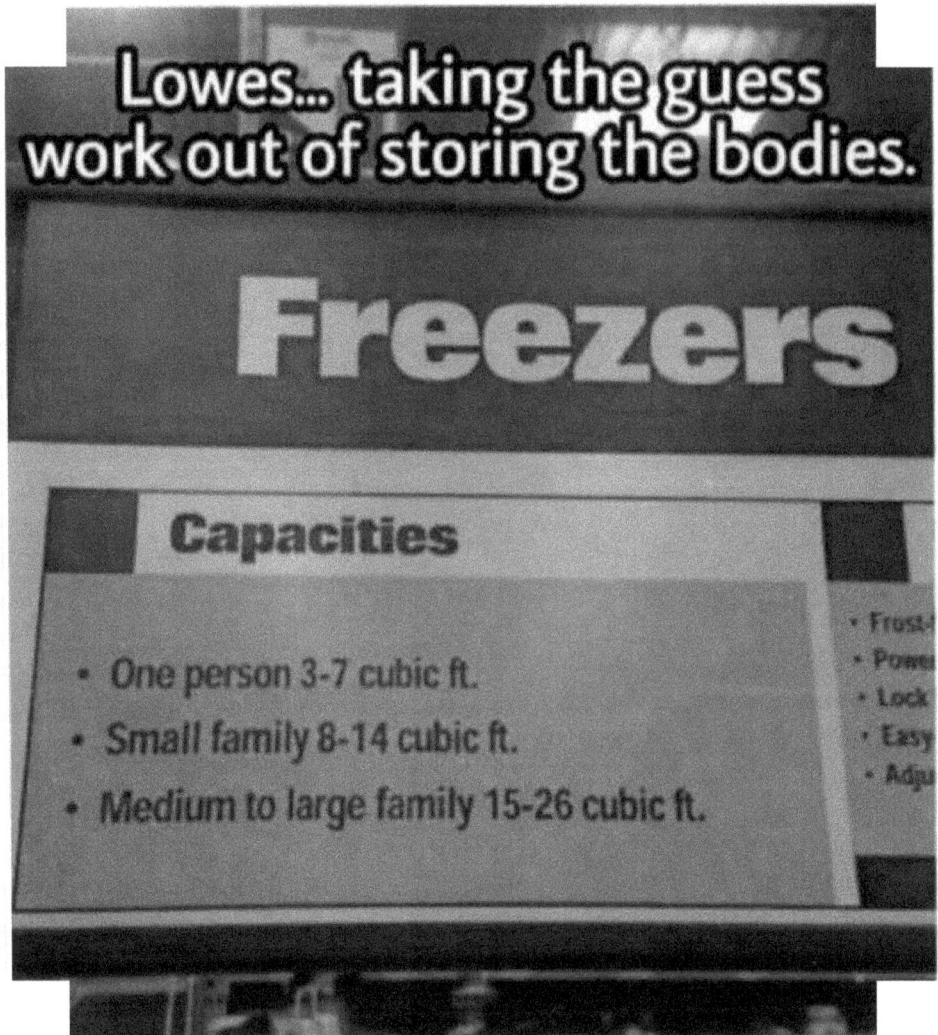

Defend Your Answer

Monday 03/25/2019 — I am in awe of minds that look on something ordinary and see something extraordinary. People who look at four answers on a multiple-choice and see a fifth possibility. People who are presented with an either-or ultimatum and discover that there's a way to avoid that kind of confrontation.

Today, I'm going to try to look at every event with an open mind, a mind ready to see alternatives, a mind ready to defend my answer in a new and refreshing way.

~ ~ ~

Removed

Tuesday 03/26/2019 — Sorry, folks. I could not – could absolutely NOT – resist this one.

Have a day filled with inner joy, and don't under any circumstance, cause a fence.

One Day at a Time

Wednesday 03/27/2019 — This fridge magnet has been greeting me each morning for I don't know how many years.

One day at a time.

It's a good precept to keep in mind.

"Sufficient unto the day is the evil thereof," sort of says the same thing, but I rather prefer "Sufficient unto the day is the goodness thereof." True, there's no sense in dwelling on the crud that's around us at times, but there's also no sense in trying to live in the goodness of the past, when there's a whole new world of goodness available to us each and every day.

Whenever I look at this green beacon on my fridge, I like to remind myself "One good day at a time."

What's on your fridge that inspires you?

~ ~ ~

Frequency

Thursday 03/28/2019 — Never means zero percent. This reminds me of the time my sister told me years ago of traveling to a beach "resort"—she used that word loosely. She asked the owner if sharks ever came into the swimming area of the secluded bay. "Never," he assured her. "Never!" Then he went on to add, "Anyway, when they come close, I call everybody out of the water."

She didn't go swimming much while she was there.

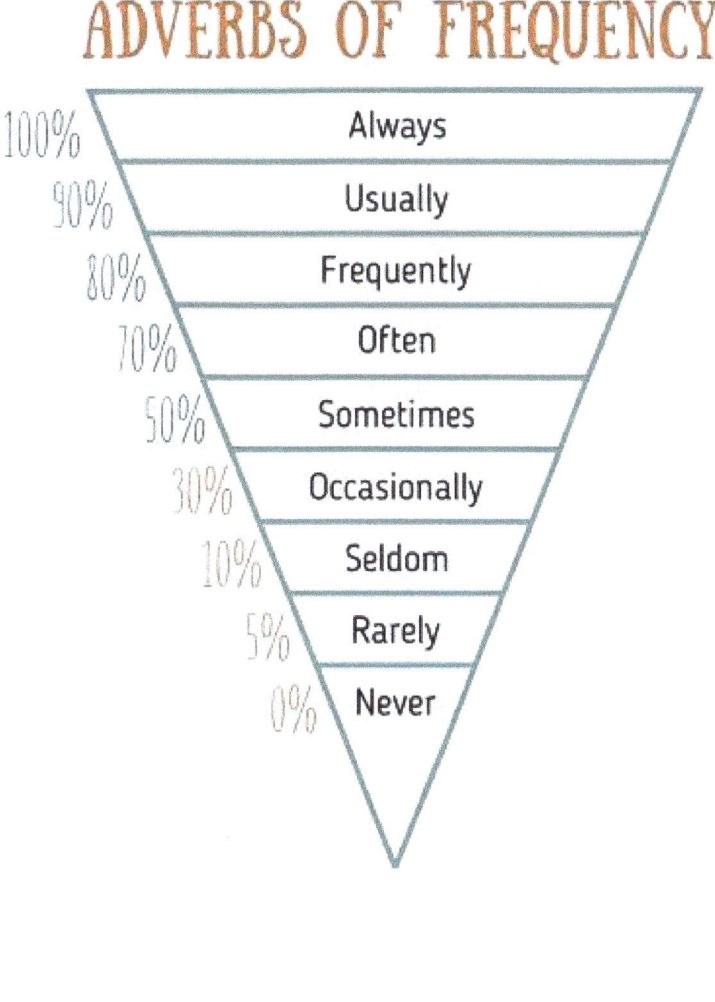

~ ~ ~

You May Not

Friday 03/29/2019 — I love this photo. I've always wondered how people manage to be in just the right place at just the right time to be able to take shots like this.

Fran Stewart

Part of it, I imagine, is that photographers are aware of their surroundings in a way that a lot of the rest of us just aren't.

Today, I'd like to pay more attention to where I am, each moment of the day.

Will you do that, too?

~ ~ ~

Madonna of the Pomegranate

Saturday 03/30/2019 — It's not often I catch a mistake in a movie (or in this case, a series), but I'm in the process of watching "West Wing" on Netflix, all seven seasons, in order. I missed it the first time around, since I haven't had a TV set for more than two decades.

I'm somewhere in the middle of season 4. They're doing flashbacks to when President Bartlet had just gotten elected, and Mrs. Landringham is trying to get his opinion on what art to hang in the oval office. "Anything from the Smithsonian or the National Archives," she says, flipping through an official-looking album of photographs, and then suggests, "Leonardo da Vinci. *Madonna and Child with a Pomegranate*."

WHOOPS! Wrong source / wrong name / wrong artist! It's *Madonna of the Pomegranate* by Sandro Boticelli. 1487 or thereabouts, in case you're interested. And the painting is in Italy, not in the Smithsonian.

Maybe this doesn't seem like such an egregious error, but I swallowed my tea the wrong way when I heard it.

I guess my inner editor operates all the time, not only when I'm reading.

April 2019

When you replace …

Monday 04/01/2019 — Five and a half years ago, I was wallowing in self-pity over a health issue. "Why is this happening to me?" was a frequent refrain.

Three months later, I came very close to dying, and everything shifted indeed. My entire perspective changed when I saw that I had a choice as to what my attitude was.

One of the lessons I teach in the memoirs classes I lead is that of how a shift of perspective can open doors, lead us to solutions, calm our frenzied minds, and turn a raging surf of rampant emotion into ripples spreading out on the surface of a quiet pool.

It's a great lesson to learn.

> @PeacefulMindPeacefulLife
>
> When you replace "Why is this happening to me?" with "What do I need to learn from this?", everything shifts.
>
> —UNKNOWN

~ ~ ~

Mindful

Tuesday 04/02/2019 — The first time I ever heard of mindfulness meditation was when I picked up a book by Jon Kabat-Zin called *Wherever You Go, There You Are*.

I was reminded of it when I saw this illustration.

I'd vote for the horse's approach to life.

Just for today, let's step aside from the chaos that we so often surround ourselves with. Let's fill our minds with the road we're on—not the one ahead of us, not the one behind us—but the steps we're taking right now.

I'd love it if you'd join me on that journey.

Needs a Cat

Wednesday 04/03/2019 — All the plants outside say spring is here. The daffodils have already finished blooming, in fact. The flowering vines are flowering, the blueberries are setting their fruit.

When I run errands, I see people walking around in tee-shirts, although many of them have goose bumps running up and down their arms.

And what am I wearing? The warmest sweatshirt imaginable. This marvelous one that my friend Linda Bell gave me. You'd think April would mean springtime. The plants believe it. But I don't. Not quite yet.

The people who service my heating/cooling system twice a year always call in February to set up the maintenance appointment for my air conditioner. "Are you kidding?" I always tell them. "Getting the A/C ready when the furnace is still pumping practically non-stop? I'd like to wait until it's a little closer to summer."

So, the furnace is still running, and I'm cozy in my soft sweatshirt, and—even though the weeds are growing almost non-stop—it ain't quite spring yet.

In the Mood

Thursday 04/04/2019 — When I get in this sort of mood, but I don't have the time to head out on the road, I can always go to the library and pick up a book I've never heard of before.

It's amazing how a new book can open up vistas I wouldn't have dreamed of. Those coffee table books, for instance, that most libraries have aplenty? I eat them up. I can go all sorts of places without leaving my living room. I can see sights I'd never see considering my limited hiking range.

Is that truly a good substitute for "the real thing?"

Well, yes and no. There's certainly nothing like being somewhere in person. I could read forever about the

Science Museum in Toronto, but unless I've been there and handled their interactive exhibits, I won't get the full flavor of it. (Here I am channeling a 1988 trip where we spent several memorable days there.)

But photographs of the lesser-traveled wild places of this country fascinate me. And not having a real destination in mind is, to my way of thinking, one of the nicest ways to take a trip.

~ ~ ~

Same Cattitude

Friday 04/05/2019 — When Wooly Bear was stalking Fuzzy Britches this morning – and when Fuzzy Britches was stalking her favorite toy yesterday, I saw the wild tiger in both of them. I love it that a cat is still so close to its wild nature. Watching my cats makes me want to go out and climb a tree.

Do You Make a Difference?

Saturday 04/06/2019 — Let's hear it for firefighters!

I love this summation of what firefighters "make."

> Oh.. you're a Firefighter?? That's cool. What do you make?" "WHAT DO I MAKE?? I make holding your hand seem like the biggest thing in the world when I'm cutting you out of a car. I can make 5 minutes seem like a lifetime when I go in a burning house to save your family. I make those annoying sirens seem like angels when you need them. I can make your children breathe when they stop. I can help you... survive a heart attack. I make myself get out of bed at 3am to risk my life to save people I've never met. Today I might make the ultimate sacrifice to save your life. I make a difference, what do you make?"

~ ~ ~

Never Wish Them Pain

Monday 04/08/2019 — I spent most of Sunday and part of yesterday in a flap over some virulent text messages and a bizarre voicemail. No need to go into the details – just suffice it to say that I wasted a lot of time dealing with the repercussions, and I kept feeling that the person who had generated those diatribes had somehow stolen that whole day and a half from me.

Then, looking back through the photos I'd earmarked for possible inclusion in these daily "mini-memoirs," I noticed this one.

I wish her healing.

Whew! That feels a whole lot better.

~ ~ ~

Stress Level

Tuesday 04/09/2019 — What wonderful therapy! When I was babysitting my grand-dog over the weekend, we discovered a new game. She sat on one side of the room while I walked behind the couch. Then I ducked down as quickly as I could. When I disappeared, she let out a squawky bark of surprise ("Where'd you go?????") and came charging around the end of the sofa looking for me. Of course, she ran right into me. Then we had to love and hug and lick. (We both did the loving; I did the hugging; she did the licking.)

We kept doing it over and over, each time with the same surprise, the same search, the same impact, the same follow-up.

And it was truly joyful.

I hope you have as much joy in your day. If not – play hide-n-seek with a pup and see what happens.

Fran Stewart

~ ~ ~

6+3=9

Wednesday 04/10/2019 — My sister and I are having an argument by telephone. I'm headed her way next month for a short visit, and we have different opinions about where I should sleep.

I'm a 7+2 person, and she's an 8+1. They both end up at bedtime, but my dear loving wonderful sister doesn't recognize anything but her 8+1.

You see, when I'm in a bed other than my own, I'm most content with two soft blankets. Preferably on somebody's couch. She doesn't like napping on her couch, so she bought one of those blow-up beds for guests. She said she'll fix it up with a fitted sheet and a regular sheet and a blanket or two all tucked in at the bottom.

What she doesn't know is that the last time I was there, she'd make up the couch the way she wanted it each evening, I'd wait until she and her husband were snug in bed, and then I'd un-tuck everything and wind myself up in the blanket. The next morning (since I was still on Atlanta time—two hours earlier than Colorado) I'd get up early, fold up the sheets and blankets, and make myself a cup of tea.

"How'd you sleep?" she'd ask me an hour later.

"Great," I'd say.

This time, though, she's bought that portable bed, and I'd still be happy with the couch. I'll give it a try the first night and see what happens.

The question is – am I being just as inflexible as she is?

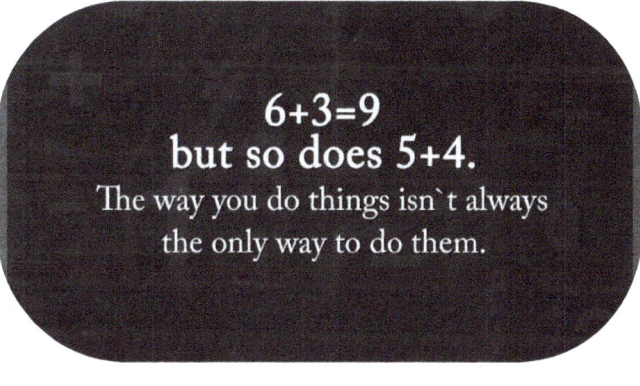

~ ~ ~

Singing in a Car

Thursday 04/11/2019 — I admit it. I love to sing when I'm driving. It doesn't matter whether it's a song from my childhood, a song I wrote, a song from a musical, blues, jazz, big band era, opera. If I know the words, I sing them. If I don't know the words—who cares? Tra-la-la works pretty well.

Nowadays, though, people who pass me by probably think I'm talking on a hands-free cellphone.

p.s. My Inner Editor can't help but mention that today's saying should read "loudly," rather than "loud." Other than that—I agree completely.

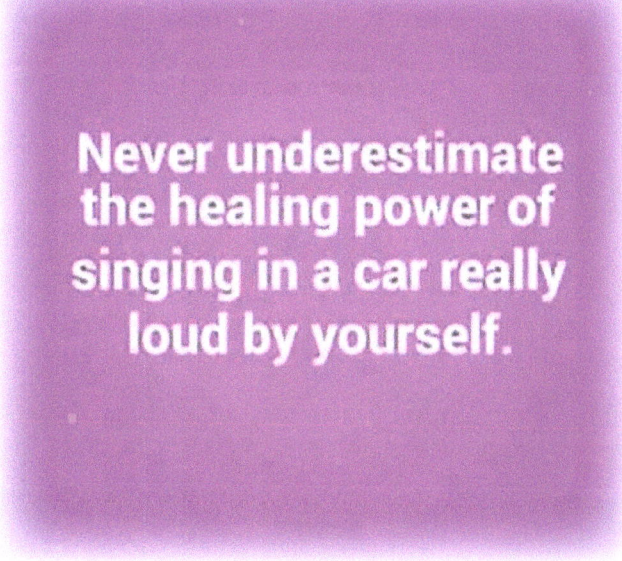

The Biggest Wall

Friday 04/12/2019 — It's amazing what sort of barriers we put up to limit ourselves, isn't it? Lately, I've found myself saying "I can't," when, if I put my mind to it, I would find that "I can" is just around the corner. Taking that early morning walk, hauling out my old-fashioned reel mower to do something about the weeds that are jumping with joy, doing the dusting and straightening that I've gotten so far behind on…

Really, Frannie—what on earth have you been thinking?

What I've been thinking is that I don't have the energy for these things. I can't—I can't—I can't.

Time to let go of that sort of negative gunk. I can—I can—I can.

I'll start with the walk. Listening to the birds' dawn chorus is more fun than dusting pollen off the floorboards.

On the other hand, maybe I'll go walking after it stops raining.

~ ~ ~

Wooly Bear

Saturday 04/13/2019 — Good morning! What's ahead of us today? It's probably something exciting. Even if it isn't to begin with, I can make it exciting just by being with my human. We can romp and play and chase a feather toy and run around the house chasing reflections.

Or maybe I'll climb the bookcase again. That was a lot of fun.

Then again, I could just settle back down here on the comforter and – well – get comfortable. Maybe that's the best idea.

Bye for now from Wooly Bear.

Brainwash

Monday 04/15/2019 — You may call this Tax Day, but I'm going to rename it Believe in Yourself Day.

Let's make "I can't" an obsolete expression.

Let's celebrate "I can."

The memoirs classes I teach help people recognize the value of their life stories. So many people are afraid to begin writing those stories. "I can't," they say. But then they take my class and start to feel they might be able to do this.

As people share their stories in class, they see that others have had similar experiences, that others have surmounted challenges, that others have laughed at the same sorts of events. That, in fact, we are all human.

Eventually I CAN'T turns into MAYBE, which soon becomes "I CAN."

And isn't that a glorious moment!

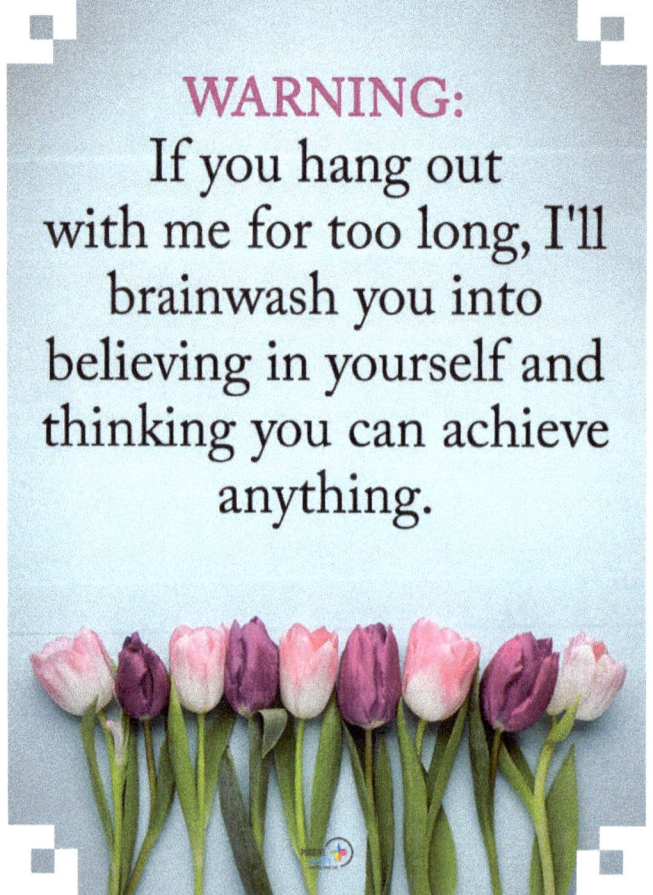

~ ~ ~

Will Age

Tuesday 04/16/2019 — Some of the best people I've ever known have been wrinkly old ladies – at least they looked old to me at the time.

My grandmother, a favorite aunt, two teachers I was fortunate enough to have. They had beautiful souls, which I suppose is the reason I thought they were beautiful, even though the world in general might not have agreed with me.

Now, I look in the mirror and I see wrinkles a-plenty—and heaven knows my body has seen enough changes over the years. But I'm working on the beautiful soul part, since that's the part that truly matters.

Won't you join me in this quest?

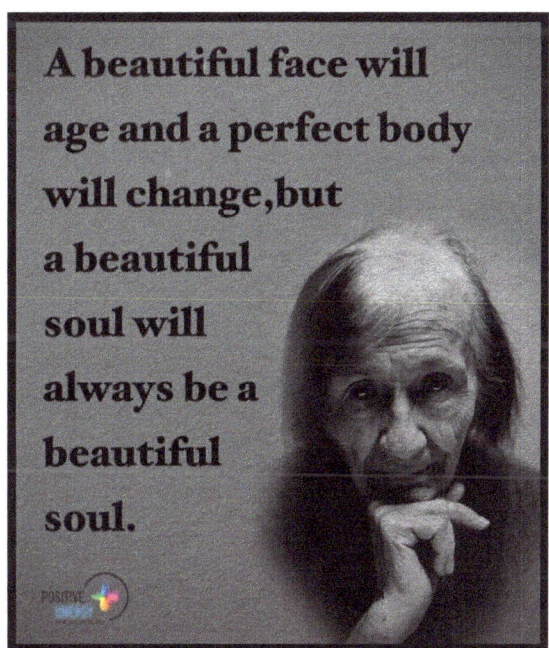

~ ~ ~

What Lies Behind Us

Wednesday 04/17/2019 — This thought for the day goes pretty well with yesterday's photo and saying.

I can't do anything about what came before—some of the dumb decisions I made, some of the less-than-stellar moves.

And I can't truly see what lies ahead—all the guesses in the world aren't foolproof; all the plans I make may somehow go awry.

But I sure can do something about what lies within. These things are, after all, my choices.

It's up to me, doggone it. Can't pass the responsibility to anybody else.

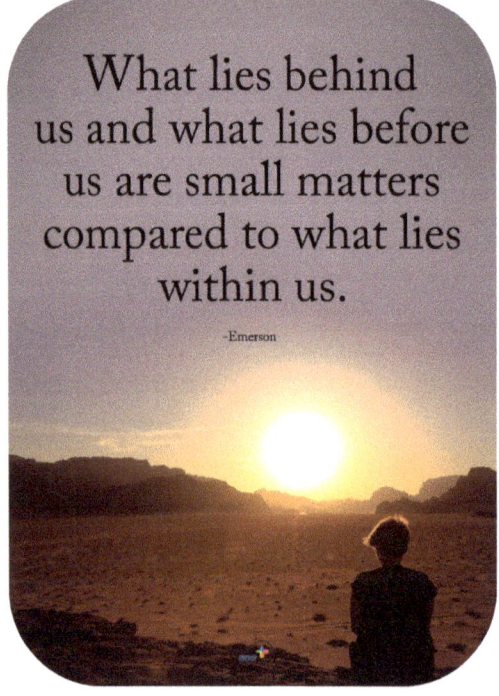

~ ~ ~

Some Days

Thursday 04/18/2019 — You may have noticed that for the past two days I've been philosophical.

Today, I'm admitting to eating fudge for supper last night. Not for dessert AFTER supper. For supper itself.

~ ~ ~

What to Carry

Friday 04/19/2019 — How much time do we waste worrying about past indiscretions, errors in judgment, stupid things we said that we shouldn't have?

I like this idea of using those events as stepping-stones. We can't undo them, but if we learn from them and turn them into a path (or a major highway!) to take us farther along our life journey, then maybe some good will come of it all.

Today, let's take the high road.

~ ~ ~

Because I Decided

Saturday 04/20/2019 — "Too bad it's raining." "Too bad it's so hot." "Too bad it's so cold." And so on.

Do you ever get tired of hearing people complain about the weather?

Do you ever tire of complaining about it yourself?

There's a big difference between reacting to something and responding to it. When we react to something—like the weather or another person's comment or a news item—we're giving that event mastery over us, saying in effect that we've given that condition, person, or event the power to control how we feel.

If, on the other hand, we respond (rather than react), it means we've put some thought into the situation and we've decided to keep our own power to determine how to feel about it, or how to act.

Too bad it's raining? My response is usually, "Come next August we're going to wish we had this."

Life IS good—in large part because my thoughts and my actions have made it so.

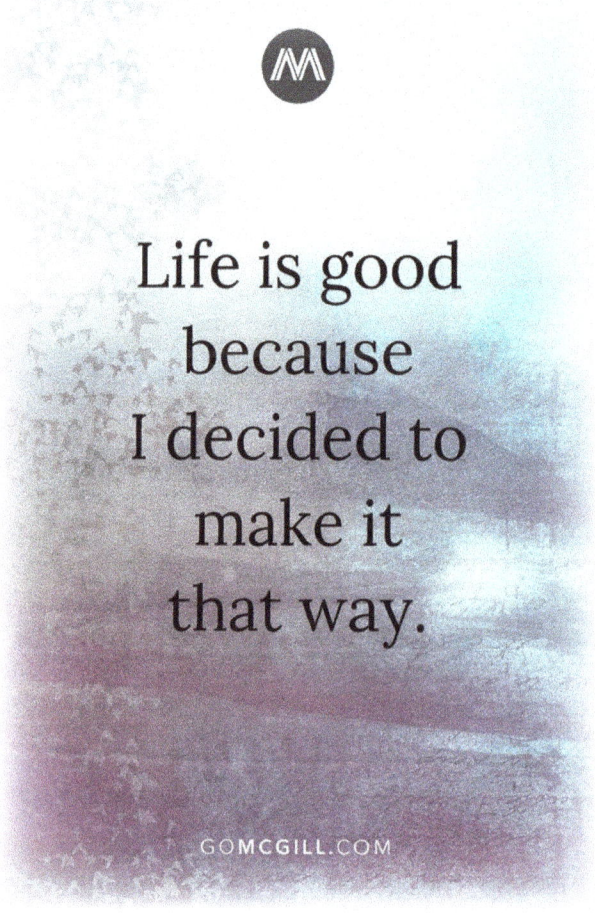

~ ~ ~

Hug a Tree

Monday 04/22/2019 — It's **Earth Day.** Since I don't have a huge tree like this in my yard, I plan to hug whatever is available – and there are plenty of those, since my entire back yard is deciduous forest.

Because the trees are on the south & west sides of my house, the A/C doesn't have to run very much in the summer – and in the winter, the leaves are down, so I get lots of warming sun coming in my windows.

But, aside from the practical value of them – I simply love trees. It seems like they would have so much to tell us if we could (if we would) listen to them.

~ ~ ~

You've Been Tagged

Tuesday 04/23/2019 — I was looking through an old photo album yesterday and came across a couple of pictures that looked disconcertingly like the lower photo in today's picture. It reminded me of a scene I wrote in WHITE AS ICE about a pregnant woman who opened a portfolio of her father's sketches after his death and—without thinking—burned some of the sketches that showed her as a gawky young girl.

You know that time of life, when knees are knobby, and arms and legs seem too long, and hair won't behave.

Only after the handful of drawings have turned to ashes does she realize that someday her daughter soon to be born may have need of knowing that her mother, too, went through that sort of phase. But it was too late to save those sketches.

I guess I'll keep the old album with ALL its photos.

~ ~ ~

Eli's View

Wednesday 04/24/2019 — My son, Eli Reiman, has an artist's eye when it comes to sharing his travels. On his way to paddle-boarding in the Pacific Ocean a few days ago, he spotted this vista.

I wonder how many people pass along that same road every day and never take the time to see the glory.

I remember being struck years ago by that now-famous line in Walker's *The Color Purple*:

> "I think it pisses God off if you walk by the color purple in a field somewhere and don't notice it. What it do when it pissed off? I ask. Oh, it make something else. People think pleasing God is all God care about. But any fool living in the world can see it always trying to please us back."
> — Alice Walker, *The Color Purple*

Wherever I am today, I plan to look for the color purple. How about you?

~ ~ ~

All the Purples

Thursday 04/25/2019 — Yesterday I talked about how I was planning to notice purple all day long.

You wouldn't believe the number of purple things I saw! Or maybe you would, especially if you saw just as many. It started with bright purple irises beside my driveway and kept going right through the day.

When I visited my dear daughter-of-the-heart Nima, who's staying with a friend in Atlanta (in a PURPLE house), we had to snap the last purple photo of the day. She wore a purple tanktop and I had purple swirls in my dress.

 On the way home, there was all sorts of purple along the roadsides, but Georgia has a no-phone-in-your-hands law, so I had to keep those riotous flowers in my mind rather than on my camera phone.

Did you have a purple day, too?

~ ~ ~

The Food Chain

Friday 04/26/2019 — Good Morning! Just stopping by to say hello.

"Hel-loooooooooooooh!"

Have a faaaaaaaaabulous day.

This burro picture, by the way, came from an article about the food chain that I read on the BBC World Service.

~ ~ ~

Self-care Isn't Always

Saturday 04/27/2019 — Twice a year a very knowledgeable, very likeable man named Sam comes to my house to service the furnace (in the fall) or the A/C (in the spring). He was here yesterday. In the process, because he had to run the A/C to be sure it was working right, the house cooled down quite a bit. Brrrr.

When he left, I turned the system completely off. Last night, I forgot to check the weather report, and didn't even think to switch on the furnace. Why would I? The weather's been so mild lately, I haven't had it on at all.

Overnight, the temp dropped into the 40s, which meant my house dropped into the low 60s. Getting up this morning was NOT easy. In fact, if I hadn't needed to get this written and posted, I might have stayed under the covers. On second thought, Wooly Bear would not have let that happen. After all, it was breakfast time.

Before I fed the cats, though, and before I wrote this post, I turned on the furnace, thereby showing at least a bit of self-care as I got up to face the COLD day.

Time to participate in life! Brrrrrrrrr!

~ ~ ~

Happy Selfie

Sunday 4/29/2019 – Sometimes I'm just happy. Not thinking about anything else. Just content and smiling. It's a good feeling.

~ ~ ~

Diana's Art

Monday 04/29/2019 — I thought I'd start the week yesterday with a happy selfie I took a couple of years ago. The background still looks the same, but I've changed a bit—longer hair, different glasses, more wrinkles.

As to what's on that wall behind me? An art piece my sister Diana Alishouse created that shows the first sentence of *Orange as Marmalade* (diagrammed over a reproduction of the first page). Remember sentence diagramming? She included four of the insides of old floppy disks, the ones on which I'd stored early versions of *Orange*. A human brain, the beginning of the Fibonacci sequence (more about that tomorrow), handprints, initials, Grecian columns, various encyclopedia pages, and—of course—a gift at the very bottom.

My sister. A work of art in and of herself.

~ ~ ~

Fibonacci Sequence

Tuesday 04/30/2019 —I did a search for "images of Fibonacci Sequence" and came up with a wealth of beauty. The sequence is a mathematical marvel that expresses natural laws. Here are just a few of the pictures I found. The first two show how each number in the sequence (the sum of the two numbers preceding it) grows from 0+1=1 to 1+1=2 to 1+2=3 to 2+3=5, and so on.

0, 1, 1, 2, 3, 5, 8, 13, 21, 34, 55, 89, 144, ad infinitum.

The next photo shows how that sequence plays out in plants (and one little chameleon tail). Then there's the Chambered Nautilus shell, reminding me of one of my all-time favorite poems.

Fran Stewart

Everybody uses sunflowers and artichokes and the nautilus shell as examples of how those spirals are formed, but what about weather? What about stars?

I hope you enjoy this array of Fibonacci wonder as much as I do.

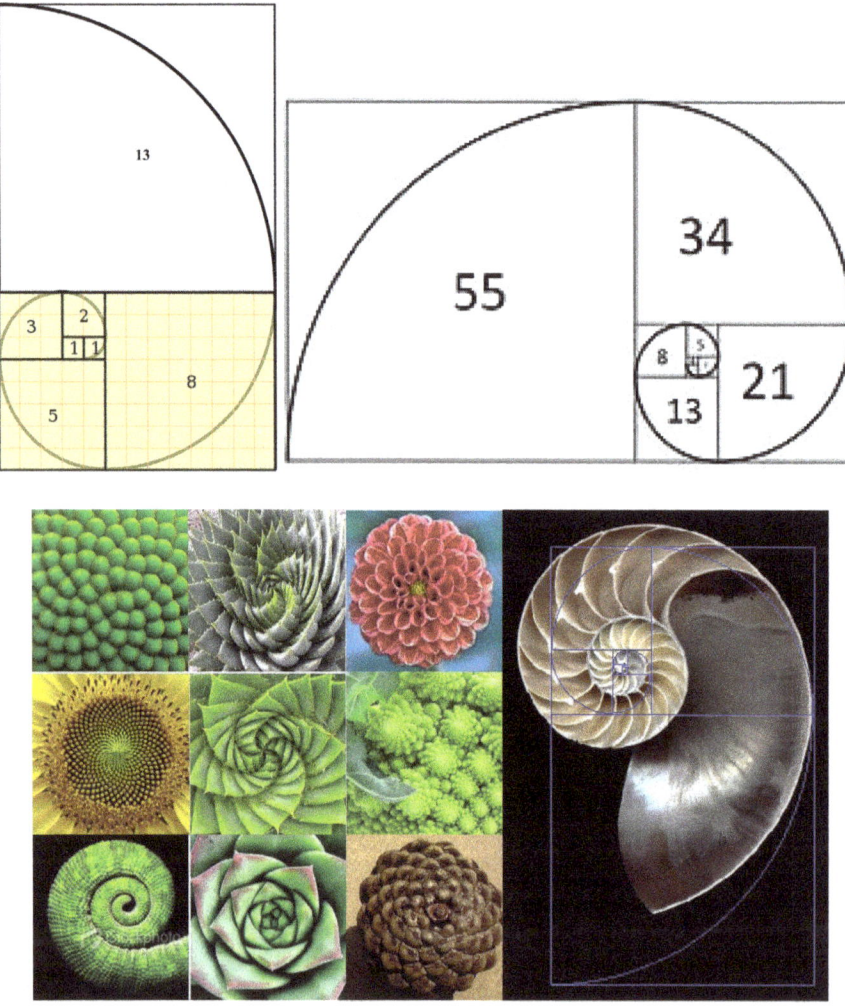

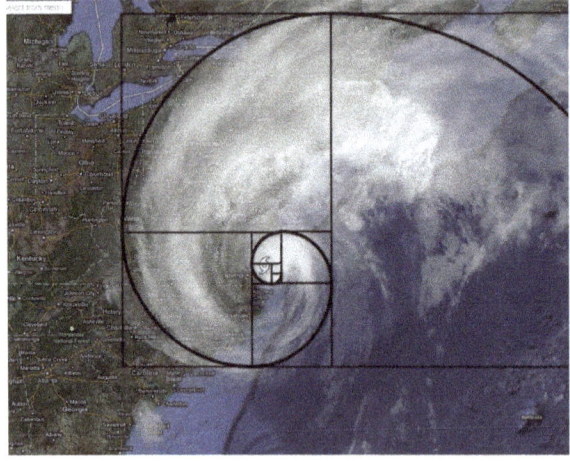

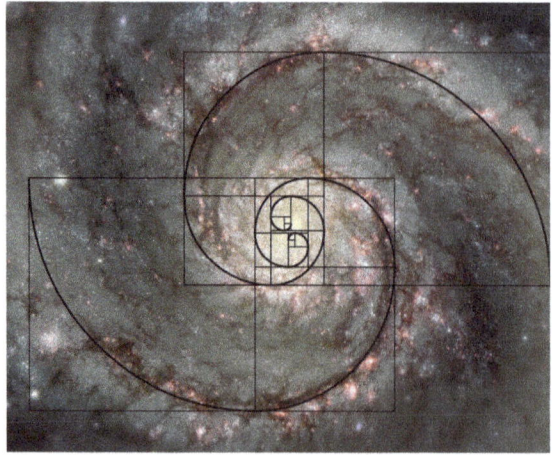

May 2019

My Natural Wonder Wall

Wednesday 05/1/2019 — Today's post is the third in a series. Beneath and beside the art piece from my sister, I have a whole wall section devoted to natural wonders. Arching over it all is a piece of baleen that my son Eli bought from an Inuit community when he worked on a barge in Alaska one summer during college. The hairy leading edge of it is what strained plankton and krill from the water as the whale swam open-mouthed through the ocean. I honor that whale, for in death it fed the people, warmed them, and helped to sustain their community.

There is a dreamcatcher from the American Southwest, a box-turtle shell a friend found in the woods near her house, a necklace made of hemp with a shell clasp and a pendant made of a petrified tooth on which my son carved an eagle in flight. Speaking of birds, there is a crane carved from a curving horn—I wish I knew its source.

There is a cornucopia basket made of—I think—palm fronds attached by leather thongs to an old gray lichen-mottled stick, and a whimsical strand of golden elephants Eli and Nima bought for me in India.

And to think this whole sequence of posts began with an old selfie.

Fran Stewart

~ ~ ~

That Earthy Smell

Thursday 5/2/2019 — How long has it been since you went walking in the rain just for the fun of it?

That used to be a favorite activity when my grandchildren visited me on Tuesdays years ago when they were young. Sometimes we had an umbrella or two with us. Sometimes we just got wet. Well, even on days WITH the umbrellas, we got pretty damp anyway.

There's something about the smell of wet earth that can't ever be reproduced in words. But when you've experienced it, you will—I guarantee—never forget it.

What are your rainy-day memories?

And, before I sign off, Happy Birthday, Veronica! You are such a blessing in my life—and to countless other people as well. Thank you for being the strong and magnificent woman you are.

~ ~ ~

Doing Your Best

Friday 5/3/2019 — My friend Linda Bell comes up with the greatest pictures and sayings on her FB posts. She found this one a week or so ago, and I had to reflect on what another friend of mine told me last year.

You see, I belong to a marvelous organization of highly creative women (AtlantaPenWomen.org and NLAPW.org). Artists, writers, musicians, we gather once a month to share with, encourage, and sustain each other. There's a newsletter, which everybody liked to read, but nobody wanted to edit, so I agreed to do it. There was the position of treasurer, which everyone agreed was vitally important, but nobody wanted to be responsible for our financial records, so I agreed to do it. There was the need to make reservations for the monthly luncheons, but the woman who'd been doing had begun traveling a lot and had to let it go. Nobody else volunteered, so I did. Then there was keeping track of the nametags for members and guests. Guess who ended up doing that as well?

Eventually my friend Peggy and I met for lunch one week when I felt particularly frazzled.

"What do you think would happen," Peggy asked me, "if you simply resigned from half these jobs?"

Duh!

Sure, I was doing my best, but I found out that when I said "no more" other people stepped up to fill in the void. It's amazing how much more time I have—and how much less frazzled I feel—now that I'm simply the treasurer of the group.

I Dusted Once

Saturday 5/4/2019 — This is a good thought for the day.

I'm very tempted to follow this advice, especially since the Atlanta area is still in the throes of the dreaded Pollen Season. If you live somewhere else in the world, you probably don't realize just how pervasive pollen is from—oh—about February through the end of May.

Around here, cars, houses, and roads turn yellow this time of year. When the wind blows, you can see drifts of pine pollen, like terrestrial northern lights, coming in curtains off the trees. Naturally, the stuff works its way inside as well.

Okay, so maybe I'll dust occasionally from February through May, if only to keep my coffee table, baseboards, kitchen counter, and chairs safe from the yellow plague. But the rest of the year, when it's only dust—let the dust settle where it will. The cats will sweep it away with their tails.

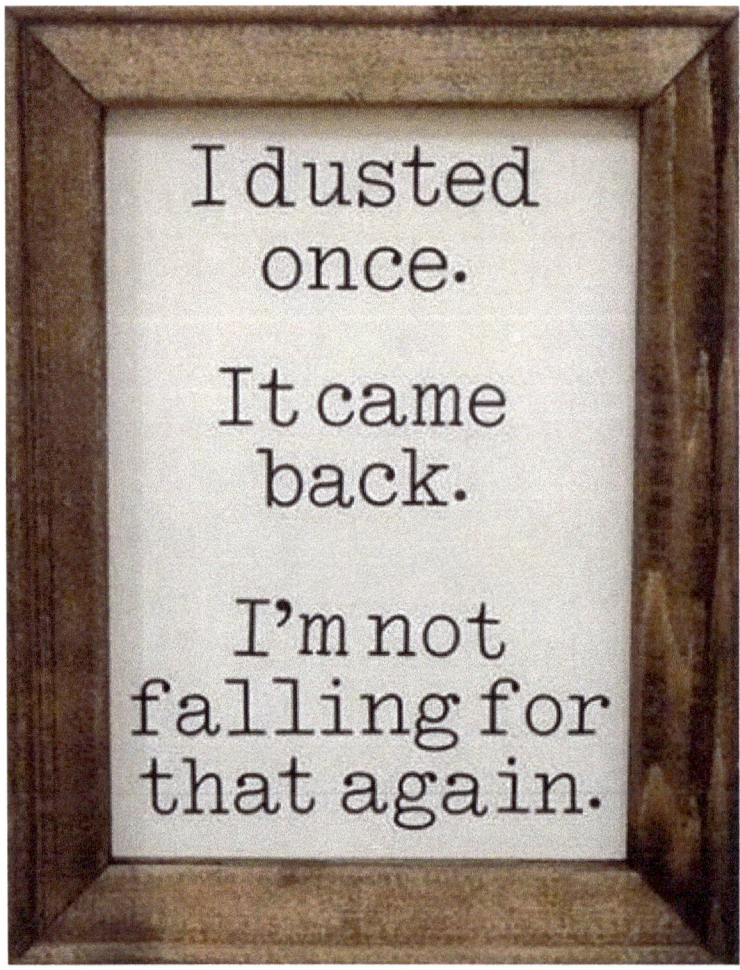

~ ~ ~

Each Other's Hearts

Monday 05/06/2019 — Wooly Bear nuzzles me each morning just like this. It's a great way to waken.

I try to remember her gentleness throughout my day and to extend it to everyone I come in contact with.

How about you? Gentle, loving, patient, tolerant, caring?

A good aim to have in mind.

~ ~ ~

Open Faces

Tuesday 05/07/2019 — When I was in the middle of taking "purple pictures" a few weeks ago, I came across this clump of flowers that springs up every year beside my front path. I have no idea what they are—some sort of wild aster, perhaps? But they grow without my having to do anything to encourage them—other than not mowing them down.

The dappled sunlight is pouring through the early spring leaves of a sassafras tree. That's another live being I didn't plant. Did the squirrels bury a seed? Did a robin poop one out just where it would land on a bit of fertile soil?

I willingly accept the morning shade from the sassafras and the bright happiness of these white and gold flowers.

Look for beauty today.

~ ~ ~

Official Flower

Wednesday 05/08/2019 — Growing up in an Air Force family means that I'm truly a military brat. When we call ourselves that, it's a term of recognition, not a pejorative. It's funny how we tend to gravitate to each other at parties. Give me a whole room full of strangers, and I'll end up talking to someone else who grew up on military bases.

Maybe this is why I like dandelions so much. In addition to the fact that bees depend on dandelion flowers and other weeds to get them through the nectar-deficient early springtime.

Let your dandelions thrive!

~ ~ ~

Rows

Thursday 05/09/2019 — Since we seem to be talking about dandelions—or at least, I was talking about them yesterday—we might as well discuss weeds in general.

I don't think I'm going to grow in a row today.

I think I'll spread out across the countryside any which way I want to.

I think I'm going to have a GREAT day!

Fran Stewart

Change that thought. I *know* I'm going to have a great day.

How about you?

~ ~ ~

Big name donors for Notre Dame

Friday 05/10/2019 — Really? They're going to rebuild it in less than a day? Even 700 million euros couldn't accomplish that.

I just returned home from a visit with my sister in Colorado. While there, her town newspaper ran a story about a local nursery that was holding "Edible Fairy Garden Classes."

I truly did not know that fairies were edible. Maybe only some types of them are (?)

Grrrr! Misplaced modifiers are a big no-no, but they keep cropping up.

Have you spotted any today?

> GLOBALNEWS.CA
> **Big-name donors pledge 700M euros to rebuild Notre Dame cathedral in less than 24 hours**

~ ~ ~

Can't Measure

Saturday 05/11/2019 — I returned yesterday afternoon from a trip to Colorado to visit my sister, and while there I saw plenty of examples of many of these qualities. Diana, as I've mentioned before in these posts, grew up with undiagnosed bipolar disorder, a condition that stops thousands of people in their tracks before they even begin to live their lives.

Diana is an artist, though. She always has been. She just didn't know it for a long time. She is one of the most creative women I've ever known—and believe me, I know a LOT of highly creative women. Her strength and determination, her work ethic and sheer grit, her fortitude in the face of almost insurmountable odds—all of these qualities, un-measurable by any standardized test—saved her life and helped to make her one of the role models of my life. She wrote a book called *Depression Visible: The Ragged Edge*. If you've ever known anyone with depression, you need to read it.

My big sister, Diana Alishouse. A true miracle.

Fran Stewart

~ ~ ~

Wake Before I Sleep

Monday 5/13/2019 — I used to send my sister "art cards" – little poems I'd written and printed on a tiny rectangle of paper. I never knew that she saved them. Never, that is, until last week when I visited her in Colorado and we browsed through some of her old photograph albums. And there was a poem I'd written in December of 2005.

I'd completely forgotten about it.

But as I re-read it, I remembered so vividly the impetus that had generated the poem. The reminder to myself that, just a decade and a half before the poem, I'd been contemplating suicide.

It took me a long time to "wake to the possibilities of my life."

I'm so glad I finally got there.

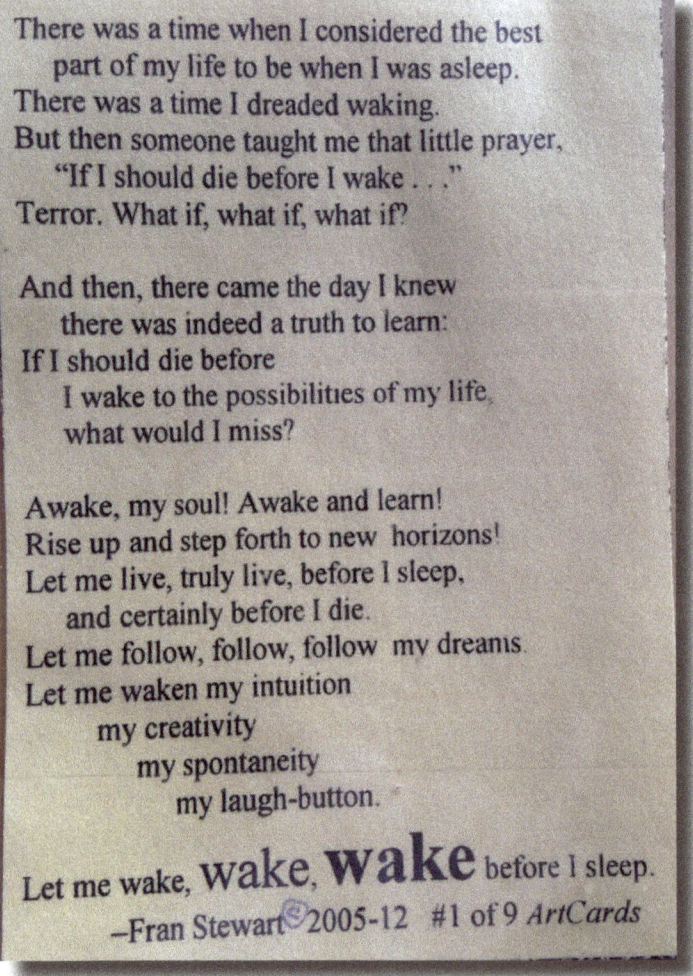

~ ~ ~

Cat Toys

Tuesday 5/14/2019 — One of Wooly Bear's favorite playthings is a long piece of crumpled packing paper that originally protected an order of books. I wonder sometimes why anyone ever buys cat toys.

It was the same with the kids when they were little. Presents were never nearly as much fun as the boxes and ribbons they were wrapped in.

This is one of those facts of life that few people ever write about. I don't think I've ever read a book where the children ignore the toys and play with the bows, but we all know it's true. Maybe someday in the distant future we will have evolved to a waste-less society in which every bit of packaging has multiple uses. What will people then think of the landfills of today?

I can just about hear them: "Look at all the toys they threw away!"

~ ~ ~

Bigger than Problems

Wednesday 5/15/2019 — Remember that old song that says, "When I'm worried and I can't sleep, I count my blessings instead of sheep"?

I was thinking about it last night and felt so overwhelmed and over-awed by all the blessings I experience every single day. I was also somewhat daunted by realizing how frequently I forget to recognize them as blessings.

Fran Stewart

Today my focus will be on seeing the miracle in each moment, including this one, in which my words reach out to you. Whether I've met you or not, you are a blessing in my life, and I delight in spending these few moments with you every morning. Today you—a blessing indeed—will stay in my thoughts.

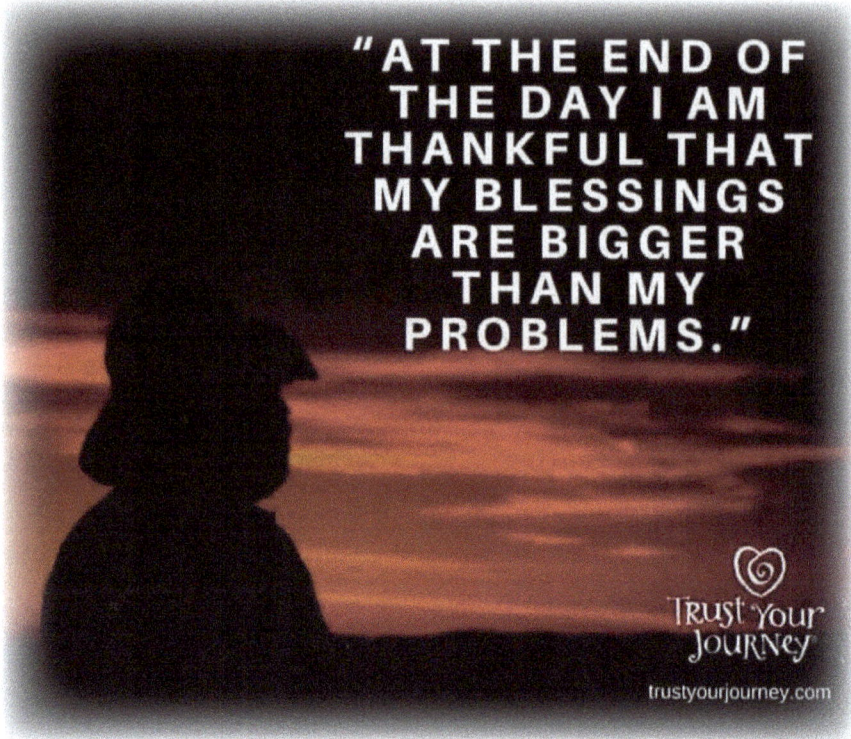

~ ~ ~

Back of my Card

Thursday 5/16/2019 — Three days ago, someone left a comment on my post about my "art card poem" asking "Have you ever done a book before?"

That was the first time it ever occurred to me that someone might have found these daily posts of mine without having come here through the route of my books. In my reply to her, I posted a photo of the back of my business card, which lists 16 of my 18 published books. [**2020 Note:** I'm up to more than 25 now.]

Since you might not like to plow through reading all the comments each day, you might have missed her question and my reply, so I thought I'd go ahead and post it for everyone to see. If you've read any of my books and like them, I'd appreciate it if you'd spread the word through a share of this post.

If you've never read any of my books, I'd love it if you'd give them a try. The two mystery series are listed here in the order in which they should be read.

If you've read only one or two, now you'll know which one(s) come next.

I love being helpful!

~ ~ ~

Out of Nothing

Friday 5/17/2019 — I'm sure this picture was photo-shopped, but I still like it. A lot.

Why am I thinking along these lines this morning? It's because of something one of my fans, an 8th-grade student, said to me a couple of weeks ago when she finished reading PINK AS A PEONY, the next to the last book in my Biscuit McKee Mystery Series. "I googled Martinsville and Keagan County, and I couldn't find them anywhere in Georgia. Did you really just create them out of nothing?"

Well, yes and no. You see, a writer is in many ways a photo-shopper. We take a mental picture we've been carrying around and adjust a little bit here, shade a little bit there, lighten this, darken that, add a whole series of elements, subtract just as many, and—Voilá—we have precisely the picture we want to convey, whether it's a town, a county, or an interloper among the meerkats.

In these daily "mini-memoirs" of mine, I'm not writing fiction, but I'm sharing with you a portion—a selected portion—of my thoughts and feelings. Much like this "third from the left" guy, you see what I choose to reveal about my day, about my life. What I write here is true; it's a reflection of how I feel right now when I'm writing it, but it is in subtle ways photo-shopped, to present just a sliver at a time. Put together, all these posts will give you a composite picture of me. That's one reason I'm seriously considering compiling all these posts into a book that will make it easier for you to see who and what and why I am, and a little bit about what makes a writer tick.

I enjoy it when you message me sharing your moments of insight. Together, even if we've never met, we can make a connection that, like a photograph, captures a moment in both our lives.

Keep in touch.

~~~

Fang Shui

Saturday 5/18/2019 – I know darn well the litterboxes in my house are in the wrong places, but—doggone it—the people who invented feng shui did so thousands of years before litterboxes were invented.

For that matter, everybody had outdoor latrines back then, didn't they, so there was no concession made for where to put the bathroom(s).

And don't get me started on the garage … Talk about the wrong placement.

~ ~ ~

Door Lock

Sunday 5/19/2019 — I've decided the litterbox for Fuzzy Britches is most definitely in the wrong place. Not because of feng shui, but because aliens invaded my house last week.

That's the only conclusion possible.

Last week I was out of town Monday through Friday, visiting my sister in Colorado. My daughter Veronica came over to the house each day to feed the cats and play with them. I told her she didn't need to clean out the litterboxes. I'd scoop them before I left on Monday and clean them out again when I returned on Friday. For just those few days, the cats would be fine.

Right.

And they were just fine. Except . . .

When I returned on Friday, I cleaned out the upstairs litterboxes, the ones Wooly Bear uses. Then downstairs to clean the one that sits outside on the "catio." This is a part of my front porch, completely enclosed with heavy hardware cloth screening, thick enough that possums and raccoons can't get into it.

There are only two ways into the catio. The cats can come and go year-round through a window cat-flap. They love sitting out there in the early morning sunshine, watching the birds at the multiple feeders, and checking out the chipmunks who scurry though the front yard. They're protected from rain by the wide overhang. They have a cat-tree to climb, scratch, and perch on. Even in the winter, they have ready access to the outside porch through the cat flap window that is sealed with weather-stripping all around.

The second way into the catio is through a locking screen door (reinforced with top to bottom hardware cloth).

Fran Stewart

Usually I take the key, which is attached to a heavy bright red carabiner, from the basket near the front door, unlock the screened door, clean the litterbox, sweep out the catio, relock the door, return the key to its basket, dispose of the litter mess, and go on about my daily life. I've had this same routine every day or two for YEARS.

But last Friday, when I went to take the key out of the basket, it wasn't there.

I've looked everywhere. Everywhere. Without exception. Except, I suppose, for the one place where the key is. Wherever that may be.

The lock is a special one that can't be jimmied.

So now, instead of easily cleaning out the litterbox every morning, I have a new routine. It started three days after I returned from Colorado when I was desperate and Fuzzy Britches was quite upset with me.

I moved the inside cat tree away from the window, shifted a nearby table out of the way, took the cat-flap window insert out, removing all the weather-stripping in the process. Then I climbed out the window (it's a sash-type, so I had to sort of bend in half to get out there), and cleaned the litterbox. I couldn't sweep, because I'd forgotten to take the broom out the window with me. Then I climbed back in, replaced the window (without the weather-stripping), replaced the table and the cat tree.

Later on today, I'm scheduled to do it all again.

Would somebody please ask those aliens to return my key?

Or—do you know how to pick a lock?

~ ~ ~

Picture of Joy

Monday 5/20/2019 — Joy! This is how I feel this morning, like spreading my arms to the rising sun. It isn't yoga, it isn't some sort of sun-worship. It's pure and simple and overwhelming happiness.

When I moved to Georgia 26 years ago, I built an arbor (complete with a bench on either side) and planted a New Dawn thornless rose. A couple of years later, this was the result.

I don't live in that house anymore, but I carry those roses in my heart.

What picture of joy do you carry in your heart?

~ ~ ~

Poison Ivy Incursion

Tuesday 5/21/2019 — I'm horribly susceptible to poison ivy. It landed me in the emergency room once a very long time ago when my daughter's dog snuggled with me after having apparently rolled in a patch of the stuff.

Over the years I've grown from being absolutely terrified of it to learning how to deal with it, so when I found this lovely vine—it IS lovely, don't you agree?—clambering up a wooden planter next to my front path, I dealt with it calmly. That's a lot better than the heartbeat-racing panic I used to experience just at the sight of those three leaves.

I save the plastic bags that my newspaper is delivered in three days each week. My hand and forearm fit nicely into one bag; I slip on another layer of plastic; I gather the vine from the top down into the dual layered plastic until I reach the ground, where I pull the roots up completely.

Then it's just a matter of slipping the rest of the bag carefully from around my arm down over the leaves, stem, and roots, making sure that none of my skin comes in contact with any part of the plant. Presto! I have a fully encased double-layer bag of poison ivy that I then dump into the trash.

Simple. No racing heart, no panic, no outrageous fear. Just a matter of seeing clearly what needs to be done and then doing it in the most efficient manner. Believe me, it's much better that way.

~ ~ ~

Squirrel Incursion

Wednesday 5/22/2019 — Okay, tell me the truth. How many squirrel-proof birdfeeders have you bought over the years?

The birds that grace my yard (and who eat a LOT of bugs and mosquitos) love peanuts. I buy the things in 20-pound bags and go through a lot of them when it's just the birds eating them. But one of the pesky gray squirrels figured out how to get up onto my supposedly squirrel-proof feeding stations. Now he's eating away at my supposedly squirrel-proof peanut feeder. This morning, when I looked out the front window, I saw that he'd managed to push open the lid. He must have gotten tired of gnawing on the bottom of it. Needless to say, the peanuts were all gone.

<<Sigh>>

A Gardener's Delight?

Thursday 5/23/2019 — Each individual leaflet is bigger than the palm of my hand. I went to the library yesterday and took the time to snap a photo of what looked like the biggest healthiest poison ivy vine imaginable. Those are my fingers in the picture to give you an idea of the size. All along the parking lot beside the library, these vines wind in and out of the trees that separate the library from the subdivision next door.

And I thought my puny little P.I. vine of two days ago was a problem.

You know what the real problem is? These plants are BEAUTIFUL. They're also very beneficial to birds, who love to eat the seeds and are not affected by the poisonous oils. In the autumn, the leaves turn a luscious red. Poison ivy grows abundantly in all sorts of soil conditions, and they can survive almost any drought. A real gardener's delight. Right?

I wrote a character into one of my Biscuit McKee Mysteries who was a lot like poison ivy. Lovely, adaptable, durable . . . and downright toxic.

[**2020 Note:** Before you have a hissy fit, I will admit that one of my readers messaged me saying that it wasn't poison ivy. I'd been so concentrating on "leaves of three" that I ignored the shape of the leaves. It's still an invasive plant, but it's not *Toxicodendron radicans.* It's kudzu!]

~ ~ ~

Edible Fairies?

Friday 5/24/2019 — Don't you love headlines? And misplaced adjectives?

I never knew fairies were edible. How about gnomes? How about sprites? How about will-o'-the-wisps?

A miniature fairy garden of edibles?

A fairy garden of miniature edibles?

An edible garden of miniature fairies?

~ ~ ~

Crying Over Breakfast

Saturday 2/25/2019 This morning as I took my early walk—before the humidity and temp made walking unbearable—this *Stella d'Oro* daylily greeted me next to my front path. It's the first *Stella* bloom of the season, and I was glad to see it, even though the daylily is not a plant bees gather nectar or pollen from. I wish I hadn't planted so many daylilies way back when.

The sad news, though, is that despite the fact that my golden rain tree has been blooming for two weeks, I have yet to see a single bee on it. Usually it's a bee magnet, and as we go into June it continues to bloom and usually attracts pollinators of all sorts. But this year? Nobody's visiting.

I'm afraid that means that someone within a three or four-mile radius of here has sprayed RoundUp, one of the worst bee-killers imaginable. It doesn't kill immediately. Instead, it is absorbed into the pollen. The bee takes that infected pollen back to the hive, and eventually every bee in the hive can be affected, i.e. killed.

I haven't seen any bees on my clover or dandelion blossoms, either. I think I'll go cry some over breakfast.

~ ~ ~

Memorial Day

Monday 2/27/2019 – So often military personnel are defined by the wars during which they served. The justification for the military is based on fighting wars that make a lot of money for a lot of companies. What would happen though if we reinstituted the draft for everyone and put those people to work—not fighting, but rebuilding America's crumbling bridges and highways, planting trees, constructing playgrounds, repairing public buildings, cleaning streets?

I went to college as an adult and therefore wasted a lot less time with partying and stressing out. I was more focused by that point. My dad served in the Civilian Conservation Corps before he went into the Air Force. Thank you, Dad, for all the things you taught me.

Two years of mandatory paid civic service might go a long way toward solving a lot of the problems this country is experiencing.

Something to think about this day.

~ ~ ~

Chipmunk Sighting (?)

Tuesday 5/28/2019 – I had to laugh at myself yesterday when I looked out at the birdfeeder and saw a chipmunk rummaging through the dropped seeds just on the other side of the big rocks at the bottom of my bird feeder. The reddish brown of his coat with those distinctive white stripes was unmistakable. But then the little fella hopped up in the air and flew off.

It wasn't a chipmunk after all. It was a brown thrasher. It wasn't a rodent. It was a bird.

Maybe I need to get my eyes checked.

Have you made any silly mistakes like this lately?

Homemade Candied Ginger

Wednesday 5/29/2019 – Yesterday someone asked me if I'd done anything special over the long weekend. Well, yes, as a matter of fact.

I've been buying candied ginger, a favorite treat with its peppery spicy tang, from a spice shop in a nearby town. But I got to wondering whether I could make my own. Amazing what one can find on the Internet.

I found a recipe that looked fairly simple.

It was simple, all right, but where it said cook for 35 minutes, it actually took 55 minutes to soften the sliced-up ginger root. On top of the twenty or so minutes it took me to peel the blinkin' thing.

Then instead of 20 minutes to crystallize, it took 30.

I don't mind spending that kind of time baking bread from scratch, but the next time I need candied ginger, I'm going back to the spice shop (even though what I created was delicious).

What would you rather make than buy? What would you rather buy than make?

~ ~ ~

Bee Happy

Thursday 5/30/2019 – My yard is the only one in my neighborhood that is inviting to bees, birds, and frogs – three species that give us a pretty good indication of just what shape our world is in. If the bees go away (that's a euphemistic way of saying "if we kill them all off") we'll lose 1/3 of our food supply. If the birds go away, there's a good chance we'll be overrun by mosquitos and other pesky insects. If the frogs go away, we'll know our water supply is in truly bad shape. Mother Earth will be crying.

Fran Stewart

As of today, I have birds and frogs, but I haven't seen a single bee so far this season. Honeybees, bumblebees, no bees. If you live within five miles of my house, and if you've used Roundup on the weeds in your yard, there's a good chance you're the one who's killed off all the bees that used to pollinate my yard.

A few years ago, after I installed two beehives on my back deck, my neighbors up the street told me they had the biggest fig harvest ever from the fig tree in their back yard. Before my bees came, they'd get just enough figs for their family. After my bees spent a few months pollinating the fig blossoms, Gene and Jan had enough figs to feed the neighborhood.

Why, why, why are we doing this to our Mother?

~ ~ ~

Becoming Dandelions

Friday 5/31/2019 – I know these little fellas aren't responsible for their hair—uh—feathers, but wouldn't life feel more whimsical if we could all run around like this occasionally without feeling conspicuous?

There's a lot to be said for spontaneity.

June 2019

GCFAAA

Saturday 6/1/2019 – I had so much fun yesterday! From 7:30 in the morning until 4:30 in the afternoon, I played the part of a patient so that paramedics-in-training could complete their final testing before heading into their firefighter training. There were ten of us from the Gwinnett Citizen Fire Academy Alumni Association who volunteered to serve as "simulated patients." Four served as runners, picking up the completed test scores, delivering them to the main staging area, and doing all sorts of paperwork. The rest of us (each in a separate room) were given individualized scripts that we had to stick to very closely.

One after another, more than a dozen paramedic students came into the room where I sat with the testing official and one helper, and had to assess what the problem was and then treat me accordingly.

I got to be a totally drunk 34-year-old who had just swallowed an entire bottle of prescription meds. I had heart palpitations and eventually had to go into a seizure and then go unconscious. I had a hard time not laughing when one of the recruits forgot to ask me my age or my weight. He estimated that I was 60 years old and placed my weight at 180 lbs. Twelve fewer years and a lot of pounds more??? And there I was "unconscious" and couldn't correct him.

We couldn't take pictures, but I doubt you'd want to see me drooling anyway!

It's good to live in a county where the firefighters are so well trained, especially since a large majority of the calls are for medical assistance rather than fires. Congratulations to all the men and women who passed their exams yesterday. I was happy to do my small part to help.

p.s. I'll have some exciting news for you on Monday. In the meantime, have a lovely weekend.

~ ~ ~

BeesKnees!

Monday 6/3/2019 – Finally! I decided it was time for me to publish the story of my journey into, through, and out of beekeeping. Tomorrow *BeesKnees #1: A Beekeeping Memoir* will be released as an e-book through all the usual e-book channels.

I'm so happy that I've put this together. It's the story of a chunk of my life beginning in October of 2010.

If you were a fan of my 600-day blog at www.beeskneesbeekeeping.blogspot.com, then you might be interested in this updated version. It's a lot easier to read this way (rather than having to scroll backwards through 600 posts!)

The best thing is, you don't have to "bee" a beekeeper to enjoy the journey.

Let me know what you think of it. I'd love hearing from you.

~ ~ ~

Eli's Gulls

Tuesday 6/4/2019 – I'm listening to the dawn chorus this morning, relishing the deep-throated music from my wind chimes on the front porch, and enjoying the cool breeze—YES! COOL!—wafting through the house from open windows on the east and west sides. The forecast says we'll be getting rain and thunderstorms for the next week, and my parched trees think that's a very good idea. I hope the rain is gentle enough not to cause damage. The ground is so completely dried up, though, it will take a while before it will be able to absorb the rain.

My dad used to call that kind of gentle rain a "Mississippi drizzle." I wrote about it, or rather I had my characters talk about that kind of rain in one of the books of my WHITE AS ICE quadrilogy.

What does all this have to do with this photo my son took of a Florida sunrise? Absolutely nothing, I suppose, except that I was talking of dawn and birds.

One good thing for which I'm grateful is that no matter what the weather, I hold joy within me. No matter what the outer circumstances, I can choose to embrace life.

I hope you make that choice today as well.

~ ~ ~

Cool Numbers

Wednesday 6/5/2019 – What, you might ask yourself, does Fran do when she has some time to wait before her daughter picks her up to attend a session of the Landmark Forum? There I was all dressed up with a few minutes to spare. I'd already done my meditations for the day; I was listening to the birds at the feeders; and I wanted something to do with my hands.

Did you know that 111,111 times 111,111 equals 12,345,654,321 – Cool, huh?

Even better yet, 111,111,111 times 111,111,111 = 12,345,678,987, 654,321.

After that, Veronica drove up, so I had to go back to doing normal things. But my jaunt into math heaven had been great fun.

By the way, while I was there last night, I signed up to do a repeat of the Landmark Forum in the fall. Looking forward to it. It's been 20 or so years since I took that weekend seminar the last time.

~ ~ ~

Women on D-Day

Thursday 6/6/2019 – I'm in awe of these women, and I'm happy to support the Red Cross for their disaster relief efforts.

One other little note of trivia: Can you imagine heading off to a war zone wearing culottes and saddle shoes?

Here's a Normandy Beach landing photo they don't show you in textbooks. Brave women of the Red Cross arriving in 1944 to help the injured troops.

~ ~ ~

Your Own Voice

Friday 6/7/2019 – Listen to your own voice, your own soul. I've been doing a lot of listening lately, and I've come to wonder about the people who do things that seem to me to be outrageous, despicable, and/or downright wrong.

Are they listening to their own voice, to their own soul? Everything in me would like to say, "Well, obviously not!" But then I have to return to the thought that we each have a journey that only we as individuals can make. What seems right (or wrong) to you may seem wrong (or right) to me.

So, do we just sit back and let people do whatever they want to? After all, it's their own soul's journey—right?

Well, no. I've come to this way of thinking because I found recently that several of my friends simply assume that I believe the same way they do. Why? Because I haven't expressed my opinions on what I believe is a highly personal matter.

My still inner voice has been telling me lately that there is an injustice rampant now that I can no longer stay silent about. I don't intend to preach about it. I don't intend to do any ranting. But tomorrow, I'd like to share with you a most thoughtful article that I hope you'll be willing at least to read. It will be my still small voice expressing (through someone else's well-written words) where I stand.

Tomorrow's post only—after that I'll go back to my daily musings. Some will be thoughtful, some will be slightly grumpy, some will be funny, some will be informational. All of them will, I hope, serve to connect us rather than divide us.

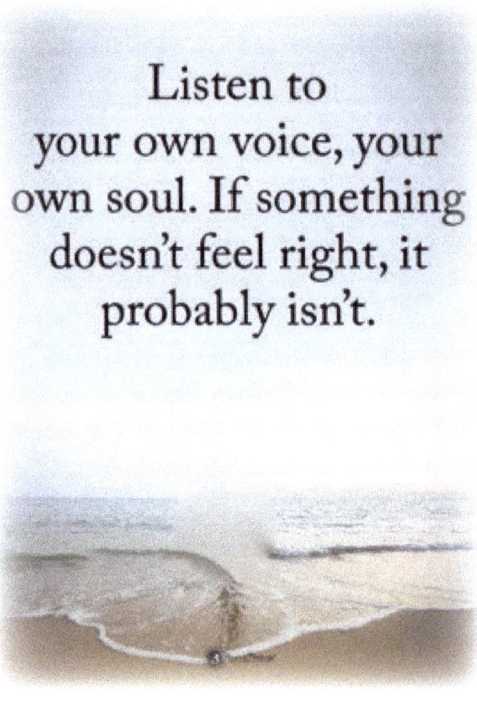

~ ~ ~

The Wrong Bodies

Saturday 6/8/2019 – As promised yesterday, I'm taking a stand to state what I believe. I'm not doing this to foist my belief on anyone else. I'm simply making it clear where I stand. If you disagree, I will respect your choice to believe what you want to believe, but I ask that you respect my choice as well. I can no longer remain silent, since silence too often implies consent.

I make this article available for you to read because it so clearly says what I feel needs to be said.

To find it online, search for *we're controlling the wrong bodies*, which is the title of the article.

Here is a small excerpt from that article from scarymommy.com:

We still don't have a birth control pill for men, largely because in clinical trials, [men] couldn't handle the same side effects we experience every day. Women can be forced to deal with side effects like blood clots, high cholesterol, weight gain, and mood fluctuations....

"The issue was that … the side effects [were] too demanding or taxing," Dr. Tomer Singer, director of reproductive endocrinology and infertility at Lenox Hill Hospital in New York City, told Healthline. …

We protect men at all costs, while constantly telling women they have total responsibility for what happens before they get pregnant, but no say in what happens after.

And here's another quote from a spin-off article on the same website:

Hormonal birth control is widely available to women, and such side effects as weight gain, depression, mood changes, and acne are considered par for the course.

~ ~ ~

Important Spine

Monday 6/10/2019 – I'm headed to my chiropractor later today for a tune-up, so I thought this little reminder was apt.

Think about it. The entire upper part of our skeleton is attached to the spine. Where would we be without it?

Here's a great big thank you to Dr. Patti Seebach, my wonderful chiropractor!

~ ~ ~

My Human

Tuesday 6/11/2019 – As I work on updating and formatting my BeesKnees Beekeeping Memoir, I've had time to reflect on the similarities and differences between cats and bees. To begin with, they're both fuzzy, but the fuzz on a bee is electrostatically charged—think of rubbing a balloon across your hair and then sticking it to the wall—so pollen will stick to the fuzz. A cat's fur becomes electrostatic only when I use certain types of brushes on her, so I avoid those types of brushes. It's no fun shocking a cat when she reaches out to sniff my finger.

The biggest difference, though, was that, although the bees from my back-deck hives were curious about me and often crawled around investigating my arms and hands, they never gave hugs, never cuddled, never were content simply to "bee" close to me. I've had plenty of lap cats, but never a lap bee.

Still, I loved going out early each morning with my cup of tea, sitting right next to the hives, and listening to the bee song as they went about their work.

Word of warning: don't ever take toast spread with honey near a beehive. They'll want to reclaim it.

~ ~ ~

Feet!

Wednesday 6/12/2019 – A whole bunch of years ago, my son took this picture of his niece and nephew. I've always loved it, and wanted to share it with you this morning just to brighten your day. And mine.

© Yelloideas Photography

~ ~ ~

More Stately Mansions

Thursday 6/13/2019 – "Build thee more stately mansions, O my soul / As the swift seasons roll." I first read "The Chambered Nautilus" when I was in seventh grade, thanks to Miss Helen Johnson, my marvelous English teacher who helped instill in me a deep love of good poetry.

One of the exercises she gave us was to compare "Thanatopsis" by William Cullen Bryant to "Do Not Go Gentle" by Dylan Thomas, and then to compare both of those poems—which deal with our attitudes toward death—to this Holmes poem, which I believed then (as I do even more so now) concentrates more on our attitude toward living than on dying.

I know you could Google it—but I'd like to give you the entire text here. Do enjoy it, my friend.

==========

"The Chambered Nautilus"
by Oliver Wendell Holmes, Sr.
This is the ship of pearl, which, poets feign,
Sails the unshadowed main,—
The venturous bark that flings
On the sweet summer wind its purpled wings
In gulfs enchanted, where the Siren sings
And coral reefs lie bare,
Where the cold sea-maids rise to sun their streaming hair.

Its webs of living gauze no more unfurl;
Wrecked is the ship of pearl!
And every chambered cell,
Where its dim dreaming life was wont to dwell

Fran Stewart

As the frail tenant shaped his growing shell,
Before thee lies revealed,—
Its irised ceiling rent, its sunless crypt unsealed!

Year after year beheld the silent toil
That spread his lustrous coil;
Still, as the spiral grew,
He left the past year's dwelling for the new,
Stole with soft step its shining archway through,
Built up its idle door,
Stretched in his last-found home, and knew the old no more.

Thanks for the heavenly message brought by thee,
Child of the wandering sea,
Cast from her lap, forlorn!
From thy dead lips a clearer note is born
Than ever Triton blew from wreathèd horn!
While on mine ear it rings,
Through the deep caves of thought I hear a voice that sings:—

Build thee more stately mansions, O my soul,
As the swift seasons roll!
Leave thy low-vaulted past!
Let each new temple, nobler than the last,
Shut thee from heaven with a dome more vast,
Till thou at length art free,
Leaving thine outgrown shell by life's unresting sea!

=========

~ ~ ~

The Art of Sleeping in a Box

Friday 6/14/2019 – As an Air Force brat, I have often described my life as a series of boxes—each one a reflection of where I've lived. I'm fairly sure I've shared that observation with you before. The whole idea is that each place I've lived has been very much like a box. All my memories of any time of my life are defined within the limits of that particular box.

Each time my dad was reassigned, I closed up the box I'd been in and moved on to a new one.

I have a lot of those "boxes" to open and review now that I'm actively writing my memoirs.

Cats are great at boxes, as you'll see from these three photos from the Everyday Cats website. Looking back, I wish I'd been able to relax into some of my boxes the way they relax in theirs. But for the first forty-some-odd years of my life, I'd never been adopted by a cat, so I didn't have the opportunity to absorb their wisdom.

~ ~ ~

Keeping Clam

Saturday 6/15/2019 – As I work on updating and formatting the next volumes of my beekeeping memoirs, I'm somewhat—okay, I'm VERY—humbled by how many typos I've found in those original blog posts.

Fran Stewart

Most people, including writers themselves, see what they expect to see on a page. That's why editing is such an important aspect of writing.

I've been appalled recently to see the number of typos appearing in my local newspaper. But I try hard not to be too critical, since a number of errors slipped through in my last four Biscuit McKee mysteries.

At least I'm pretty sure I'm catching all the ones in *BeesKnees*.

After all, I'm keeping clam.

~ ~ ~

Who's Banned Plastic Bags?

Monday 6/17/2019 – I love CBC News. A couple of days ago they published a list of countries that banned plastic bags, along with the years in which they banned them.

So, how come we're so far behind a lot of the rest of the world?

I have a collection of canvas totes in my car that I take with me whenever I enter a store. Three of those bags came from Vermont—and I moved away from that state almost 27 years ago, which means I've been using those bags for more than 30 years, and they're holding up just fine. Sure, they have 30-plus years of stains on them. So what? Think of all the plastic bags that haven't gone into a landfill (or into the ocean) because of me.

Impressive, wouldn't you say?

How long ago did you decide not to accept any plastic bags? If you haven't made that choice, why not?

Photo Credit: 1 CBC News - Who's Banned Plastic Bags

~ ~ ~

Don't Disturb the Cat

Tuesday 6/18/2019 – This is what I felt like last night. It was bedtime; I'd reached a good stopping point in the book I'd been reading for the past hour; my legs felt like they were going to sleep, but the rest of me couldn't. Why not?

Fuzzy Britches had settled in for a lap nap—a L O N G one.

Of course, I finally just picked her up for a good snuggle. She put up with it for a few minutes and then

Fran Stewart

hopped off to head for her cat tree.

Did I feel put upon? Nope.

People who've never been owned by a cat probably won't understand.

~ ~ ~

significant otters

Wednesday 6/19/2019 – Good morning. I'm running a little late today. We had a great book club meeting last night, ending up with toasting marshmallows (indoors over candles) and then pairing them with chocolate and graham crackers. Has there ever been a better combination of tastes than those found in s'mores?

The upshot of it all, though, was that by the time I got home, the sugar and chocolate had worked their hyping effects on my system, and I wasn't at all sleepy. I picked up a puzzle book and started on crosswords and cryptograms. Three hours later I was still going strong.

So, this morning, Wooly Bear tried to wake me up at the usual time. I did manage to open one eyeball and saw a bright-eyed face peering at me over the comforter, rather like the little fella on the right of this first photo. You'll just have to use your imagination to substitute a black cat for a brown otter.

~ ~ ~

opened two gifts

Thursday 6/20/2019 – I'm feeling a need for a big dose of gratitude this morning. And this is a good place to start.

The miracle of sight! It deserves its own exclamation point. Even before I opened my eyes, though, I experienced the miracle of touch—when Wooly Bear nuzzled my face; the miracle of sound—when her purr resonated through the room; the miracle of smell—when she placed her front foot right beside my nose (yes—I do like the smell of kitty paws); the miracle of imagination—as I thought about what the day was going to bring.

I'm sure you'll have your own list of miracles. Now, let's just be sure we take the time to appreciate them.

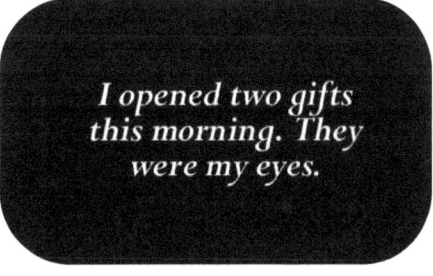

~ ~ ~

Idaho

Friday 6/21/2019 – I'm not sure my family know how very much I enjoy the photos they post on Facebook every few days. My daughter posts pictures of her with her children – and I duly copy them, title them, and save them in a photos folder called "family." She seldom forwards them to me—probably because she's never realized just how much the pictures mean to me.

My son posts photos and videos of his travels across the US. I feel like I travel virtually with him, and I certainly enjoy the trip(s).

Today I'd like to share with you one of Eli's striking photos of the Sawtooth Range in Idaho. Each morning when I check his FB page, I pull out my trusty atlas to pinpoint approximately where he is. Yesterday he was in the dark green spot, lower center.

Yes, I still have a printed AAA Atlas ©2004. It's eleven inches wide and seventeen inches tall. So much more satisfying than a cyber map.

 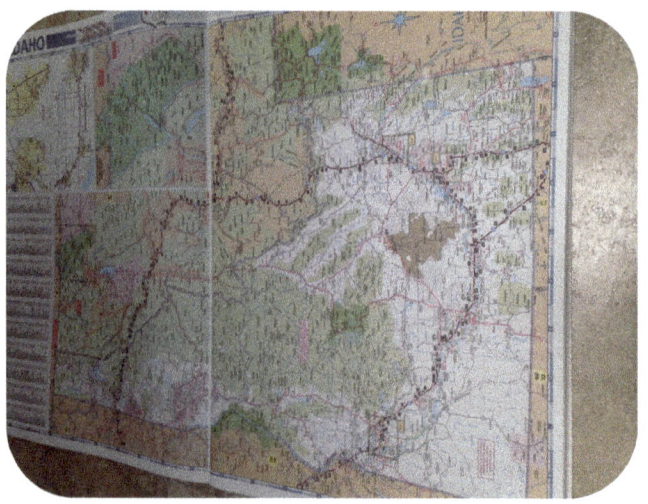

~ ~ ~

Jessa's Tea Parlor

Saturday 6/22/2019 – Guess what I did yesterday? My friend Polly Craig celebrated her 92nd birthday with high tea, hosted by Diane Staubus (2nd from the right in the photo). **Jessa's Tea Parlor** in Woodstock GA is a delightful venue, and we made great inroads on the meal. Everyone else had a chicken salad croissant, while I chose the Tomato-Basil Soup. Yum, yum, yum! The salad featured heirloom tomatoes grown in Jessa's own garden. Quadruple-yum! And we each had our own personal pot of tea. I tried the Rooibos Chai; Mozelle and Diane had BlueLady, Polly chose Jasmine, and Frances had . . . I can't recall, but there was a whole page of choices.

Check it out. You'll be glad you did.

Cat's Whiskers

Monday 6/24/2019 – Puns simply are not translatable. Dos batidoras are here shown lying on un gato – a far cry from "whiskers" on a cat.

I love English puns. I used a lot of plays on words in *Violet as an Amethyst*, my sixth Biscuit McKee mystery, never even thinking that it might be hard to translate.

I'm old enough to remember how a translation taken out of context in 1956 brought the US and Russia to the brink of a confrontation. The translated words were, "We will bury you," which Americans took to mean that Khrushchev threatened to annihilate us. In the context of the speech, however, his words meant, "We will survive you—when your way of life is long gone, we will still be around."

Fortunately, I doubt this cat's whisks (or whiskers if you will) could ever spark an international incident. Let's hope not, at least.

~ ~ ~

full groan

Tuesday 6/25/2019 – While we're talking about puns, here's the ultimate one—a pun about puns.

For some reason it reminds me of *paraprosdokians*. Don't you love that word? It comes from the combination of two Greek words. One means "against," and the other means "expectations." So a paraprosdokian is a sentence in which what you think is going to be said after the beginning phrase turns out to be pretty much the opposite to your expectation.

Like: "I used to be indecisive, but now I'm not so sure," a witticism from Welsh comedian Tommy Cooper.

Or "Where there's a will, I want to be in it."

Or "Americans can be counted on to do the right thing . . . after they'd tried everything else." That one was first said by Abba Eban (1915-2002), Israel's former Minister of Foreign Affairs. It's widely attributed to Winston Churchill – but either of those men had good reason to say it. Churchill did say, "If I agreed with you, we'd both be wrong."

Paraprosdokians and puns. You may groan, but you've gotta love 'em!

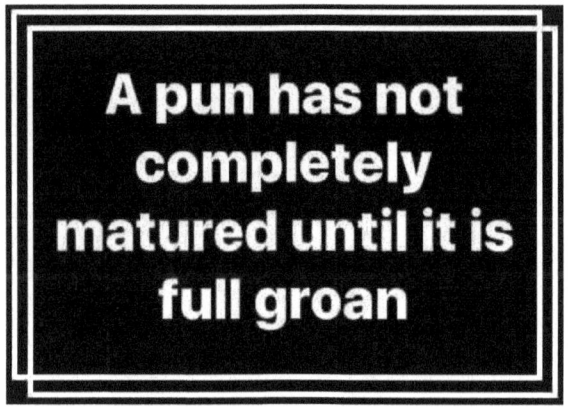

~ ~ ~

2004 Atlas

Wednesday 6/26/2019 – Maps. Did you ever really sit down and think about them?

My son posted a comment a couple of days ago thanking me for inculcating him with a love of maps. The funny thing is that it wasn't anything I was consciously trying to do. Sure, I do believe that instilling an appreciation for maps is important—although how parents do that nowadays I have no idea. How does one come to love a map app?

But a book of maps? Or one of those marvelous folded-up treasures that service stations used to give away for free? Now those are marvels if I ever saw one.

But let's think about the real marvel behind a map. Think about the first map ever drawn. How on earth did someone who had never seen the earth from a thousand feet overhead ever come up with the idea of drawing hills and rivers and settlements in spatial relationship to each other?

I can imagine a woman sitting beside a river trying to tell her friends just where she had found a particularly rich bed of edible roots. "Downriver," she'd say. But how to describe exactly where? Taking up a stick, she'd draw it in the sand: "Here the river bends in that direction, and beyond that a ways it takes a big turn the other way where this hill looms up." She draws the stick through the sand to indicate a barrier of some sort. "Just beyond that" — here she makes a mark with her stick, sort of an X-marks-the-spot — "you'll find the richest gatherings we've ever seen."

Voilà! The first map.

p.s. The Fuzzy Britches paws in this photo are an extra bonus.

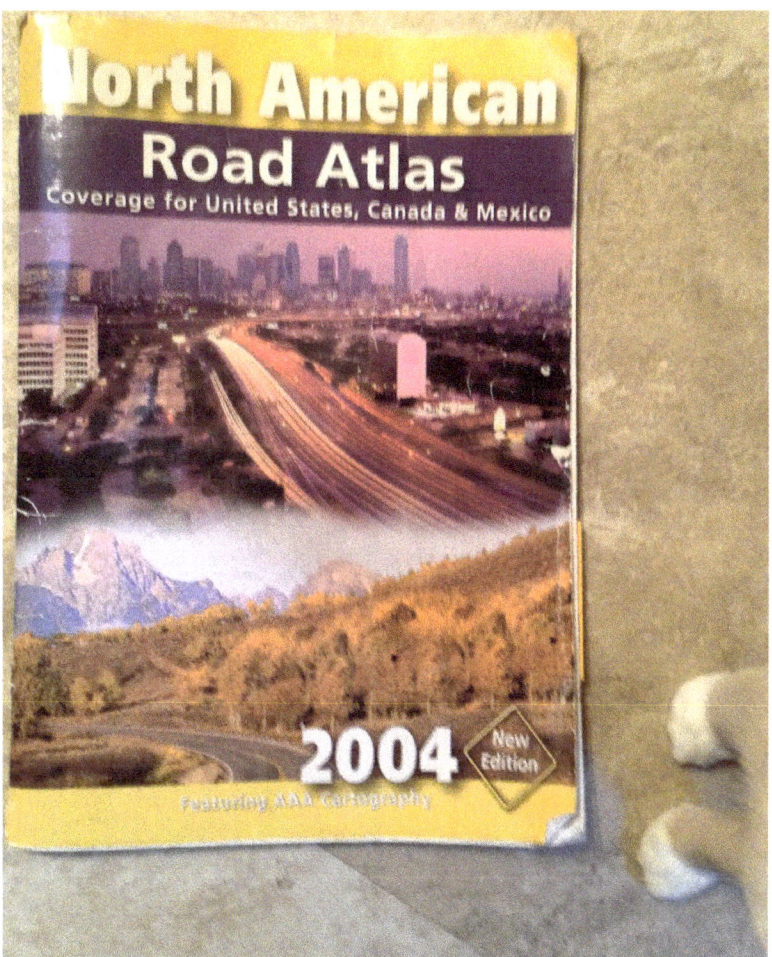

~ ~ ~

Idaho Pictures #2

Thursday 6/27/2019 – Speaking of maps, as we were yesterday, there's another component to maps that the increase in technology has made more available: the ability to tie a photo to a particular place. Now, I didn't do that with these photos that my son, Eli Reiman, took while hiking through the Sawtooth Range in Idaho, but I'm fairly sure that he has some sort of techno-labeling doodad that allows him to pinpoint exactly where each of his pictures originated.

Think, though, of what it was like before cameras. You've seen reproductions of old maps, I'm sure. The ones where the oceans are inhabited by fearsome sea monsters?

Fran Stewart

I like sunsets and wildflowers better.

~ ~ ~

The purpose of life

Friday 6/28/2019 – Despite what it says here, sometimes the purpose of life is simply to enjoy a cup of hot tea first thing in the morning.

Yeah, yeah, yeah. I'll get around to saving me and the rest of the world later.

~ ~ ~

600,000 plastic bottles

Saturday 6/29/2019 – Wouldn't it be wonderful to use plastic bottles—the one-use kind—for something else? Yesterday I saw a report on CBC News about a house built using 600,000 recycled plastic bottles.

Makes a lot of sense. Hopefully, if there turns out to be a demand for such technology, the costs will go down.

And don't you wonder what else entrepreneurs out there are dreaming up to help save us from our own garbage?

The biggest part of *Reduce, Reuse, Recycle* ought to be the first R. But if we don't reduce drastically, then why not figure out ways to use what otherwise will just fill up our dumps?

Wouldn't you agree?

To find the article, search for *CBC plastic bottle home nova scotia.*

July 2019

Asparagus

Monday 7/1/2019 – It's Asparagus Day!

I'm pretty sure I've shared this story with you before – in fact, I probably did it last July 1st. But I haven't shown you these other two pictures, the ones of me just before my son was born more than 4 decades ago.

One was taken on our dock leading out into Lake Iroquois. The next one was on the back deck after I'd gotten all dressed up to go to dinner at a neighbor's house.

It was at that dinner that I first tasted fresh-picked asparagus. How did I make it all those years without ever having had that experience? Well, I don't know exactly, other than that I had a mother whose idea of asparagus was to buy it in a can. No wonder I hated it.

But the fresh stuff? Wow!

The next day I went into labor, so I've always thought of July 1st as Asparagus Day.

Once it's a more reasonable hour out in Idaho, I'm going to call my son and wish him a happy one.

 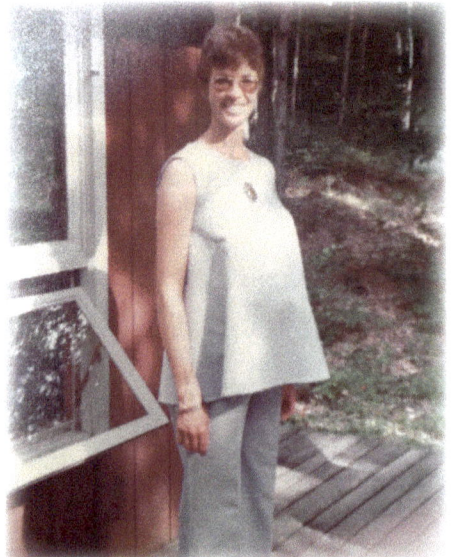

~ ~ ~

Vegan Meals

Tuesday 7/2/2019 -- Happy Birthday, Eli!

My son changed to a vegan lifestyle a number of years ago, and it's served him well ever since.

I used to have the idea that vegetarians (and vegans) must be missing a lot – but look at these photos of a couple of vegan meals (taken from a royalty-free website called pexels).

Hard to feel deprived when you're eating such beauty.

~ ~ ~

9 Days Difference

Wednesday 7/3/2019 – Nine Days. Can you believe it?

What am I talking about? I'm glad you asked.

The bees, both honeybees and bumblebees, love the bright yellow flowers of the *Koelreuteria paniculata* (Golden Rain Tree) that grows beside my driveway. It was easy for me to take a picture of this particular flowering branch since it hangs right down to nose level.

Exactly nine days later, I took the second picture, showing the abrupt change from flowers to seed pods.

As lovely as it is, I'd recommend that you DO NOT PLANT ONE in your own yard. At the time I planted it, I had no idea it was considered invasive. Every one of those green pods holds multiple seeds. Once the pods turn brown, they burst open and scatter the black ball-like seeds across my drive (and everywhere else they can reach). Then the rain disperses them downhill. I'm constantly digging up sprouts, not only around the tree itself, but all over the lower reaches of my yard.

Still, the honeybees and bumblebees do swarm around it while it's flowering.

<<sigh>> Guess I'll just keep digging up the extras.

~ ~ ~

Liberty and Justice for All

Thursday 7/4/2019 – I've been reading a number of documents lately, one of which has been an eye-opener.

In 2003, political scientist Dr. Lawrence Britt wrote an article called "Fascism Anyone?" It was published in the Spring 2003 issue of *Free Inquiry* (page 20). He studied the fascist regimes of Hitler (Germany), Mussolini (Italy), Franco (Spain), Suharto (Indonesia), and Pinochet (Chile), and found they all had 14 elements in common. He calls these the identifying characteristics of fascism. You may Google them, but I'd like to list them here in accordance with the Fair Use terms of the copyright laws.

The 14 characteristics (© 2003 *Free Inquiry magazine*) are:

1. Powerful and Continuing Nationalism: Fascist regimes tend to make constant use of patriotic mottos, slogans, symbols, songs, and other paraphernalia. Flags are seen everywhere, as are flag symbols on clothing and in public displays.

2. Disdain for the Recognition of Human Rights: Because of fear of enemies and the need for security, the people in fascist regimes are persuaded that human rights can be ignored in certain cases because of "need." The people tend to look the other way or even approve of torture, summary executions, assassinations, long incarcerations of prisoners, etc.

3. Identification of Enemies/Scapegoats as a Unifying Cause: The people are rallied into a unifying patriotic frenzy over the need to eliminate a perceived common threat or foe: racial, ethnic or religious minorities; liberals; communists; socialists, terrorists, etc.

4. Supremacy of the Military: Even when there are widespread domestic problems, the military is given a disproportionate amount of government funding, and the domestic agenda is neglected. Soldiers and military service are glamorized.

5. Rampant Sexism: The governments of fascist nations tend to be almost exclusively male-dominated. Under fascist regimes, traditional gender roles are made more rigid. Opposition to abortion is high, as is homophobia and anti-gay legislation and national policy.

6. Controlled Mass Media: Sometimes [the] media is directly controlled by the government, but in other cases, the media is indirectly controlled by government regulation, or sympathetic media spokespeople and executives. Censorship, especially in wartime, is very common.

7. Obsession with National Security: Fear is used as a motivational tool by the government over the masses.

8. Religion and Government are Intertwined: Governments in fascist nations tend to use the most common religion in the nation as a tool to manipulate public opinion. Religious rhetoric and terminology is common from government leaders, even when the major tenets of the religion are diametrically opposed to the government's policies or actions.

9. Corporate Power is Protected: The industrial and business aristocracy of a fascist nation often are the ones who put the government leaders into power, creating a mutually beneficial business/government relationship and power elite.

10. Labor Power is Suppressed: Because the organizing power of labor is the only real threat to a fascist government, labor unions are either eliminated entirely, or are severely suppressed.

11. Disdain for Intellectuals and the Arts: Fascist nations tend to promote and tolerate open hostility to higher education, and academia. It is not uncommon for professors and other academics to be censored or even arrested. Free expression in the arts is openly attacked, and governments often refuse to fund the arts.

12. Obsession with Crime and Punishment: Under fascist regimes, the police are given almost limitless power to enforce laws. The people are often willing to overlook police abuses and even forego civil liberties in the name of patriotism. There is often a national police force with virtually unlimited power in fascist nations.

13. Rampant Cronyism and Corruption: Fascist regimes almost always are governed by groups of friends and associates who appoint each other to government positions and use governmental power and authority to protect their friends from accountability. It is not uncommon in fascist regimes for national resources and even treasures to be appropriated or even outright stolen by government leaders.

14. Fraudulent Elections: Sometimes elections in fascist nations are a complete sham. Other times elections are manipulated by smear campaigns against or even assassination of opposition candidates, use of legislation to control voting numbers or political district boundaries, and manipulation of the media. Fascist nations also typically use their judiciaries to manipulate or control elections.

Copyright © 2003 *Free Inquiry magazine* Reprinted for Fair Use Only.

If you don't know what "fair use" means, I suggest you Google it.

Meanwhile, as soon as I sign off here, I plan to read the Declaration of Independence and then the U.S.

Fran Stewart

Constitution. That's something I do every year on this day. Are you willing to join me in that tradition?

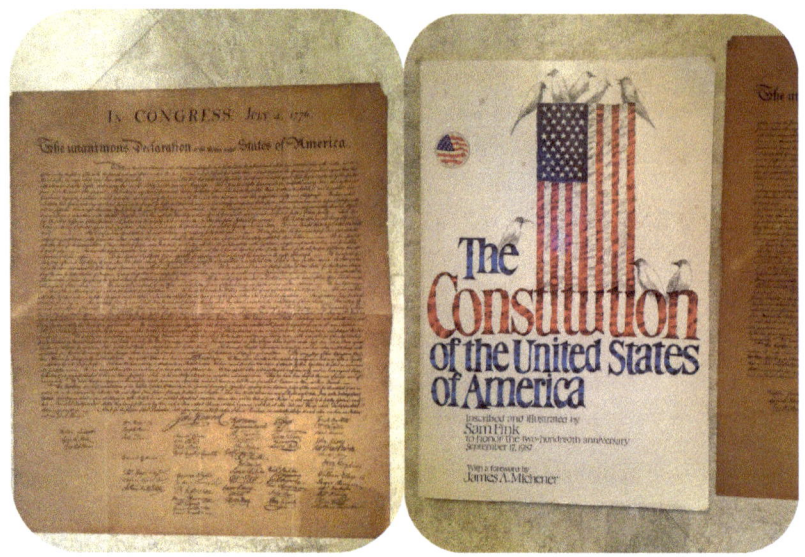

~ ~ ~

Carrots, Eggs, and Coffee

Friday 7/5/2019 – Volume #2 of my *BeesKnees Memoirs* was released yesterday as an e-book. I've had a lot of people ask me if and when a print version will be available. Thanks for asking. You've spurred me to do it, so I promise you, I'm working on it.

In the meantime, I thought you might like a little preview. This was an entry from Volume 5, which will be available in early October. It's a timely story, one that we all can take to heart. And, I must admit, I'd forgotten about it until I re-read it while I was preparing the manuscript for publication. Who knows how many other wonderful stories I've forgotten along the way?

= = = = = = = = =

Day #451:

A friend of mine in Australia shared an interesting story with me recently about a wise old woman who helped a younger woman deal with adversity. "Dig up some carrots," she said, "and gather some eggs, then bring me some ground coffee beans."

The young woman did as directed, and then was instructed to put them all in boiling water. So she took three pots, brought water to boil, and put the carrots in one, the eggs in another, and the coffee in the third.

"Look at them," the older woman said after a while. "What do you see?"

The young woman replied, "They've all cooked."

"Yes," said the wise woman, "but look at the differences. The **carrots** were hard and resistant when they were put in the water, but they softened up and gave in to the heat. The **eggs**, with their soft vulnerability, became hard in the boiling water. As for the **coffee**? Well, it changed the water!

We all have adversity. But how each one of us reacts to that adversity is up to us. Will we be carrots, eggs, or coffee?

= = = = = = = = =

What, you may ask, does this story have to do with bees? Well, not a lot, except to note that bees have lasted millions of years. I have to wonder what their secrets are.

~ ~ ~

If the Ocean …

Saturday 7/6/2019 – Just a passing thought for this weekend.

Salt water mixed with air.

I like that idea.

Calm myself? I like that even better.

Puppies Arrested

Monday 7/8/2019 – One of my favorite FB pages is "Captain Grammar Pants." She derives an inordinate amount of pleasure from newspaper headlines that ignore rules of grammar. The woman who writes the daily posts is an English professor named Sean Williams, and she recently released a book (I've ordered it, of course) called *English Grammar—100 tragically common mistakes and how to correct them*. Once I've read it, I'll be sure to let you know more about it.

Last month she posted this headline, bemoaning the fact that those little bitty puppies had been arrested. Hardly seems fair.

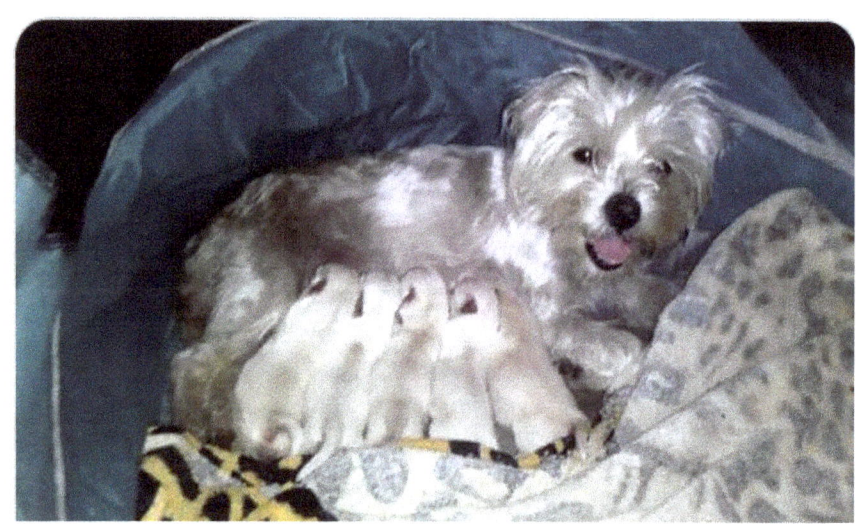

~ ~ ~

Aftermath

Tuesday 7/9/2019 – A few days ago, I had occasion to talk with someone a lot younger than I am. I wish I'd thought to show her this poem I wrote a dozen years ago. Reminiscing about childhood angst can get a woman so wrapped up in misery, it can turn debilitating.

But learning the lesson—that this, too, shall pass—frees one to love what is.

Of course, I'm not sure that my poem would have made any difference to her. After all, there's a long road between 5th grade and senior-hood. At least I remembered to tell her that we tend to compare our own perceived weaknesses with what we perceive as other people's strengths. I certainly did that with Dolores Foland, my 5th-grade nemesis.

I do wonder whatever happened to Dolores, or Dodie as she was known then. Anybody out there know her?

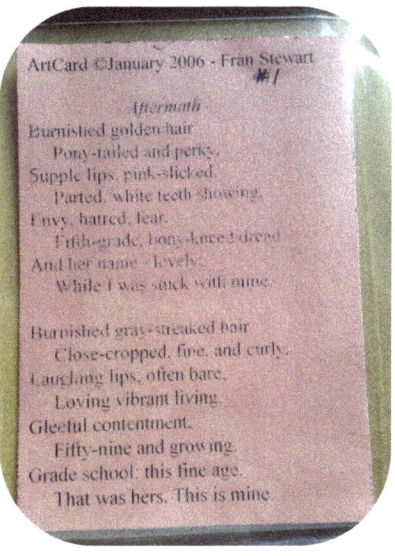

~ ~ ~

Rug to match the cat

Wednesday 7/10/2019 – I can certainly identify with this off the mark cartoon.

The other day Fuzzy Britches threw up her entire breakfast on the ramp that leads from one of the cat trees to the cat-flap door that gives her access to the "catio," the porch with heavy metal screening that allow her to sit outside but prevents raccoons from getting into the house.

Trouble is, the ramp is made of one of those corrugated cardboard scratching thingies (which, as you can see, she loves to scratch), so it looks rather ratty. I found out that you can't completely rinse partially-digested breakfast out of thick cardboard.

So, what did I do?

I'm glad you asked.

I lifted the whole thing and set it outside by the front stairs for the rest of the day. By late afternoon, hundreds—thousands—of teeny-weeny ants had cleaned it up completely. They got into all the furrows and crevices and did a lovely job. All I had to do was thump off the remaining ants, and the ramp was good to go.

Maybe I'll hire them. After all – they'll work for leftovers.

Fran Stewart

~ ~ ~

Calming Shelter Dogs

Thursday 7/11/2019 – Here we are again – my usual yearly diatribe against loud fireworks. I always stay home every evening from the 30th of June to the 5th or 6th of July, because a number of people in my neighborhood insist on loud firecrackers that begin booming at twilight and often keep on until almost midnight. My cats are fairly calm – but I think that's only because I remain with them.

This idea to calm shelter dogs sounds like a real winner. (Do a search for "people comfort shelter dogs July 4") Too late for this year, but wouldn't it be great if something like this sprung up at every shelter around the country?

Would you volunteer this way?

~ ~ ~

not my job

Friday 7/12/2019 – If you've been reading these posts of mine for any length of time, you've probably figured out that I'm an inveterate list-maker. Lists with—preferably—little check-off boxes to one side.

There's something so satisfying about making that little V with one long arm. That's a perfect description of a checkmark, wouldn't you say?

Well, here's another type of list: one that gives yes/no options. Here's a good one: *Not My Job* compared to *My Job*.

I was trying this morning to choose which is my favorite item from the right-hand list. I've decided it's all of them.

~ ~ ~

Didn't Like It

Saturday 7/13/2019 – See you on Monday.

Hint: You DID like the Monday one.

~ ~ ~

Fill the World

Monday 7/15/2019 – If you're a daughter, or you have a daughter, this one's for you.

p.s. See? I told you. You liked it.

Indigo, Violet, Gray

Tuesday 7/16/2019 - I'm embarrassed to admit that I just last weekend noticed for the first time that there's a box off to the side of this FB author page that contains something called "visitor posts." So I went looking through it Saturday morning. I'd just about given up scrolling down through it when I noticed one comment (from 9/21/2018). I did a copy and paste so you could see it:

= = = = = = = = =

> Horrible way to end indigo as an iris. What happens to boy or who susan's dad is. Probably won't read any more of your books. People like to know endings.

= = = = = = = = =

I realized that the woman who wrote this may have assumed I was too arrogant to have answered her—when the reality was that I hadn't yet completely figured out the ins and outs of Facebook. I wonder what else I've missed???

Anyway, here's my reply to her:

= = = = = = = = =

> Margaret - I have to apologize for not having replied to this. Today (almost a year after you wrote it) is the first time I've seen your message.
>
> I certainly understand your frustration. If this were a "stand-alone" novel, I'd agree with you 100%. The Biscuit McKee Mystery Series, though, was designed right from the start to be one sweeping story, as if each book were really simply a V-E-R-Y long chapter. They all hinge on the fact that Martinsville was founded in ways that nobody ever suspected—until the final four books (chapters??) of the 11-book series, when Biscuit and her friends finally begin to investigate the attic that she's been threatening to clean out in each of the previous seven books.
>
> If Susan and little Willie had shown up halfway through a six-inch-thick book, most people would see it as adding to the suspense. Believe me – the answers do come, but Susan's father isn't identified until the following book, *VIOLET AS AN AMETHYST*, and little Willie plays an important part in book #7, *GRAY AS ASHES*.
>
> This whole idea of one very long tale is the reason the book covers are designed the way they are, with the stripe at the top of each book showing the color of the next book – *ORANGE AS MARMALADE* has a yellow stripe; *YELLOW AS LEGAL PADS* has a green stripe, and so on.
>
> So, when all is said and done, I appreciate your comment. It would be lovely if at

some later date you decided to try all my books – in order. If not, thank you for having at least read one—and for having cared about the characters enough to be so thoroughly incensed.

I appreciate you.

= = = = = = = = =

[p.s. to my FB Followers: If you've sent me a message to which I didn't respond, would you send it again? Now I know how to find the darn things!]

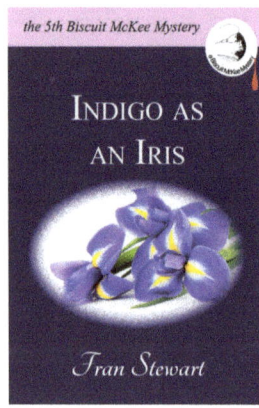 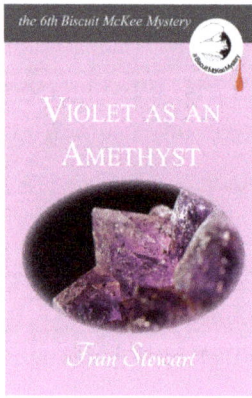 

~ ~ ~

e-books

Wednesday 7/17/2019 – While I'm admitting to being completely inept about various FB doodads (see yesterday's post), I might as well tell you I goofed when I started publishing my BeesKnees memoirs.

I used a marvelous site called Draft2Digital—check it out if you want to publish e-books—but I assumed that listing the book titles as **BeesKnees: A Beekeeping Memoir** and then noting the volume numbers would allow you to tell them apart. [#3 will be released on August 4th].

Only trouble is – They don't differentiate between volumes if the title is the same. And I wondered why people were having trouble ordering my books…

Luckily, when I asked, a kind person at D2D gave me the steps to follow, so now my titles are:

BeesKnees #1: A Beekeeping Memoir,

BeesKnees #2: A Beekeeping Memoir, and

BeesKnees #3: A Beekeeping Memoir.

Four, five, and six will follow at monthly intervals.

Whew!

Also, I found (all on my own!) a link D2D makes available so you can easily sign up to be notified each time I have a new book coming out. Here it is:

https://books2read.com/author/fran-stewart/subscribe/1/114185/

And if you'd like to see the gorgeous covers, I'm including those as well.

Fran Stewart

~ ~ ~

Complete Sentences

Thursday 7/18/2019 – At book club the other night, we were all set to discuss *A Glass Ocean*, historical fiction based on the sinking of the Lusitania. We'd been invited to "dress as poshly as possible," so of course I wore a gorgeous custom-made sequined outfit I'd had hanging in my closet for years. And pearls. Everybody else dressed comfortably, as usual. I rather stood out.

We dined, our usual potluck style, except that Ingrid had set the table with her best china, and there was gold flatware and real napkins, and lovely goblets for water or wine (or both).

Before we started, though, one of the women (almost 20 years younger than I) showed us an app that "ages" a photo, showing herself as what she'll look like when she's old. Then, of course, she showed "aged" pictures of her teenage children. "Here he is when he's old!"

Of course, I had to point to my own face, not a photo, here and now—and I was feeling very glamorous in my sequins—and proclaim, "Here I am when I'm old."

Sometimes being old feels VERY good!

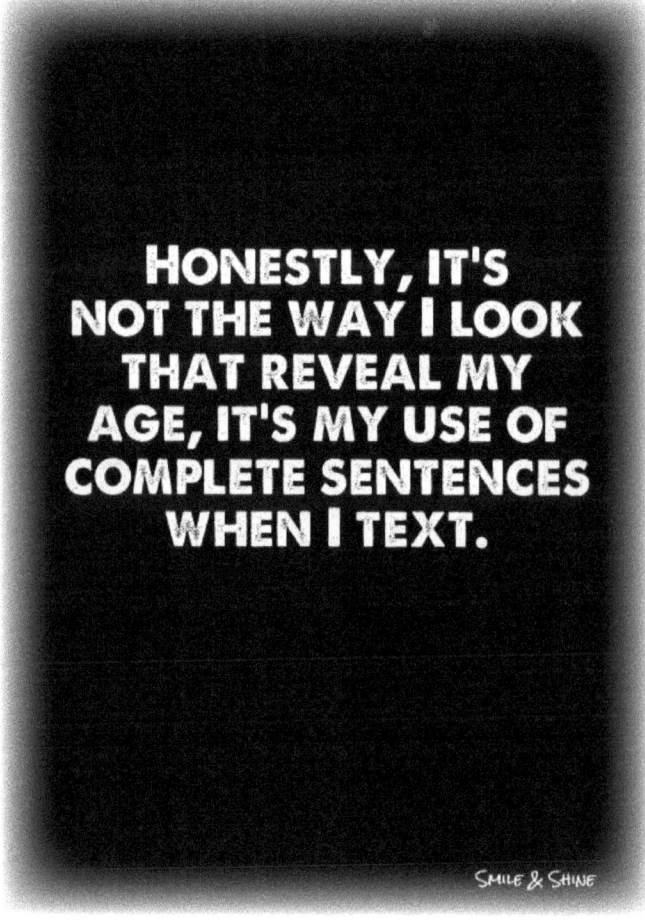

Solar Panels for Xmas

Friday 7/19/2019 – I've told you often how very glad I am of the forest in my back yard. Three sides of my house are tree-protected.

Only trouble is – that means solar panels won't work here. Phooey. I'd love to live mostly off-grid.

Still, I conserve electricity as much as I can. Last month, my electric bill (for an all-electric house) was $41.

Not bad, eh?

Dory in Gray

Saturday 7/20/2019 – Do you love scary movies? Scary books? Scary haunted houses in October?

Not I.

When I was a kid, the first scary movie I ever saw was *THEM*, about ants that had grown as big as houses after exposure to radioactivity. It terrified me. It was years before I could go to bed without checking underneath to be sure there weren't any ants there.

I was a teenager when I watched *The Picture of Dorian Gray*, and I had nightmares for weeks.

I like this Dory in Gray version better!

Have a joyful weekend, and I'll see you again on Monday.

Almond Deserts

Monday 7/22/2019 – Some time ago, a friend of mine posted a link to an article about the incredible feat of transporting bees across the country to pollinate almond groves in California.

This is the comment I posted on her site:

=========

Does anyone ever wonder WHY the bees have to be transported to pollinate the almond so-called "groves"? It's because almond growers have created virtual deserts, in which their trees are the only living entity. While the trees flower, bees can gather pollen and nectar, but once the flowering is over, any bees left there would die of starvation.

It would have been a lot smarter if almond growers left one acre out of ten to blossom with wildflowers and native flowering trees, and if they'd plant clover between and under the trees. Sure, it would take more time/money to harvest, but they wouldn't have to pay commercial beekeepers all that money to transport the bees once a year. And the local bees could survive year-round that way.

It's not just almonds, either. Those poor bees get hauled around the country to every major crop as it flowers.

Whenever will we smarten up?

= = = = = = = = =

~ ~ ~

Morning Views

Tuesday 7/23/2019 – Last Sunday morning turned out to be blessedly cool and not too humid. When I went out for my walk at 5:45 the moon was bright enough to cast distinct shadows. I tried to take a picture of my shadow waving at you, but what resulted was a basically solid black screen. So instead, I took a picture of the moon hiding behind a tree.

I thought I'd share with you what my morning walk is like. I used to try to keep track of the number of steps I took, but I quickly gave up on that for two reasons: a) my cheapo pedometer kept either skipping or adding steps. Plus it has an annoying click with each step. Irritating. b) Counting the steps myself didn't work because I kept forgetting whether I was on the seven hundreds or the eight hundreds or whatever.

Fran Stewart

Anyway, now I just walk for a certain length of time, and I use that time for meditation. It takes 16 steps to go through the words I repeat over and over as I walk (4 steps per line).

Here   Now

Walking, Breathing

Happy   Feet

Peaceful Heart

How many times do I have to repeat it? I have no idea.

It never ceases to amaze me how centered I feel and how quickly the time passes. After the walk last Sunday I sat on an old green chair beside my driveway and took the second photo of the sky above me through the trees. I kept sitting there as dawn gradually evolved. I listened to the birdcalls. Eventually I was rewarded when a hummingbird hummed right up next to my head, checked me out, decided I was neither threatening nor worth trying to sip, and she zipped over to breakfast at the white phlox and orange butterfly weed.

~ ~ ~

If you want a different life

Wednesday 7/24/2019 – Sometimes choosing a different path can seem like an insurmountable obstacle – but sometimes it's as simple as turning around. I had a professor once who detested the poetry of Robert Frost. Although I admired her exceedingly, that was one opinion I couldn't fathom. Frost's assertion that taking one road rather than the other "has made all the difference" is a reminder we all could take to heart.

The important point, to me, is that the "other road" Frost took was the one he <u>chose</u> to take.

Which path will you choose today?

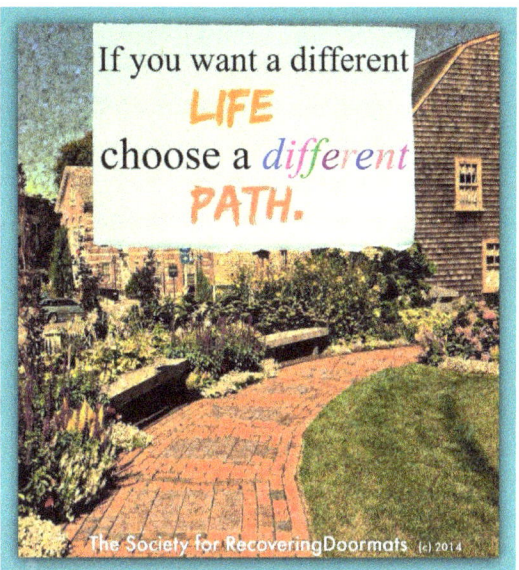

~ ~ ~

Time of Use – Old Clock

Thursday 7/25/2019 – A few days ago I wrote about my $40/month electric bill, and Marcia Dunscomb commented, asking "How do you do it?"

How do I do it? I'm glad you asked. Here's my reply to her. I copied and pasted it because I believe few people go through and read the comments or my replies to comments, and I didn't want you to miss this.:

Jackson Electric Coop has a program called "Time of Use," designed to encourage people to avoid electricity use during peak hours, which are defined as 3pm to 8pm, Monday through Friday, from June 1st to September 15th.

The way it works is that Jackson EMC charges Time of Use members an extremely high rate during those peak summer hours—punitively high, in fact. At ALL other times, the rate is very, very low. Even with a $25/month service charge for Time of Use, I still make out quite well. My $40 last month meant that I really only paid $15 in electric usage.

It requires a lot of discipline to follow such a schedule, but over the years I've worked out a good system. I have a programmable thermostat that in effect shuts off my A/C from 2:45 to 8:15 Mon-Fri. I cool the house enough before that so I don't bake in the evening. From June through mid-September, all my evening meals are cold – salads, pasta dishes, even meat dishes I've prepared during the early morning when it won't heat the house too much. I never do laundry during the high-use hours. Nor do I use the stove. And I avoid opening the fridge as much as possible.

Fran Stewart

It helps that I work from home, so I don't have to jam all my home chores into the afternoon/evening hours.

It helps, also, that I don't have a TV set. My computer is a Mac laptop that I can easily unplug during those times. In fact, I have a timer set on my phone to remind me each day to turn off as many circuit breakers as possible so that I can't turn something on without thinking. I leave on the circuit breakers for the water pump, the fridge, and the garage (in case there's an emergency and I have to take the car somewhere). At 8:01pm Mon-Fri another alarm goes off and I flip all the circuit breakers back on.

The trees are a huge help. By shading the house from the afternoon sun, they contribute to a huge cooling effect. I doubt I could manage this if I lived in a sterile subdivision with one or two lollipop trees per house. In the winter, because the trees are deciduous, I get afternoon sun through the bare branches. Lovely!

I admit the rooms do get a bit dark by 7:30 in the evening, so reading can be a challenge, but knitting works fine and I can play my piano by feel without having to look at music. My laptop is lighted from within, so I can write all I want to. I have skylights that let in enough daylight, even at 7pm, so I never feel like I'm living in a dungeon.

I have a celebration every September 16th when I can light my evenings once again.

As I said, it takes discipline to follow a program like this, but I've found over the years that it's well worth it. My neighbors seldom pay less than $300 each month, but they all say they don't want to give up the convenience of what they have. It's their choice. But "Time of Use" is my choice.

~ ~ ~

Drive Carefully

Friday 7/26/2019 – In a couple of weeks it's going to be time for me to give blood again—every eight weeks for dozens of years—so I've started my usual routine of being sure to eat iron-rich foods. If I don't do that, my hemoglobin tends to be on the low side.

Here's an 86-year-old Canadian guy, though, who's made 1,000 plasma donations. Ewen Stewart (not related to me as far as I know) gave his first donation in November of 1951. Pretty impressive.

Do you donate blood?

If you don't, you'd better drive carefully. My blood and his will only go so far.

Photo credit Tom Steepe/CBC

~ ~ ~

Turn Off the News

Saturday 7/27/2019 – This is my plan for the weekend. Thought I'd share it with you.

Enjoy the music!

~ ~ ~

Boneless

Monday 7/29/2019 – What about you? Have you had any boneless watermelon lately?

'Tis the season.

~ ~ ~

The Buzz

Tuesday 7/30/2019 – A neighbor recently clued me in to KUSC, a classical music radio station that I can listen to on my laptop. She listens on her phone, but I don't do that sort of thing.

Anyway, there's a KUSC blog entry about a colony of bees hived in a repurposed cello (tuned to the key of C)

To find the blog, search for "what's the buzz kusc." And be sure to listen to the *Flight of the Bumblebees* performed by two cellists.

Note: If you don't add *KUSC* to the search, you'll get something about Jesus Christ Superstar—at least, that's what happened to me when I looked up the website again.

~ ~ ~

Wasps

Wednesday 7/31/2019 - The BBC posted a news story on May 20th about the benefits of wasps.

I have a paper wasp building a paper nest behind the bench on my front porch—where I often to sit to read when the weather is cool enough. They're quiet and rather sedate. I enjoy watching them each time I enter or exit. It started with just one wasp, building up the paper cells with great deliberation. Now there are about fifteen of them that sit around on the nest all day and don't do much. I find myself wondering what they're thinking.

Now, if these were an aggressive sort—like yellow jackets—I'd sic my son-in-law on them, but for now, we have a gentle truce going. My daughter thinks I'm nuts, but I'm on the side of the pollinators.

[**2020 Note:** The wasps didn't return this year. I rather miss them.]

August 2019

New Dawn Rose on Arbor

Thursday 8/1/2019 - Happy first day of August. I was looking through an old photo album and found this picture of the New Dawn Rose I planted shortly after I moved to Georgia in the 90s. One of my first construction jobs in my new house (new to me, that is) was to build an arbor with a bench along each side. The rose was delighted with it, as you can see.

I also built a three-bin compost pile, which provided marvelous compost over the years I lived there. Maybe that's why the rose grew so prolifically. Compost and joy. A combination that can't be topped.

~ ~ ~

Librarians Answer

Friday 8/2/2019 – I've been reading a spate of excellent non-fiction books recently, and I'm always in awe of how these authors can take so much research from so many books—their bibliographies are often pages and pages long—and weave all those disparate facts into a coherent whole.

Yes, I've done a lot of research for my mysteries, particularly the Biscuit McKee series, but my endeavors pale in comparison to the amount needed to shape the histories I've been reading. In each of the author's notes at the end of the books, I find praise for the librarians and archivists who aided the writers, steering them to obscure publications they might not have found otherwise.

Have you used the resources of a library lately? If not, why not? Find a subject you're vitally interested in, and see what the library has to offer.

~ ~ ~

Yawning

Saturday 8/3/2019 – How long has it been since you've indulged in one of those enormous stretch-your-whole-face yawns?

We spend so much energy trying to cover up a yawn—attempting to keep our mouths closed, doing our best to pretend we're not really yawning, or at least hiding our half-hearted yawn behind a hand.

I get it. I know we consider a wide-open yawn to be impolite. But, let's face it, yawns are a part of life.

Fran Stewart

When we're tired or when we're bored, we tend to breathe shallowly, which means less oxygen to the brain. Hence—an oxygen-infusing yawn.

I suggest we see yawning as a healthy thing to do. In public, you can place your hand over your mouth; after all, nobody wants to inspect your epiglottis. But when you're home, feel free to indulge yourself and imitate this lion.

Feels good, doesn't it?

~ ~ ~

My books on library shelf

Monday 8/5/2019 – Look what I saw on a shelf at my local library a while back! I was so excited about it, I had to take a picture. This was in advance of the month they'd invited me to be a guest author at their monthly Mystery Book Club to discuss *Green as a Garden Hose*.

I can't help it. I still get excited whenever I see my books on display, whether in a library, a bookstore, or someone's home. Maybe the authors whose books sales number in the millions get used to it, but I like feeling that thrill.

The third volume of my beekeeping memoir (*BeesKnees #3*) was released yesterday as an e-book. I'm still working on getting the print versions ready. Hopefully before the end of 2019.

~ ~ ~

Put in the Comma

Tuesday 8/6/2019 – I get tired of having to back up when I'm reading a book in order to check the meaning of a sentence. All because of a missing comma. If it happens once, okay—I get it. Authors don't always have control over how their books get printed.

But when it happens four or five times, I get suspicious.

After number six, I give up on that author. My inner editor is too powerful for me to relax and enjoy a poorly punctuated story.

I never bad-mouth other authors online, so I won't tell you who I'm talking about. After all, those missing commas might not bother you.

Maturing is Realizing

Wednesday 8/7/2019 – Sometimes it's enough simply to listen and then to cry along with the one who's speaking.

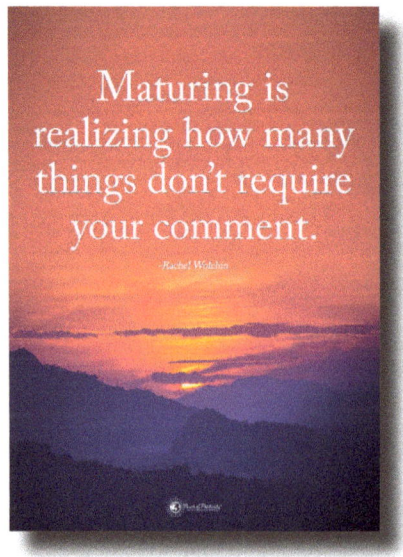

~ ~ ~

Clear Your Path

Thursday 8/8/2019 – A couple of days ago when I was teaching a Memoirs Class at the local library, one of the students shared her story of the way in which what had seemed a storm in her childhood.(dealing with a predicted life expectancy of no more than 18 years) prepared her for the role she now has taken on as a caretaker for her husband during his medical challenge. She said the hospital staff told her, "Your husband's room is the happiest one on the cancer ward."

Can you imagine what a role model this 33-year-old woman can be to others? Not only to those who are dealing with disease issues, but with anyone facing seemingly insurmountable obstacles.

After her sharing, I felt not only uplifted, but incredibly humble.

~ ~ ~

Scottish Hummingbird

Friday 8/9/2019 – I get a great deal of joy watching the birds fluttering around the feeders throughout the day. One of my favorites, though, is the rarely seen Plaid Hummingbird, whose ancestors are thought to have hitched a ride on a schooner from Scotland in the 1700s.

When it flies, what grace!

Truly amazing.

And its hum? How sweet the sound.

~ ~ ~

Fran Stewart

Off on my Own

Saturday 8/10/2019 – Why do I post only six days each week rather than seven?

I'm glad you asked.

If you've been following my author page for more than a couple of years, you may recall that I used to post every single day. The writing is simply a part of my morning routine. First I feed the cats. Then I walk. Then I refill the birdfeeders. Then I feed myself. Then I write the morning post and send it into cyberspace.

Sometimes I choose the photo the evening before. Most often, though, it's a spur-of-the-moment decision based on what I'm thinking about right then. It was the middle of last year, I think, that I came to see that no matter how much I enjoy sharing my thoughts with you each day, I needed one morning each week when I could avoid the computer completely for a couple of hours at the start of the day.

I picked Sunday for no other reason than Sunday was the morning I made that decision upon waking.

Have a joy-filled Saturday today, and I'll rejoin you on Monday, after I've recharged my internal batteries. While we're at it, why don't you recharge yours as well?

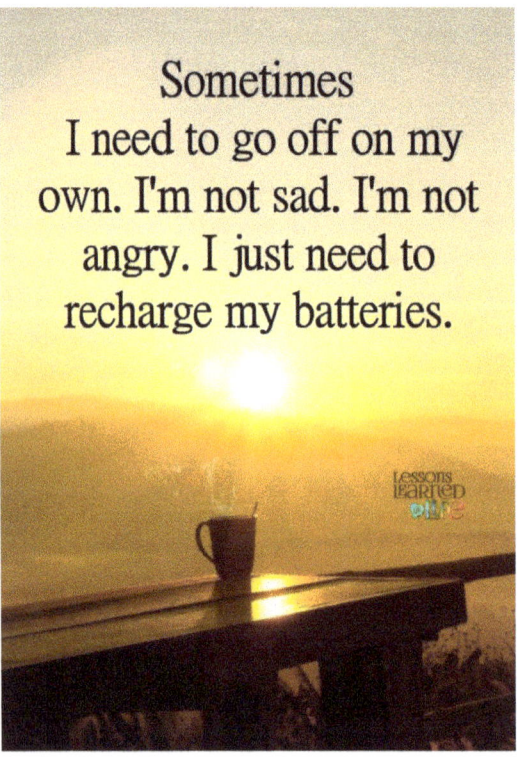

~ ~ ~

Erasers are made…

Monday 8/12/2019 – I love erasers. And pencils. That's why I always start writing a new book in longhand on a yellow legal pad. With a pencil. And an eraser.

In my non-fiction book *From the Tip of My Pen: a Workbook for Writers* I have an essay about pencils. I'd like to share it with you:

=================

We did it! We lived through another summer. I may have thought I'd never stop wilting when I walked out into that wall of humidity that lurked outside my door, but—lo and behold—it's coming up on autumn and my windows are open again.

This is a good time to take up where I left off last spring and begin to write outdoors. Even if you have a laptop, why not try stepping outside and writing with a pencil, just for the fun of it? It's a truly marvelous invention, and it's been around since 1565. Anything that's lasted that long must have a few things going for it.

Let's see . . .

1. It's portable.

2. Runs without batteries. For that matter, it can run without brains, but I hope that's not the case here.

3. Has an eraser, the 1565 version of a delete key.

4. Provides a handy canvas for tooth imprints. I've never known anyone who hasn't occasionally chewed on a pencil. What computer gives a frustrated writer that kind of alleviation? I don't group solitaire, Pac-Man, or minesweeper in the same league with a yellow number 2 Ticonderoga.

5. Can be thrown across the path / room / deck when simple deletion or chewing is not active enough (see numbers 3 and 4 above).

6. Can be sharpened without a fancy gadget. My Swiss Army knife works just fine. In a pinch I can even sacrifice a fingernail to tear the wood back away from the graphite.

7. Can be broken in half to fit in a tiny notebook or a small pocket. Of course, this eliminates the delete function of one-half of it, but I can use the bare half for my *Journal of Work in Progress.* That *Journal* isn't edited, after all. It just gets me rolling and gives me a chance to air those vague ideas. And the just plain stupid ones that will never show up in my finished manuscript, but need to be released from my psyche before the good ideas can roll out.

Go ahead. I dare you. Try writing outside, under a tree or on a deck or next to a lake, and see how your writing blossoms. And all because of a simple pencil.

~ ~ ~

Dawn Thoughts

Tuesday 8/13/2019 – I've been thinking a lot recently about dawn. Part of this is just that I've been outside to see the sunrise more frequently than I used to. As the Georgia summer weather gets warmer and muggier, I've started walking earlier and earlier.

Also, early August is the time to see the Perseides meteor shower pre-dawn. The last time I saw the Perseides was when I lived in Vermont, but I remain hopeful that somehow or other one or two meteors will outshine the city lights.

But why, you ask, have I been thinking about dawn? It comes every day, right? (Unless one lives near the North or South Pole.) So, what makes it special?

Well, try to picture this: When I step outside as the light is just beginning to increase—any earlier and I can't see where I'm walking—all the colors are muted, grayed, dulled. All the different shades of green in my yard, coming from each different variety of tree, shrub, weed, groundcover, show up only as variations on the gray scale. The flowers look like they have no colors at all.

Pretty soon, though, "rosy-fingered dawn," the same dawn that Homer saw and wrote about in the *Odyssey*, begins to send its tendrils over the trees at the top of the hill to the east of my house. By the time I head back down toward my house, I can see the orange butterfly weed and the magenta butterfly bush, the yellowed seedpods on the golden rain tree and the purple liatris.

There's something else about dawn that I've come to see over the past few days. It may seem obvious, but I guess I'd never really thought about it before. Dawn comes slowly. There's no exact dividing point. At 5am it's still nighttime; by 7:30 it's definitely daytime. But what about those hours in between?

Life is kind of like dawn. When I was five, I was a kid. When I was thirty-five, I was an adult. But where did the change happen? Why did I never see it coming? Like the emerging dawn, my life has oozed imperceptibly from one stage to the other.

I wouldn't have it any other way.

Comment from **Erica Jensen**: Maybe we start at the gray scale because when we're brand new we have no experience to color our beliefs.

~ ~ ~

Pollen-laden Honeybee

Wednesday 8/14/2019 – As you look at this public domain photo of a honeybee laden with pollen grains, think about the miracle of pollination.

Fran Stewart

It's not only plants that are pollinated in order to allow fruits and veggies to thrive.

Think about how much you try without results to conquer a fear or develop a new habit or release yourself from anger or disappointment—but then you see something or hear something or read something that brings your trials into focus, and you see the way to the solution.

Think about how often you've been talking to a friend and have suddenly grasped an idea that's been eluding you.

Without all these kinds of pollination we'd starve physically, emotionally, and intellectually.

p.s. If you'd like to know more about what we can learn from bees, the first three volumes of my beekeeping memoirs are available as e-books. The print versions will be coming out soon. The titles? *BeesKnees #1*, *BeesKnees #2,* and *BeesKnees #3*. Guess what the final three volumes are going to be called …

~ ~ ~

800X magnification

Thursday 8/15/2019 – Take a moment to study this piece of incredible art. Can you even begin to grasp the intricacy of it? I know I can't look at it without wonder. Each fold, each projection, each texture is simply stunning.

Care to guess what it is?

I'll give you a hint. It's a photo that's magnified 800 times.

Still not sure? Okay. It's at the bottom end of somebody's leg.

What kind of creature?

I'm glad you asked.

It's a mosquito's foot!

Just imagine how much sensory information they can absorb through those folds. And with the red barbs, it's no wonder they can hang on so well.

I love everyday miracles like this.

~ ~ ~

Water Reclamation Plant

Fran Stewart

Friday 8/16/2019 – Here in Gwinnett County Georgia we don't have a sewage treatment plant. We have a water reclamation facility.

A couple of days ago, the Citizen Fire Academy Alumni Association members had a chance to tour the plant. We watched an informative video and then loaded ourselves onto a cart that held all fifteen of us plus four or five plant personnel. They drove us from building to building, where we could watch the movement of sewage through filters and sorters and squishers and stirrers and – well, I don't recall all the names. Squishers and stirrers weren't on the list, but I wasn't taking notes, so I have no idea what they're really called. There were also things they called the bug tanks. Really. Bug tanks. Where good bugs break down the solid waste.

Why is it called water reclamation? Great question. It's because this plant takes millions of gallons of wastewater (i.e. sewage) and removes EVERYTHING from it. Once it's clean, the pristine water is returned, forty million gallons per day, back into Lake Lanier. And twenty million gallons (I think that's the right number) into the Chattahoochee River.

This photo is one I took of one of the tanks where the water waits for one last process before being emptied back into the lake. At this point in the process, the water's in great shape. It's visited regularly by ducks who enjoy what must look to them like a big fat pond. I counted a dozen or so of them (most of which are off-camera to the right).

This plant produces as byproducts both soil that is used in the county landfills and fertilizer pellets. They also have a section of the plant that takes FOG—fat, oil, and grease—from area restaurants and processes it into useful goodies.

I like the fact that I live in a county that takes such effort to treat the environment gently. Now, if only people would quit flushing so-called "Flushables. "They're NOT FLUSHABLE," our tour guide told us. "THEY'RE NOT FLUSHABLE!!! Please remember," he practically begged us, "They're NOT flushable!"

I got it – but since I've never bought the things, I thought I'd pass on the message.

~ ~ ~

Boil a Funny Bone

Saturday 8/17/2019 – I just finished listening to a marvelous interview on WABE, my local public radio station. Normally I have complete silence in the mornings, except for cat squeaks from inside the house and bird songs from outside, but this morning I made the (happy) mistake of saying, "Alexa, good morning."

Yes. I have an Alexa. It's not something I'd ever consider buying for myself—although I have had fun asking her to play KUSC (classical music station) when I do dog sitting at my daughter's house.

Well, lo and behold, she (my daughter, not Alexa) gifted me with my very own Alexa, and I've spent the past few weeks telling Alexa to turn on WABE or KUSC or turn them off or turn the volume up or down. That's about the extent of my interaction with her, other than saying good night when I head to bed. She tells me to sleep well or have a nice night. She hasn't repeated herself so far.

Anyway, about an hour ago I said good morning and she replied with a funny thought for the day. Then she asked if I'd like to hear another one the next time I say good morning. "Sure," I told her. I was giggling about that interchange and decided to listen to WABE news while I was feeding the cats. That's when I heard a fabulous interview – which is why I'm later than usual this morning. I'll tell you about the interview sometime next week, but for now, here's my own happy thought for the day. Well, not my own—I snitched this from somebody else (wish I could remember who)—but I hope it brings a smile or a chuckle to you. It pulled a guffaw from me.

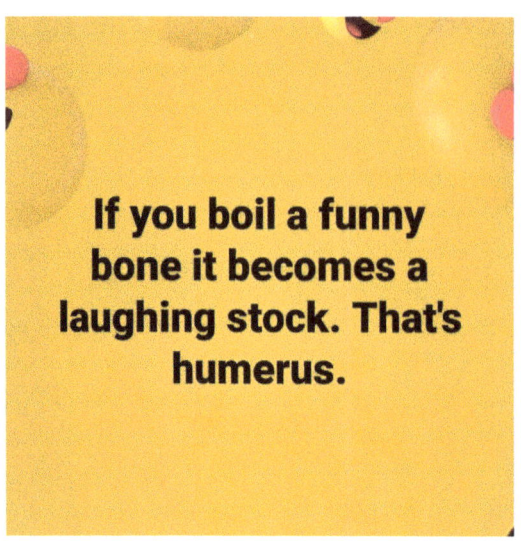

~ ~ ~

Morning Puzzle

Monday 8/19/2019 – This morning I have a good thought for you and a fun challenge.

First up is this definition from the World Health Organization in 1948. Let's take a moment or two just to absorb the implications. What would the world be like if we not only believed this, but we lived it as well?

Health is a state of complete physical, mental, and social well-being,

and not merely the absence of disease or infirmity.

~World Health Organization, 1948

And now the challenge: any guesses as to what this photo shows? I'll give you the answer tomorrow.

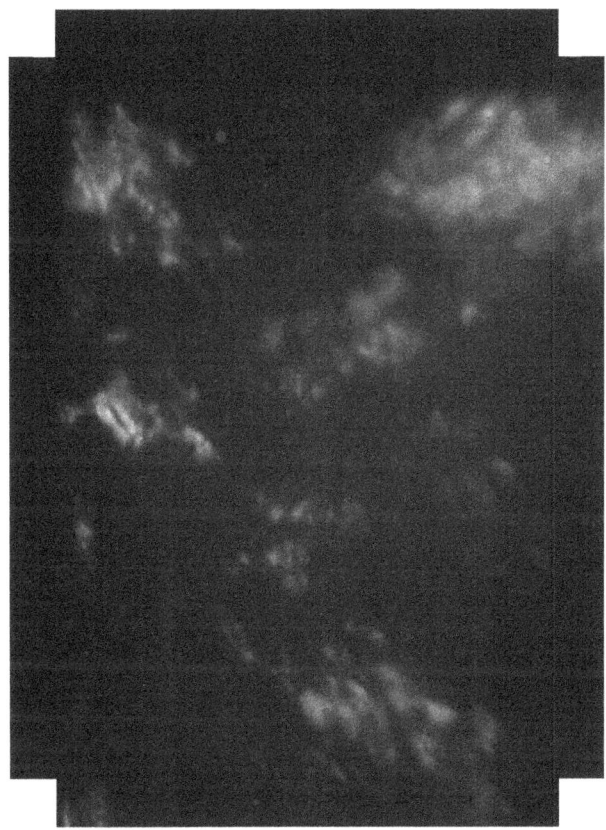

~ ~ ~

Bugs 101

Tuesday 8/20/2019 – The answer from yesterday: Early morning sunlight filtering through the trees outside one of the windows on the east side of my house and landing on a wall in my hallway. Why does the fairly light-colored wall look gray here? I have no idea.

At any rate, Karen – you win! You're the only one who figured it out. Most everybody else guessed clouds, but several said that this looked so much like clouds it couldn't possibly be clouds.

And now, on to other exciting topics. I just completed a 12-week course from the University of Alberta called *Bugs 101*. It's an introduction to the world of insects, taught by University of Alberta staff and grad students. I had great fun learning a whole lot more than I thought I would about bugs – and I certainly have a greater appreciation now for their importance in our entire ecosystem.

What's next?

I'm glad you asked.

Dino 101. I enjoy watching the dinosaurs at my bird feeders each day, so I figure it's time to learn more about their saurian ancestors.

Fran Stewart

You didn't know that birds are dinosaurs? They most certainly are. And I can't wait to delve into all the details!

Check out the University of Alberta. If you want a certificate of completion, you pay a modest fee for the online course. If you don't need the certificate as proof that you've taken the course, then there's no charge.

~ ~ ~

Seasonal Bookworms

Wednesday 8/21/2019 – It's getting almost too muggy for my morning walks. If I go out early enough to be able to walk comfortably, it's so dark (even with the light pollution from Atlanta) I can barely see where I'm stepping. If I wait for the predawn semi-light, I can barely breathe for the mugginess.

What to do instead? Well, there's always reading.

~ ~ ~

2 birds

Thursday 8/22/2019 – This morning I sat on my porch for a while watching the dinosaurs flitting around the feeders.

Dinosaurs???

I'm having great fun with my Dino 101 course from the University of Alberta. This is one of the many fascinating things I've learned so far:

"Birds are a kind of theropod, making theropods the only group of dinosaurs that is not completely extinct."

I'd heard years ago that birds are descended from dinosaurs, but it never ever occurred to me that birds ARE living dinosaurs. Makes me think twice about the chickadees, hummingbirds, nuthatches, woodpeckers, tufted titmice, blue jays, crows, wrens, sparrows, and squirrels that live close by.

Wait! No! Squirrels are not dinosaurs. They're simply imitating those other theropods by flitting from tree to tree and landing smack dab on my feeders to steal the peanuts and sunflower seeds.

Still, dinosaurs or not, I enjoy them all.

Medieval Teeth

Friday 8/23/2019 – When you think about illuminated medieval manuscripts, you think about monks sitting hunched over oak tables, right?

Scientific evidence has come to light, though, to show that it wasn't only monks turning out those exquisitely decorated books. The nuns were doing it as well. How do they know this?

I'm glad you asked.

A researcher named Anita Radini found bright blue lapis lazuli particles stuck in dental plaque, the gunk we brush off our teeth every day. Artists apparently use their teeth to sharpen the points of fine brushes, and the almost prohibitively expensive lapis lazuli pigments lodge between their teeth.

The funny thing is that Radini was studying starch granules in dental tartar on ancient teeth so she could figure out the diet of people who died a thousand years ago. Those blue particles stood out, though, so she went looking into what they could be.

Fascinating and serendipitous indeed!

What wonderful things have you found when you were looking for something else?

~ ~ ~

Assembling a Skeleton

Saturday 8/24/2019 – Did you ever put together a skeleton? When I lived in Vermont, I knew a woman who was quite an expert on birds of prey. She took me through a raptor exhibit once and let me pick up a whole bunch of owl pellets. Owl pellets are NOT poop. They are the regurgitated indigestible stuff. My children were in elementary school at the time, and we had great fun taking apart the pellets, picking out all the teeny bones, and trying to reconstruct a mouse.

So, when my Dino 101 online course from the University of Alaska asked me to put together a Parasaurolophus skeleton, I felt fairly confident. The first photo is what they started me with. The left rear leg was fixed in place, but all the rest of the pieces could be dragged around to wherever I thought they belonged.

The second picture is what I finally ended up with—all the pieces in the correct places. I don't want to admit how long it took me. A dinosaur has different angles than a mouse, and those front legs just seem to hang on to nowhere and nothing.

As I was out walking this morning, I couldn't help but think about how this process is a good metaphor for my life. I spent a good chunk of mine feeling scattered and went through a lot of oops moments as I tried to put myself together into a cohesive whole.

It finally worked, so the process was worth it.

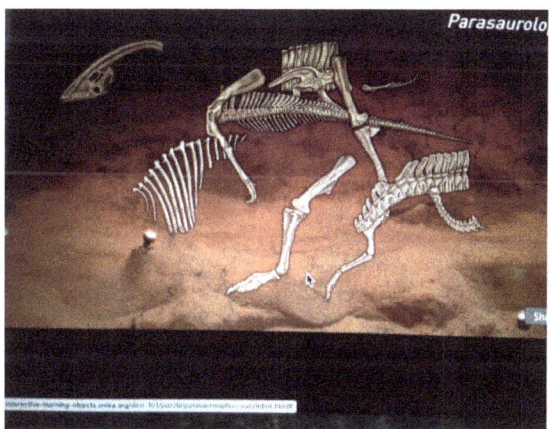

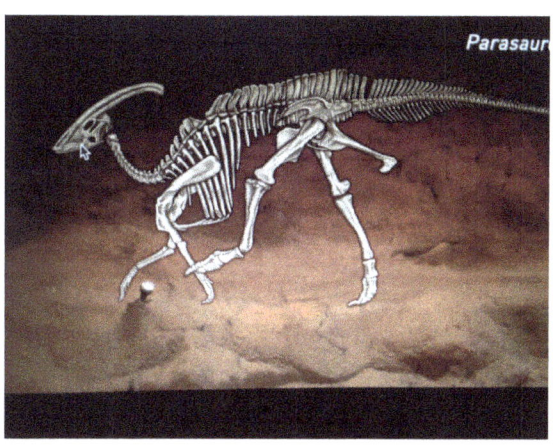

Osteoderms

Monday 8/26/2019 – So, who invented solar panels? How long have they been around?

Would you believe 75 million years?

In case you hadn't guessed, I'm truly enjoying the Dino 101 online course from the University of Alberta. A couple of days ago I found out that those bony plates on the back of stegosaurus (and smaller flatter ones on the backs of various other dinosaurs like the edmontonia ankylosaurus in this photo) had a number of useful purposes. It's believed that they served as a storehouse for calcium that the dinosaur could draw on when needed to help repair bone.

The plates, called osteoderms (bones that form underneath the skin), were naturally good for protection.

And they were most likely used as distinguishing characteristics between dinosaurs of the same species, much the way we might identify someone we'd just met as "the one lots of freckles" or "the one with the elaborate hairdo."

But – am I ever going to get around to the point of this post? Well, yes. It's believed that those bony plates absorbed the heat of the sun.

Voilá, solar panels.

You always wanted to know that, didn't you?

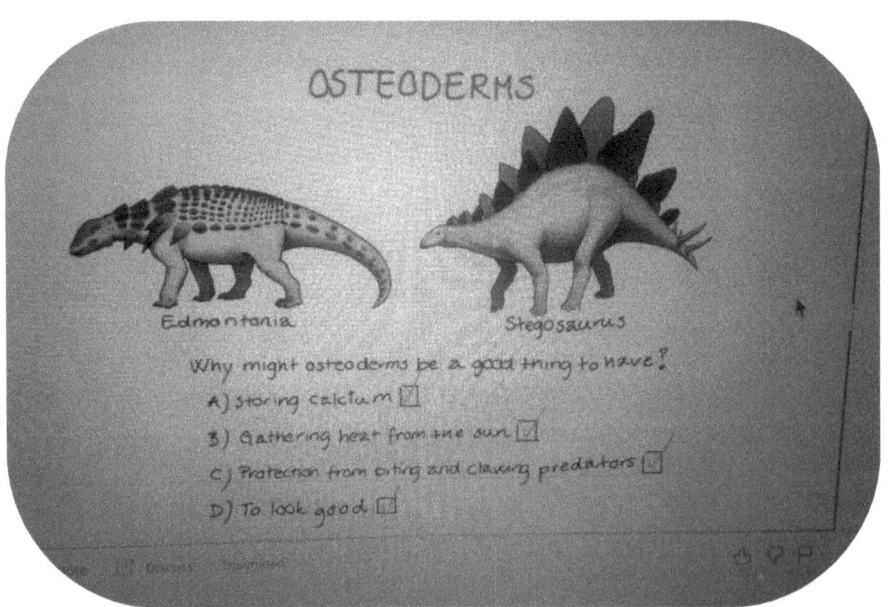

Photo credit: University of Alberta Dino101 Course

~ ~ ~

Tagged

Tuesday 8/27/2019 – I spent (all right – I wasted) a good deal of time yesterday trying to take a flattering selfie. I'm so happy my phone has a virtual trashcan. I have a great deal of compassion for this particular pup.

Just to be sure, though, I emptied my trash file.

I've done that with a lot of my less-than-stellar poems and drafts of other writing. My sister thinks I should save all my old book drafts. "Someday," she has insisted, "scholars will want to see how Fran Stewart developed a story."

Sorry 'bout that, but scholars are going to have to guess. There's a great deal I simply don't want to share with anybody. Not just typo-ridden chapters, but downright stupid ideas for story lines that I thankfully thought to revise or delete before they advanced too far.

Even the BeesKnees memoirs I'm in the process of publishing – the first print volume will be available in the next couple of weeks, and I'll be sure to tell you when it's ready – has gone through another round of editing.

My BeesKneesBeekeeping blog had some entries that came out more like this dog's second photo. The book version will, I hope, emulate the first pic.

No sense in leaving a book that will hopefully be around for the next three or four hundred years if it's full of nonsense. Or typos.

Martin's shopping bag

Wednesday 8/28/2019 – Now, why on earth would I show you a picture of one of my shopping bags?

As usual, I'm glad you asked.

This sturdy canvas bag is right around forty years old. You can probably tell it's an old lady because of all the wrinkles. You can tell it's been well used by noting all the various stains. You can't tell how many times it's been washed (lots) or what all it's carried over the years. Not just groceries, but kids' toys, beach supplies, books [of course], gardening stuff, and most recently supplies for the memoirs class I teach.

It has served me well and will continue to do so for many years to come, I'm sure.

Talk about Reduce, Reuse, Recycle. This old bag (you can interpret that pronoun any way you want to) is good at it!

~ ~ ~

Myth

Thursday 8/29/2019 – I say amen to this. How many times have I been asked to do something I didn't really want to do? How many times have I said, "I'm so sorry, but I just can't. I'm way too busy at the moment"?

Not any more. I've decided from now on, "too busy" will never be an excuse. Admittedly, there are times when I AM too busy, but at those times I have the choice of stopping some other task to take on the one that I'm being asked about, the choice to rearrange my priorities.

This reminds me of a sonnet I read and memorized years ago. I've heard it attributed to "Carol Coombs," but have never been able to verify that authorship. Anyway, here's the poem as best I remember it. I hope you enjoy it as much as I have over the years.

= = = = = = = = =

"Importance"
I've mending I must do, and beds to make.
I should not sit and watch the red sun set
Behind the hills of afternoon, nor take
This time to dream when I have work. And yet
Supposing that I go at duty's call
To make the beds and sweep the floors? What then?
These things have no real value after all.
Tomorrow they must all be done again.
I have too many of such tasks to do.
Therefore I shall forget them, every one.
And I shall sit and feel the rising dew
And watch the haze around the setting sun.
And I may find time for the housework too,
When this, the more important thing, is done.

= = = = = = = = =

By the way, you do recall—don't you?—that a sonnet has 14 lines, usually with 10 syllables per line. And the final two lines always sum up the message of the previous twelve.

Right.

> **"Too busy" is a myth.**
>
> People make time
> for the things that are
> important to them.

Fran Stewart

~ ~ ~

Sprawling Upward

Friday 8/30/2019 – When I return from my morning walk, this is part of the sight that greets me.

That's a Sweet Autumn Clematis that started out as one teeny weenie hopeful I planted 14 years ago in what used to be a fairly bare spot of yard off to the right of this photo. Now the yard is overgrown with a (delicious) blackberry thicket. And the clematis, which wasn't content with inhabiting the berry bushes alone. No, it had to clamber up a tree in the vicinity and then down the other side to engulf the mailbox.

It perfumes this entire end of the cul-de-sac. I see people walking past periodically and stopping to simply breathe and appreciate the beauty.

Tomorrow I'll show you one of the other many visitors who enjoy it immensely.

~ ~ ~

Corbiculae

Saturday 8/31/2019 – Yesterday I promised to show you some of the other, i.e. non-human, visitors who are enjoying the Sweet Autumn Clematis.

The vines are swarming with bumblebees and honeybees. I was delighted to see one that cooperated long enough for me to get this shot of her displaying the corbicula on her left hind leg.

What are corbiculae? I'm glad you asked.

If you read the first volume of my beekeeping memoir, *BeesKnees #1*, which is now available not only as an e-book, but also in a beautiful print version (!), you'll find out a lot about corbiculae, but for now suffice it to say they're the built-in pockets on the hind legs of honeybees, sort of like saddlebags, where they pack the (usually golden) pollen as they collect it. I've also seen a photo of a honeybee with red pollen in her corbicula.

I hope you can see how deliciously fuzzy this bee is.

And—happy final day of August.

Fran Stewart

September 2019

Parts of Speech

Monday 9/2/2019 – Monday seems like a good day to get our grammar up and running with this delightful *parts of speech* poem. I wish I knew the name of the clever person who wrote it.

Why am I talking parts of speech? Because yesterday I went to see a matinee performance of "The Complete Works of Shakespeare (Abridged)" at The Shakespeare Tavern in Atlanta. The three starring actors, usually played by men, were this time played by three women. It was witty, crazy, and so much fun.

One of the (many) funny lines was when "Romeo" called out to "Juliet," "Call me but love, and I'll be new baptized."

"Butt Love?" Juliet queries. "You want me to call you Butt Love?"

One little indication of how important it is to recognize the correct parts of speech.

Just thought I'd mention it to start your workweek off the right way.

THE PARTS OF SPEECH POEM

Every name is called a noun,
As field and fountain, street and town.
In place of noun the pronoun stands,
As he and she can clap their hands.
The adjective describes a thing,
As magic wand or bridal ring.
The verb means action, something done,
As read and write and jump and run.
How things are done the adverbs tell,
As quickly, slowly, badly, well.
The preposition shows relation,
As in the street or at the station.
Conjunctions join, in many ways,
Sentences, words, or phrase and phrase.
The interjection cries out, "Hark!
I need an exclamation mark!"

~ ~ ~

Confused

Tuesday 9/3/2019 – Just for today, think about this. Then, just for tomorrow, think about it again. And the day after that, and the day after that.

Who knows? After a little while, you may come to absorb this thought and then to believe it.

Has a bee ever landed on you, and instead of getting scared, you appreciate the possibility that you got confused for a flower

~ ~ ~

Frustrated

Wednesday 9/4/2019 – I'm so glad the Shakespeare Tavern in Atlanta has decided to have 2pm Sunday matinees periodically.

Why?

Because I have chosen no longer to drive between dusk and dawn, so unless I have someone who is willing to pick me up, take me to an evening event, and deliver me home again, I stay here and read.

Was this self-imposed reduction easy? No.

Has it been hard to ask for help? Yes.

If there were an absolute emergency, could I drive? Probably. But I would be putting not only myself at risk, but others as well.

Thank goodness for my friend Ingrid Krein who totes me to and from the Shakespeare plays we both love. Thank goodness for Barbara Hanville who ferries me to and from our monthly book club. Thank goodness for Amy Woodrick who is willing to cart me to CFAAA meetings. (In case you didn't know, that's the Gwinnett Citizen Fire Academy Alumni Association.)

Thank goodness for Skype and Facetime and Zoom, so I can "attend" evening book clubs when they invite me to be the guest author.

I still consider myself hale and hearty. I try not to dwell on limitations. And I truly appreciate the compassion and helpfulness of others.

~ ~ ~

Stone Soup from *BeesKnees #4*

Thursday 9/5/2019 – In case you're wondering about this 6-volume beekeeping memoir I've published, I thought I'd share one of the entries with you. It's from *BeesKnees #4*. Here it is:

Day #350 – Tuesday, September 27, 2011

I used to subscribe to an e-service called the Daily Om. Each day I'd receive an inspirational email, and I particularly enjoyed this one. Years ago I read the children's book, *Stone Soup* by Marcia Brown, without realizing that it was based on a very old folk tale that seems to have shown up in the oral traditions of many countries.

Here's what the Daily Om said about it. The first paragraph summarizes the story. The second paragraph is what I really want to share with you, though.

= = = = = = = = =

>There are many variations on the story of stone soup, but they all involve a traveler coming into a town beset by famine. The inhabitants try to discourage the traveler from staying, fearing he wants them to give him food. They tell him in no uncertain terms that there's no food anywhere to be found. The traveler explains that he doesn't need any food and that, in fact, he was planning to make a soup to share with all of them. The villagers watch suspiciously as he builds a fire and fills a cauldron with water. With great ceremony, he pulls a stone from a bag, dropping the stone into the pot of water. He sniffs the brew extravagantly and exclaims how delicious stone soup is. As the villagers begin to show interest, he mentions how good the soup would be with just a little cabbage in it. A villager brings out a cabbage to share. This episode repeats itself until the soup has cabbage, carrots, onions, and beets—indeed, a substantial soup that feeds everyone in the village.
>
>This story addresses the human tendency to hoard in times of deprivation. When resources are scarce, we pull back and put all of our energy into self-preservation. We isolate ourselves and shut out others. As the story of stone soup reveals, in doing so, we often deprive ourselves and everyone else of a feast. This metaphor plays out beyond the realm of food. We hoard ideas, love, and energy, thinking we will be richer if we keep them to ourselves, when in truth we make the world, and ourselves, poorer whenever we greedily stockpile our reserves. The traveler was able to see that the villagers were holding back, and he had the genius to draw them out and inspire them to give, thus creating a spread that none of them could have created alone. [© *The Daily Om*]

= = = = = = = = =

I have to admit, I've always thought that this was what really happened with the loaves and the fishes—people were drawn out of their self-centered hoarding, and all were fed with plenty left over. And *that* is a miracle indeed.

This is what the bees do. They make enough honey for themselves, but then they keep right on producing. It's the excess honey, honey the hive doesn't need but creates anyway, that beekeepers take. I'm going to think about that the next time I spread honey on my biscuits. And I'm planning to share the honey I'll get from my hives.

~ ~ ~

Cover & Logo

Friday 9/6/2019 – Okay, I admit it: I'm so excited I can barely contain myself.

This week, the very first print book I've published through my newly formed publishing company, My Own Ship Press, is available through all the places you usually get your books. If you've followed these FB mini-memoirs of mine for any length of time, you'll already know that I began publishing the six volumes of my beekeeping memoirs as e-books last June, releasing one volume per month. There are four of them currently, with the last two to come out on October 4th and November 4th.

I had so many requests for print books, though, that it seemed the perfect time to take over complete ownership of the books I've written, beginning with the BeesKnees series.

What does this mean?

Gradually, over the next year or so (once all six BeesKnees volumes are in print), the independent press I've been working with, Journey of a Dream Publications, will take the 15 books they've published for me out of print, and I will re-publish them under my own imprint with new ISBNs, my own logo—isn't it gorgeous?—and slightly redesigned covers.

Why?

Well, it has to do with ongoing concerns about royalties that will still be due my estate long (hopefully) after I croak.

I'm simplifying my life to make things easier for my daughter and son years from now. Although this re-publication process is going to take a tremendous amount of effort (and a whole lot of money) from now into 2020, it will be worth it for my own peace of mind.

~ ~ ~

Bubble Bath

Saturday 9/7/2019 – Let's end this week with a laugh, shall we?

Baby Blue Heron

Monday 9/9/2019 – For anyone who wonders what happened to the dinosaurs, here's a baby blue heron. It's pretty obvious this little fella is a theropod, isn't it? I'm continuing my Dino 101 course from the University of Alberta, and enjoying it thoroughly. What on earth do people do when they stop learning?

Thanks, Kaysie, for sending me the link to this picture.

Photo credit: Quartzsite Happenings

~ ~ ~

Fingers

Tuesday 9/10/2019 – This morning I got to thinking about various body parts. That's not too strange a hobby for someone who's written a whole string of murder mysteries. But this time I wasn't thinking about how to go about killing someone.

This time I was marveling at the sheer ingeniousness of fingers. Take a look at your own. Hold your hand up in front of you with your fingers sticking straight up. It doesn't matter which way your palm is facing. I'd be willing to bet that one of those four fingers is a lot longer than the others. Of course it is.

Now, curl your fingers in to make a fist. Look at what happens when the comparative lengths of your metacarpals adjust their relationship to each other: the tips of all four fingers form a straight line and nestle right into the palm of your hand. If they'd all started out the same length, you'd stab your palm every time you tried to form a fist. In fact, you wouldn't be able to make one.

What's the purpose in my mentioning this?

Well, it's occurred to me that we humans spend a lot of time wishing our lives had been planned differently—that this or that had (or hadn't) happened. But thinking that way would be like wishing we could have fingers of equal length.

Then, when we needed to curl our hands up, we wouldn't be able to.

So, for today—and maybe for the rest of my life—when something doesn't seem to go my way, I hope I'll remember to say, "Unequal fingers!" That should bring me back around to a better attitude.

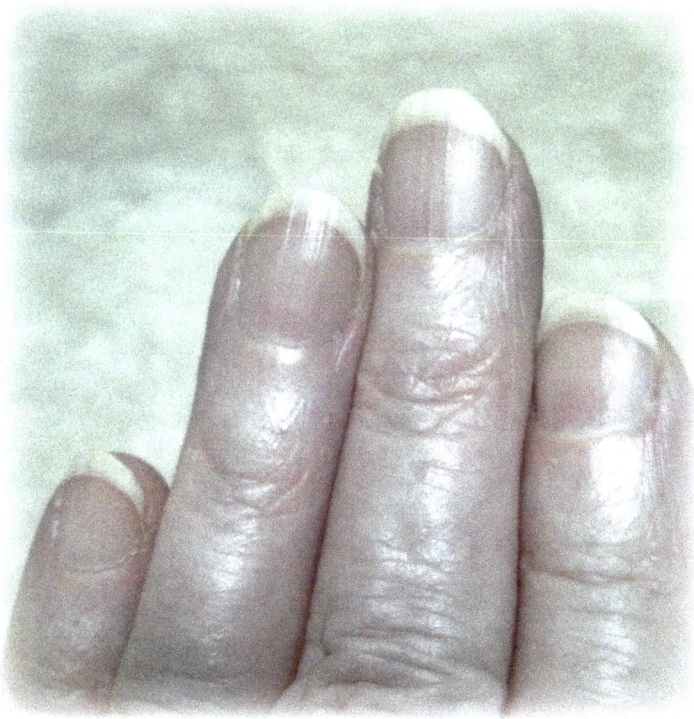

~ ~ ~

P.E.N.C.I.L.

Wednesday 9/11/2019 – Computer glitch? Not a problem. Pick up this handy lifesaver.

I wish I'd had this photo to illustrate the essay I wrote about pencils in *From the Tip of My Pen: A Work-*

book for Writers. It expresses my thought precisely. The only thing the photo is missing is evidence of the built-in stress-reliever every pencil has. I refer, of course, to tooth marks.

If you say you've never bitten on a pencil, I won't believe you.

~ ~ ~

Self-service

Thursday 9/12/2019 – I was looking at my well-loved loveseat yesterday evening and began to wonder why I still hung onto it. It became thoroughly disheveled after Waldo joined the family. Waldo wandered into my garage one day a number of years ago, bleeding and starving and covered with fleas. My free cats always seem to end up costing me at least five hundred dollars in vet bills not only for spaying or neutering, but also for extensive surgeries. I never knew whether it was a big raccoon, a dog, or a misguided human who inflicted Waldo's wounds, but he turned out to be one of the most loving cats imaginable.

He was also a furniture shredder. Before he came, my other two cats would never have thought of using anything other than a scratching post for—well, for scratching. But Waldo introduced them to the glories to be found in stretching one's claws pretty much everywhere.

After having gone through a number of years of rescuing cats, I'm finally down to just two again, and I feel like I'm almost back to where I started. Wooly Bear and Fuzzy Britches both believe that scratching posts are for scratching, that furniture is for sleeping on, and that my lap is for curling up in.

Meanwhile, I still have the loveseat. It's sort of like an elderly aunt. I can't give her away or lock her in a closet, so I drape various throws over her corners and (mostly) disguise the places where her stuffing is falling out.

Maybe someday, somebody will do the same for me.

~ ~ ~

Interview

Friday 9/13/2019 – My friend and fellow writer Doug Dahlgren is going to be interviewing me today on his live Internet radio show.

I'll be talking about the memoirs classes I teach, the backyard beekeeping memoir I've published, and whatever other subjects happen to come up. I've been on Doug's show several times before talking about my various mysteries, and I can attest to his being a marvelous interviewer who brings out the best in every one of his guests.

There's something about a good interview that energizes everyone involved. Doug asks the kind of questions that make me think—and I always find myself caught up in the back-and-forth discussions we end up having.

So many conversations are simply a matter of one person waiting for the other to stop talking, but I've always tried to have discussions where each person has a chance to express their point of view (even when those points of view differ from my own).

Try a good conversation (or two or three) today. And enjoy them thoroughly.

Pre-Dawn Wonder

Saturday 9/14/2019 – After my usual pre-dawn walk this morning, I sat on my porch and just listened. The wind high in the trees, the soft breeze that wafted down occasionally and stirred my hair, crickets, tiny splashes from the leopard frog in the birdbath I placed right down on the ground in the shade a few months ago, the soprano song of a solitary mosquito that zeroed in on me for a breakfast feast, the hush-hush wing flaps of a bat (who probably ate that mosquito as soon as she left my arm), and a general background groaning of bugs. It was a full twenty minutes later before the first bird got around to calling out, and another ten before a sparrow dropped by for some safflower seeds. What a marvelous way to start the day.

Have a joy-filled weekend, and I'll be back on Monday.

~ ~ ~

If There's a Book

Monday 9/16/2019 – This really is why I started writing my Biscuit McKee mysteries. There simply weren't any books like them. Oh, there are plenty of books with librarians, with small-town cops, with cats – but none that had quite the combination I wanted to see in those characters, so I had to write them myself.

And I'm so glad I did.

As I work toward republishing all my books (except the ScotShop mysteries, since I don't have the rights to those), I've necessarily been re-reading them and discovering yet again how easy it is to fall in love with Martinsville.

What about you? Do you have a book (as yet unwritten) that you want to read?

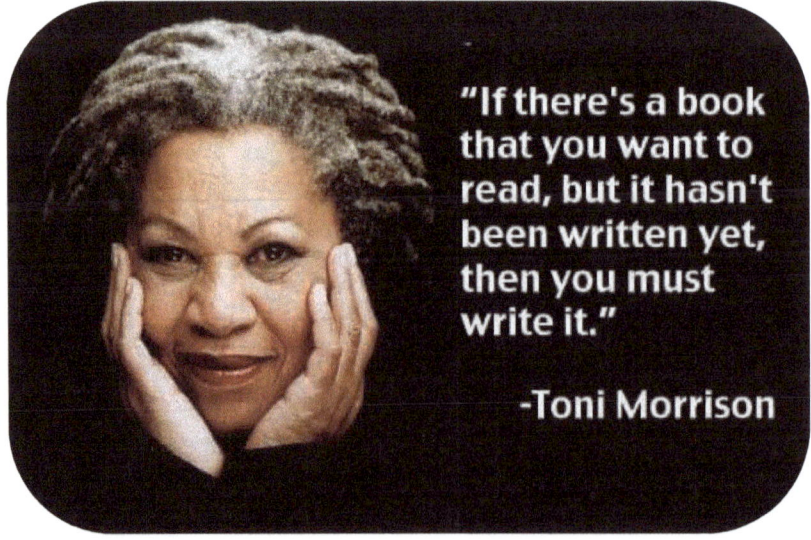

~ ~ ~

Finally!

Tuesday 9/17/2019 – This is about what my own sock-knitting efforts turned out to be. I've tried so many times, and they've been such a disaster. So I've given up. My daughter's a whiz at knitting socks. I'm happy to let her be the expert in the family.

After all, happiness is finally admitting that some things are just too much effort.

Isn't that right?

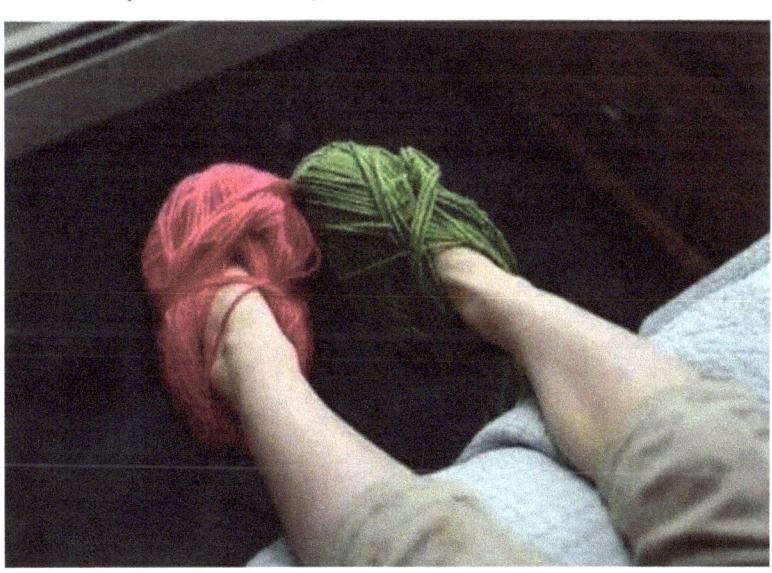

~ ~ ~

Cokie Roberts RIP

Wednesday 9/18/2019 – One of the finest journalists I have ever followed died yesterday. I listened to her reports on NPR ever since she started there as a congressional correspondent in the late '70s.

She was just so darn good at explaining what was going on. Her reports combined pinpoint accuracy with down-to-earth common sense. If you haven't read her book *Capital Dames: The Civil War and the Women of Washington, 1848-1868*, I'd like to encourage you to do so. It certainly opened my eyes to a lot of new info about the women who were instrumental in the shaping of this country. Just as Cokie herself (along with Linda Wertheimer and Nina Totenberg) was instrumental in shaping the development of National

Fran Stewart

Public Radio.

She once gave advice to new journalists: "Just do your work and get it on the air."

She certainly did her work, and I'm richer for having heard a great deal of it.

Rest in Peace, Cokie. I'll miss you.

~ ~ ~

Garden Gate

Thursday 9/19/2019 – When I look at this picture, I'm struck by how very much I would love to have a garden like this one – and how far I am from having anything like it. My vines have run rampant. I can't stand to cut down weeds, even the towering ones like the poke salad, because I see the hummingbirds drinking from their white flowers, and later I see birds investigating their fruits. I know they're eating those dark blue berries, because the birds then fly over my porch and leave purple poop where I can see it.

Not exactly a romantic image, is it? I daresay it's one a lot of gardeners deal with, but they just don't talk about such things.

Reminds me of a bunch of years ago when I was having some physical ailments and the surgeon said I needed a rectocele repair. "Very common surgery," he assured me. "I do these all the time."

"I've never heard of a rectocele repair," I countered. "Nobody I know has ever mentioned such a thing."

He skewered me with a penetrating glare. "How many people do you know who are willing to talk about their rectum in public?"

I guess he had a point.

So I'm here to tell you that rectocele repair can be a very good thing. And that purple poop isn't so bad either. As long as it's coming from the birds and not from me.

~ ~ ~

A Simple Life

Friday 9/20/2019 – Some years ago I read a book by Carol Pearson called *The Hero Within*. Marvelous book. I'd like to re-read it someday.

One of the things I remember most about it, though, was that she was talking about dealing with our dragons—the things that terrify us. "I'm going to let my dragons toast my morning bread," she wrote. (Or something very much like that—I'm writing this from memory, after all.)

I have a dragon that lives on the wall above my fireplace. One to serve as a toaster would be good, too. And one to curl around my feet while I sit reading in the evenings.

Yes! A simple life.

Fran Stewart

> I want a simple life. I want to get up late, drink tea, and read old books. I also want a spaceship and a pet dragon.

~ ~ ~

Meditation Shirt

Saturday 9/21/2019 – I like my new shirt and the message it carries: "Meditation is the best medication."

That said, I saw the cardiologist last Monday. He did all his tests and proclaimed that the regular medication I've been on for the past four years is doing the trick. I'm not against the pharmaceutical industry. When I needed meds four years ago when I came "this close" to a fatal heart attack, I was grateful they were available.

I DO, however, have a problem with the attitude that everything can be solved with a pill. Pain is available to call attention to something that needs our attention. If we insist on blocking every single pain imaginable, then we're going to miss what the Universe (through the vehicle of our body) is trying to tell us.

I still meditate. I still take the med. I'm okay with both of those statements.

~ ~ ~

Below Knee

Monday 9/23/2019 – I'd like to start this week with a funny.

Why?

Why not?

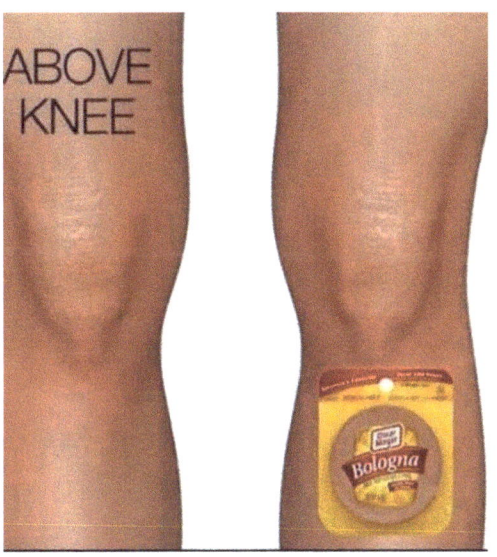

~ ~ ~

Shakespeare's "clichés"

Tuesday 9/24/2019 – They weren't clichés when they were first written. Shakespeare injected the English language with exciting exhilarating freshness. These are only a few of the phrases he coined. It's a shame, in a way, that words that were so new four-hundred-plus years ago, are now the very same words that editors tend to redline.

"Makes your hair stand on end," for instance. Think about how your heart must have lightened when—for the first time ever—you heard an actor proclaim the very feeling that you yourself had experienced, but had never been able to put into words.

Universal experiences brought into language. That's so much what Shakespeare was all about. The fact that we consider these phrases common today says a great deal about just how perceptive William was.

Let's hear it for the Bard!

Things We Say Today, Which We Owe to Shakespeare:

"Knock, knock! Who's there?" • "Heart of Gold" • "In a Pickle" • "Set Your Teeth on Edge" • "Faint Hearted" • "So-so" • "Good Riddance" • "Send Him Packing" • "Lie Low" • "Fight Fire with Fire" • "Baited Breath" • "Come What May" • "The Game is Up" • "Wear Your Heart on Your Sleeve" • "Not Slept One Wink" • "Full Circle" • "Out of the Jaws of Death" • "Too Much of a Good Thing" • "What's Done is Done" • "Naked Truth" • "Break the Ice" • "Wild Goose Chase" • "Laughing Stock" • "Breathed His Last" • "Heart of Hearts" • "Vanish into Thin Air" • "Seen Better Days" • "Makes Your Hair Stand on End" • "Dead as a Doornail" • "For Goodness' Sake" • "Love is Blind" • "Fair / Foul Play / Play" • "Off With His Head" • "Green Eyed Monster" • "The World is My Oyster" • "Brave New World" • "Be All / End All" • "A Sorry Sight"

p.s. My only correction to this is that *baited breath* should be *bated breath*. It comes from the word "abate," which means to lessen something, so a *bated breath* is one that you're holding.

~ ~ ~

Without Rain

Wednesday 9/25/2019 – My dear friend Petie is dealing with flooding in her Houston home, while here where I am, the plants around my house are gasping for rain. I wish we could average the two.

I've started taking an umbrella with me wherever I go. Why?

I'm glad you asked.

Twenty or so years ago, when Georgia was still in the "hundred-year drought," I began taking my umbrella with me. After all, why pray for rain if you aren't prepared to deal with it? I walked into the post office one sunny day to find a VERY long line, with only one harried postal worker behind the counter. As we all inched forward, someone told a joke and we all laughed. Someone else remarked on the weather and most of the people groaned. I held up my umbrella. "It's going to rain," I said. The man in front of me scoffed, but the woman behind me said, "Looks like you're prepared for it."

As we waited—and waited—and waited, the skies began to darken just a bit. I was probably the only person who noticed it, but I didn't say anything. Finally, I reached the counter. As I was paying to mail my package, the woman behind me stepped forward and tapped me on the shoulder. "Look!"

I smiled, accepted my change, went outside, and opened my umbrella. Everybody else just got wet as they ran for their cars.

~ ~ ~

Wooly Bear in the Desk

Thursday 9/26/2019 – I have a sneaky feeling that everybody has a bookcase hidden away somewhere that looks as messy as this one.

But you have to admit, those chaotic areas make a great place for somebody like my soft black Wooly Bear to hide away. Can you see her golden eye peeking out at you?

~ ~ ~

i before e

Friday 9/27/2019 – While we're talking about the English language (as we were just three days ago), here's a thought-provoking mug.

Why thought-provoking?

As I so often say, I'm glad you asked.

When I was a kid and first learned "i before e except after c, or when sounded like A as in neighbor and weigh," it never occurred to me to question that dictum. Never. I could spell as well as anybody and better than most—including all those "ei" words—but I'd been taught that teachers were always right, that people in authority always knew what they were talking about, that adults always needed to be listened to, that news items had always been well-researched, that we children could depend on the big folks to tell us what was true. And, up until Richard Nixon, I believed presidents were men of integrity.

I'm so glad that people like Greta Thunberg speak out now, as I never would have had the courage to do when I was her age. I never even considered the possibility.

I'm glad people make mugs like this one, but I'd like to see one that—like Greta—says, "How Dare You?"

~ ~ ~

No Excetions

Saturday 9/28/2019 – This one speaks for itself, but I'm going to say some more about it after you read the sign.

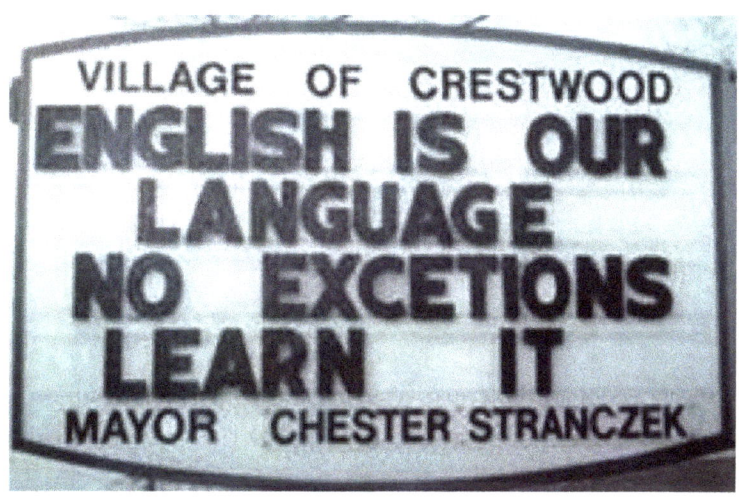

I love public radio because I hear so many different accents. I loved living in Europe as a child, because I met so many people who spoke two, three, or four languages (and nobody thought that was a strange thing).

Fran Stewart

Learning a new language helps us to understand the world from a different viewpoint—like the languages (Inuit, Swedish, Sami, Icelandic, Scots) that have multiple words for snow, or the one spoken by the Bedouins that contain 74 different terms related to camels.

Of course, we have more than a dozen words for a big sandwich, depending on where in the USA we live – hoagie, hero, sub, grinder, spukie, wedge, po'boy, zep, blimpie … Says a lot about where our national focus lies.

That's it, folks – no excetions.

~ ~ ~

GA Aquarium

Monday 9/30/2019 – Saturday my friend Millie and I went to the Georgia Aquarium. We wandered through it until we got to the Beluga Whale viewing window. There we stayed for almost an hour, watching the aquatic acrobatics and downright shenanigans of those five magnificent critters.

One of the trainers eventually threw a large square of bright red cloth in the water, and it was promptly claimed by one of the females. She tugged it around, sometimes wrapping it around her fluke, sometimes nosing into it so it covered her entire head. Another of the females made a few tries at grabbing it, but she always yanked it away in time.

Then—thank goodness I was watching the two of them at that instant—the second whale grabbed the cloth and ran [uh…swam] for it. The chase was on!

I tried a number of times to get a picture of them, but between the low light level, my old camera, and the swirliness of the water, nothing turned out. That's okay, though. I have my memories of that perfect hour. And this picture of an obliging Sea Dragon seahorse, which posed without moving. I wish the photo did justice to the brilliant yellow of the dragon's coloring.

October 2019

A Great Fall

Tuesday 10/1/2019 – I can't help it. I still think October should be Autumn-ish. Not the late-summer it is here in the Atlanta area.

This picture shows the kind of Fall we ought to have.

I know. I know! Love what is. Accept the weather whatever it may be.

But the part of me that lived in Colorado for five years and in Vermont for twenty-six years still somehow believes that this is the time to get out my turtlenecks.

~ ~ ~

Old Growth Forest Network

Wednesday 10/2/2019 – A dozen years ago, I bought and read a book by Joan Maloof called *Teaching the Trees*. She soon began the process of establishing an Old Growth Forest Network, with the aim of preserving, protecting, and promoting the country's few remaining stands of old-growth forest. Take a look at the website (oldgrowthforest.net). You might even find an old-growth forest near you. If so, try visiting it.

Fran Stewart

If you don't have one nearby, you can read about old-growth forests not only on Maloof's website, but also in *Indigo as an Iris*, my fifth Biscuit McKee mystery. The fictional town I created has three stands of original trees that were saved from being clear-cut back in 1745 when the town was founded. To find out why, you'll have to read the White as Ice quadrilogy (the last four books of the Biscuit McKee series).

Walking among trees—any trees—is good for the soul. Walking among ancient trees heals in a very special way.

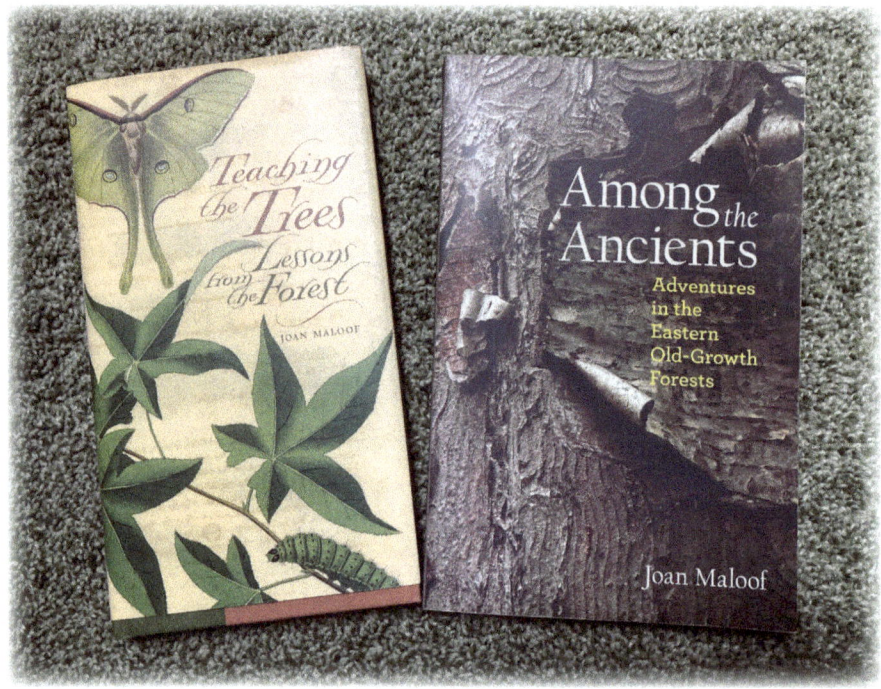

~ ~ ~

3 frogs

Thursday 10/3/2019 – Look who showed up in my former birdbath!

When the post supporting this old birdbath broke last winter, I placed the top of it down on the ground next to my "Do Good in the World" pole, wondering if the birds would continue to use it. They did. I see them sipping water there every once in a while.

Then, early this summer, a frog showed up. One frog.

Frog number one must have spread the word. Now there are three. Can you see them there?

I guess when it comes down to the bottom line, we're all looking for a puddle to cool off in. Sometimes it's not perfect, but we make the best of it. After all, if we have friends in there with us, even a leftover, half-broken cast-off will feel like sheer heaven.

~ ~ ~

3D Beak for Karl

Friday 10/4/2019 – I decided some time ago to subscribe to a daily email from Smithsonian Magazine. They send out a list of interesting stories, some of which I check out and others I ignore, depending on the amount of time I have available to me. The same with the NatGeo Pictures of the Week. I very seldom click on a link to take me elsewhere. Ditto the e-newsletters from my alma mater and the daily news digest from the CBC.

Nothing but links, links, links. I usually check my emails twice a day—early morning and late afternoon. In the evening, when I'd have time to check out all those links, my computer is generally turned off, I have a cat in my lap, and a book is much easier to pick up. Why would I want to disturb Fuzzy Britches just so I could go to my laptop?

Today's emphasis on linking things is a far cry from the days of my childhood when my parents received a big yellow *National Geographic* each month, and I spent hours poring over every issue, reading it cover to cover and then going back to re-read it several times. It was always there on the coffee table for me to pick up whenever I had a chance. Have I ever told you that I learned to read because a) my father read to me regularly, and b) the *National Geographic* was there to help me hone my skills?

I choose not to do email or Internet stuff on my phone. It was a conscious decision a number of years ago. I don't object to technology. I do object to the tendency to think that more and more data more and more of the time means more and more knowledge.

Do I miss some very good stories? Probably. Do I regret the way I've arranged my life? Not at all.

So why am I encouraging you to find this Smithsonian article?

I'm glad you asked.

This is one of the few stories I followed through the Internet maze this week. All because an artist colleague of mine, Joyce Ryan, has experimented with 3D printing her sculpture, and I wondered about the scientific practicality of creating a new lower beak for a bird using 3D technology.

If you're interested in that—and have the time—do a search for *3D Bill for Karl* and enjoy the story. If you're not—or you don't have the time—just know that Karl, an Abyssinian ground hornbill, now has an artificial beak that works beautifully. A happy story, even without the links.

~ ~ ~

The Old Red Barn

Saturday 10/5/2019 – When I moved to Vermont back in 1968 just shortly after I was married, there was an intersection between the towns of Williston and Essex Junction where a big old red barn dominated one corner. It was a handy structure, in that anybody could give directions based on it. "Head out Williston Road," they'd say, "and turn left at the red barn."

I've known people like that old barn. People who have helped to give my life a sense of direction. Most of them, now that I think about it, were teachers. Mr. Connor, 10th grade social studies. Miss Helen Johnson, junior high school English. Mrs. Martha Van Aken, 12th grade English. Mrs. McChesney, 6th grade at Jefferson Elementary. Mr. Cooley, 7th grade math. And the one whose name I can't remember—10th grade driver's ed.

So often, when I'm faced with a difficult decision, their words or actions offer me guidance even before

I'm aware of having asked for it.

"But," I can hear you asking, "aren't they dead by now?"

"Sure," I say. "Just like the big old red barn."

"Huh?"

You see, that barn burned down one year, but that never stopped anybody who lived in those parts from still giving directions. "Turn right at the red barn," they'd say. The fact that the red barn was no longer visible made no difference whatsoever. We all knew where it was.

So, Mrs. Van Aken, I'm still turning left or right or going straight ahead when your sturdy presence in my life suggests that THAT's the best way to go.

I hope that someday I'll be a red barn kind of person.

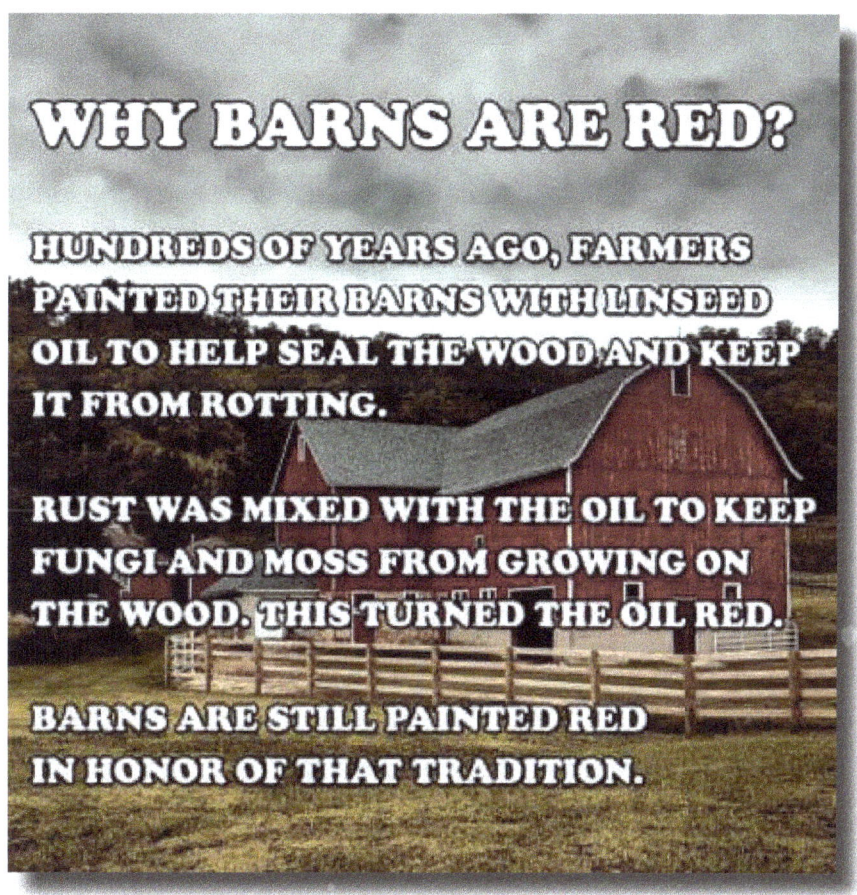

~ ~ ~

Tree Meditation

Monday 10/7/2019 – I thought this tree meditation was a very good thing to think about today. Why? Well, yesterday afternoon a friend of mine picked me up and took me to a concert given by the Gwinnett Sym-

Fran Stewart

phony Orchestra and Chorus.

On the way there, her husband, who was riding in the passenger seat, mentioned how much he enjoyed my posts. He pulled up Saturday's post on his phone and read aloud the text on the photo. "Mixed with rust?" he said. "Didn't know that."

"Did you read what I wrote about it?" I asked.

No, he hadn't. "A millennial," he told me, "would probably just comment TMT DNR."

I had no idea what that meant, so he explained. "Too much text. Did not read."

Oh.

Something in his tone told me that he agreed with that point of view.

That gave me something to think about. You see, the value of these daily posts, as far as I'm concerned, is in the text. Sure, the photos are sometimes amusing, sometimes thought provoking, sometimes informative, sometimes a bit silly. But there are hundreds—thousands—of people out there posting entertaining photos every day, just as there are authors out there churning out two, three, or four books a year because that's the best way to make money as a published writer.

I'm not one of those.

If all you do is look at the picture every day, that's like walking by the open door of a restaurant and just sniffing the air. It's like jogging by a towering oak and not even noticing the dappled sunlight through its leaves.

I would invite you to slow down—step into the restaurant or rest a while beneath the tree—but then again, if you don't read this invitation, you'll miss the point. Still, even if you DNR my posts, I wish you well. Of course, without reading what I've written, you'll never know that.

And thanks to Jeri Eset for sharing this tree meditation with me. The photo is rather fuzzy, so in case you can't read it, here's what it says:

>There is more to life
>than measuring its speed.
>Let me look upward into
>the branches of the towering oak
>and know that it grew great and strong
>because it grew slowly and well.
>Slow me down, Lord, and inspire me
>To send my roots deep into the
>soil of life's enduring values.
>*Author unknown*

> There is more to life
> than measuring its speed.
> Let me look upward into
> the branches of the towering oak
> and know that it grew great and strong
> because it grew slowly and well.
> Slow me down, Lord, and inspire me
> to send my roots deep into the
> soil of life's enduring values.
>
> — Orlin L. Johnson

~ ~ ~

Where the Sun Shines

Tuesday 10/8/2019 – Georgia has had entirely too much sunshine lately. We need some rain.

I'm quite capable of finding happiness where the sun shines, as this photo (and this cow) urges me to do. But I'm also capable of appreciating a rainy day (or two or three.) When the very trees around me appear to be gasping for moisture, I find it hard to appreciate the weather forecasters who are bleating, "Another fine day coming up!"

Let's hear it for rain—ample gentle rain for the trees (and rain for me, too).

Fran Stewart

And if you're in one of the flooded areas of the US, feel free to substitute sun for rain and rain for sun.

~ ~ ~

find the time

Wednesday 10/9/2019 – I've made time recently to do something really fun. It's also really helpful, but the reason I began it was because of the fun element.

The Gwinnett Citizen Fire Academy Alumni Association (GCFAAA) agreed to help out with our county's paramedic training for firefighters. How? By volunteering to be "patients" during their training period. It's one thing to work on a dummy, but no matter how technologically advanced the thing is, it's quite another experience to be confronted with a live human being.

They sent out a list ahead of time, so we'd know what we're suffering from and what we have to act like. This week I got to be a pretend stroke victim. The person in the next room was having chest pain; the one down the hall had congestive heart failure. Next week I'll have a pretend bloodstream infection, while the other two GCFAA volunteers will have pneumonia and asthma.

No idea what the week after that will bring for the three of us. But it's sure to be fun.

What sort of special moments have you taken time for lately?

~ ~ ~

Don't sit on the cactus

Thursday 10/10/2019 – Have you been sitting on a cactus lately? Every once in a while over the years I've found myself doing that, and it's darned uncomfortable.

Fortunately, the older I get, the less inclined I am to wallow in self-pity. Or self-flagellation.

Yesterday, as I met with a number of other Pen Women at our Stone Mountain Pen Women Nature Garden, I felt nothing but joy. The weather was cooler than it usually is, but I simply wore a jacket. The day was cloudy, and I gloried in not having to look for shade to avoid the direct sun. My back had a few proclamations to make, but I just said, "Thanks for sharing, spine. Now I'm going to walk the paths and enjoy myself."

No cactus sitting yesterday. None today, either.

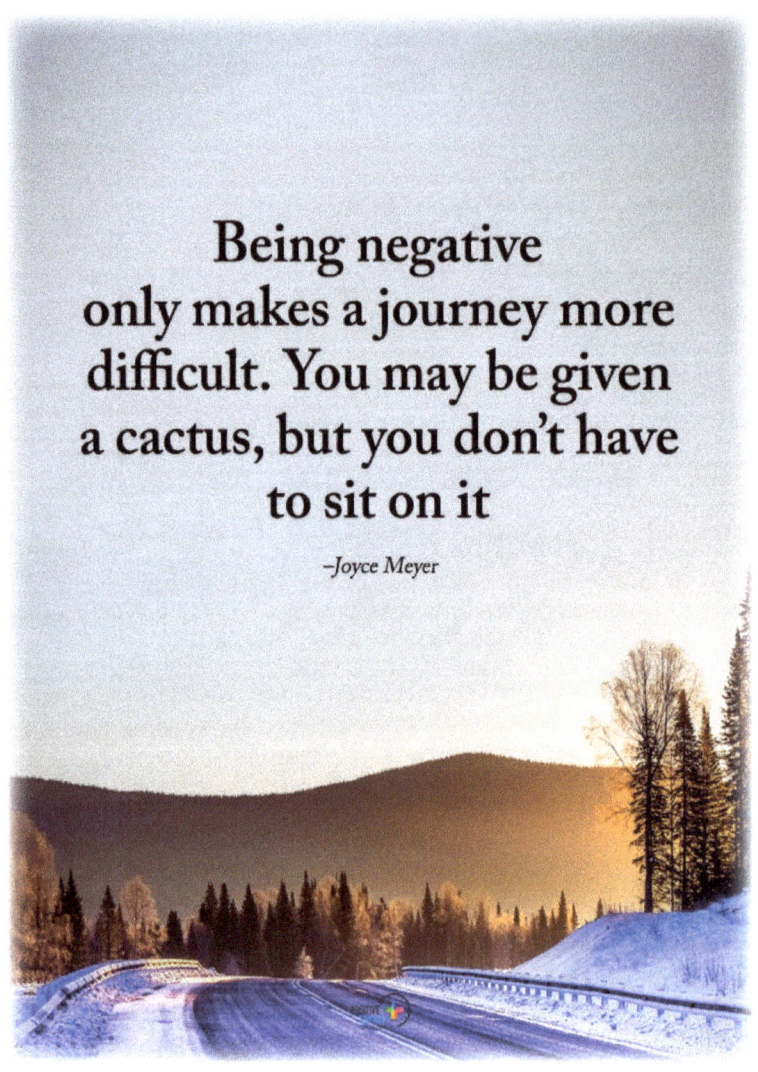

~ ~ ~

Prisoner of Your Past

Friday 10/11/2019 – In the memoirs classes that I'm teaching, we talk a lot about how writing the stories of our lives can help us to put our life in perspective, to see the value of all the various experiences we've had (or endured).

Sort of like the message in yesterday's post, we talk about how there's no need to sit on a cactus. Instead of dwelling on past mistakes, we can acknowledge them and then—the important part—figure out just what we learned from those detours in what we thought should have been our path.

Just a lesson. Not a life sentence.

~ ~ ~

Ravenmaster & Ravens

Saturday 10/12/2019 – I just finished reading *The Ravenmaster* by Christopher Skaife. I've been spending a lot of time over the past few years reading memoirs, and the good ones give me a chance to use great examples in the memoirs classes I'm teaching. The not-so-good ones I just ignore.

The Ravenmaster is one of the good ones. I've long been entranced by ravens, and thoroughly enjoyed learning more about them. Combine the birds with the Tower of London—how can you go wrong? There's even a ghost story or two in the book. The White Tower is where I saw two ghosts when I was in London many years ago. I assume they're still roaming the place. Along with the ravens.

[I took these photos from the Ravenmaster Facebook page.]

~ ~ ~

Autumn's Coming

Monday 10/14/2019 – love it when Orion shows up in the northern hemisphere. That's the harbinger of fall, and I always feel like I'm greeting an old friend when I walk outside after dark or before dawn and see that belt of three stars.

I'm afraid a lot of the color now is caused by the drought here in Georgia, not by the onset of autumn. But since fall brings not only Orion, but sometimes a bit more moisture to the land—to say nothing of the cooler temps—I'm ready to embrace it.

Especially the hot cocoa.

~ ~ ~

quiet courage

Tuesday 10/15/2019 – I have a friend who, over the last five months, managed to make it through intensive chemotherapy and a 12-hour surgery, only to have fallen last week. She had to go through an operation last Friday to repair a broken hip.

My heart aches for her.

I wish there were more I could do to help.

I applaud her quiet courage.

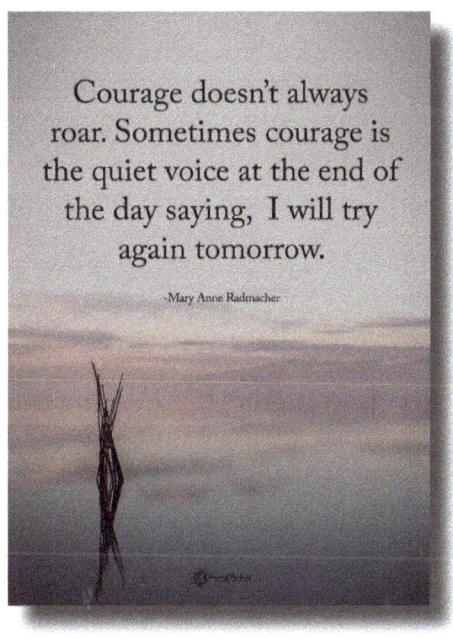

~ ~ ~

Alcohol and Fats

Wednesday 10/16/2019 – I've never trusted fads. Fads in clothing, diet fads, self-care fads.

They strike me as being more market-driven than sense-driven.

I've eaten and loved butter all my adult life. When "everyone" started saying it was bad for the body, I ignored them. Then, a few decades later, margarine was on the no-no list.

Eat more protein. Eat less protein. No fats. Only good fats. Lose weight fast. Lose it slowly.

Blah-blah-blah.

Fran Stewart

I say, love what you eat. Love what you wear. Love what you say. Love those you associate with. If you can't love it, do without it. Your life will be richer.

Alcohol & Fats

It's a relief to know the truth after all those conflicting medical studies.

The Japanese eat very little fat and suffer fewer heart attacks than the British or Americans.

The French eat a lot of fat and also suffer fewer heart attacks than the British or Americans.

The Japanese drink very little red wine and suffer fewer heart attacks than the British or Americans.

The Italians drink excessive amounts of red wine and also suffer fewer heart attacks than the British or Americans.

The Germans drink a lot of beer and eat lots of sausages and fats and suffer fewer heart attacks than the British or Americans.

Conclusion: Eat and drink what you like. Speaking English is apparently what kills you.

~ ~ ~

downy woodpecker in my house

Thursday 10/17/2019 – Yesterday afternoon I heard an unusual commotion upstairs. When I went to investigate, I found that Wooly Bear had cornered a female Downy Woodpecker on a bench in my bedroom. As I pulled the cat away, the bird fell to the floor and squeezed behind a curtain. I reached in and grabbed her as gently as I could, being sure I'd trapped her wings against her body so she couldn't flap them and injure herself.

Although I wanted to take the time to examine her for blood, injuries, or other problems, I knew she was terrified, so I took her outside as quickly as I could, opened my hand, and—within about a second and a half—watched her fly to the thicket that fills the northern corner of my front yard.

Downies are the smallest of the woodpecker varieties, and the females have no red on their heads. I know they're very good at getting into small crevices in trees to root out tasty bugs.

I also know that in the Native American totem, woodpeckers are connected to the rhythm, the heartbeat of Mother Earth. So my SECOND question was what on earth was the message she was trying to convey to me by coming so dramatically into my space? One of the spirit messages of woodpeckers is to look more clearly—in black and white so to speak—at what's going on in one's life.

There will be time over the next few days to reflect on that second question. But my FIRST question was how the heck did she get inside my house? I certainly would have noticed if a woodpecker, even a small one, had flown in as I walked through a doorway. Anyway, I'm always very careful about doors, simply because Wooly Bear and Fuzzy Britches are both 100% inside cats.

Yes, they have a catio they can get onto by creeping through a cat flap in a living room window, but that catio is completely enclosed in hardware cloth to keep them safe from predatory dogs (or people). No woodpecker, even a little Downy, could squeeze through the half-inch openings in that heavy wire screening.

So I searched my entire house. Every window was closed. The opening to the attic space was still fully blocked by its wooden door. There aren't any holes in the walls anywhere. Every furnace vent is intact. My skylights haven't been breached.

And a further indication that I don't have any clear openings to the outside is that my furnace isn't working overtime (as it would have been if there'd been a hole somewhere letting in the 40-degree weather).

There is, however, one other little clue (besides the woodpecker) that something somewhere in this house is letting in the outside. I've been inundated with flies over the past three days. In the fifteen years I've lived here, I've seen maybe three flies, each one of which flew into the house when I opened a door. But in the last three days I've evicted almost three dozen of the things. After 30 or so, I pulled out an old hardly-ever-used flyswatter and started executing them.

Fran Stewart

The spirit meaning of the housefly is a reminder that I have the ingenuity to see things through and the power that means nothing can stop me. It's also a reminder to root out any negativity in my life.

Fine.

I just want to root out the flies.

And no more woodpeckers inside, please.

(Photo credit: Audubon Society - James M. Wedge/VIREO)

~ ~ ~

Honeybee fossil

Friday 10/18/2019 – Once upon a time, a bee was trapped in a shale formation in what is now Nevada. The recognizable vein patterns in the wing (and various other body parts) proves that honeybees existed in North America 14 million years ago

In another 14 million years, what will be the legacy we've left behind?

I hope one of the things that remains is the US Constitution.

~ ~ ~

English pronunciation

Saturday 10/19/2019 – Let's end the week marveling yet again at the vagaries of the English language.

I've been foiled by so many of the languages I've tried to learn. I take that back. I've been foiled by my lack of follow-through in trying to learn them. At any rate, people who start with one language and learn another are to be applauded. I am in absolute awe of anyone who manages to learn English as a second language.

Then again, it would be admirable if we'd learn to speak our own language properly. I'm getting tired of

Fran Stewart

reading books in which the author doesn't know the difference between peek and peak and pique. Or lie and lay. Or access and excess. Or . . .

Well, I'm sure you get the idea.

> If you can correctly pronounce every word in this poem, you will be speaking English better than 90% of the native English speakers in the world.
>
> crimsun
>
> Dearest creature in creation,
> Study English pronunciation.
> I will teach you in my verse
> Sounds like corpse, corps, horse, and worse.
> I will keep you, Suzy, busy,
> Make your head with heat grow dizzy.
> Tear in eye, your dress will tear.
> So shall I! Oh hear my prayer.
> Just compare heart, beard, and heard,
> Dies and diet, lord and word,
> Sword and sward, retain and Britain.
> (Mind the latter, how it's written.)
> Now I surely will not plague you
> With such words as plaque and ague.
> But be careful how you speak:
> Say break and steak, but bleak and streak;
> Cloven, oven, how and low,
> Script, receipt, show, poem, and toe...

~ ~ ~

Cover

Monday 10/21/2019 – *BeesKnees #2: A Beekeeping Memoir*, the second volume of my latest book series is available now in print. I'd like to share one of the chapters with you, just because it seems like a good way to start the week. And if you go searching for the book online, be sure you type BeesKnees as one word—and add the #2 to the title. Amazon keeps trying to correct the search to Bees Knees (two words), so you may have to jump through hoops to find it. Try including the colon and the subtitle, or putting quotation marks around the title. [The easiest way to find a correct link is to go to my website franstewart.com].

Day #134 Civilization - Wednesday, Feb. 23, 2011

I keep saying that bees haven't really changed since their beginnings. Well, guess what? I'm not too sure people have changed much either. We have increased our technology and our languages. But have we changed in any substantive way? Are human beings any different than they were a couple of million years ago?

I once was asked in a class to explain how people have changed over the course of history. My answer, I'm sorry to say, was that as people became more "civilized," they simply increased the distance over which they could hurt each other.

Think about it. A bee butts a person to scare him away from the hive. As a last resort, the bee will sting, thereby killing herself. This has been true for more than 140 million years. Now think about people. We, like bees, used to be able to hurt people only if they were close by, within an arm's length of us. Then, with such tools as language and weapons, we gradually extended the range over which we could cause pain.

On the other hand, we've also increased the distance at which we can cause joy. A phone call from my sister or a dear friend can brighten my day considerably, no matter how far that person is from me geographically. A well-written book brings me joy even if the author is on the far side of the country—or the globe—or on the far side of the grave.

Bees still have to "bee" right next to each other to communicate, but we humans can reach each other happily at any distance. What a relief. Maybe there's hope for us humans after all.

BeeAttitude for Day #134: *Blessed are the children, for they shall be the harvesters of tomorrow.*

Comments:

    Pete Ogg I have loved your bee pages for years !!! This is a keeper for sure !!

~ ~ ~

the emptier the wagon

Tuesday 10/22/2019 – I'd like my wagon to be full. Full of:

> ideas
> good thoughts
> wonderful family
> great friends
> open-mindedness
> thoughtful memories
> peaceful evenings
> kind words
> willingness to learn
> loving communications
> the courage of my convictions
> helpfulness
> inspiration

What's in your wagon?

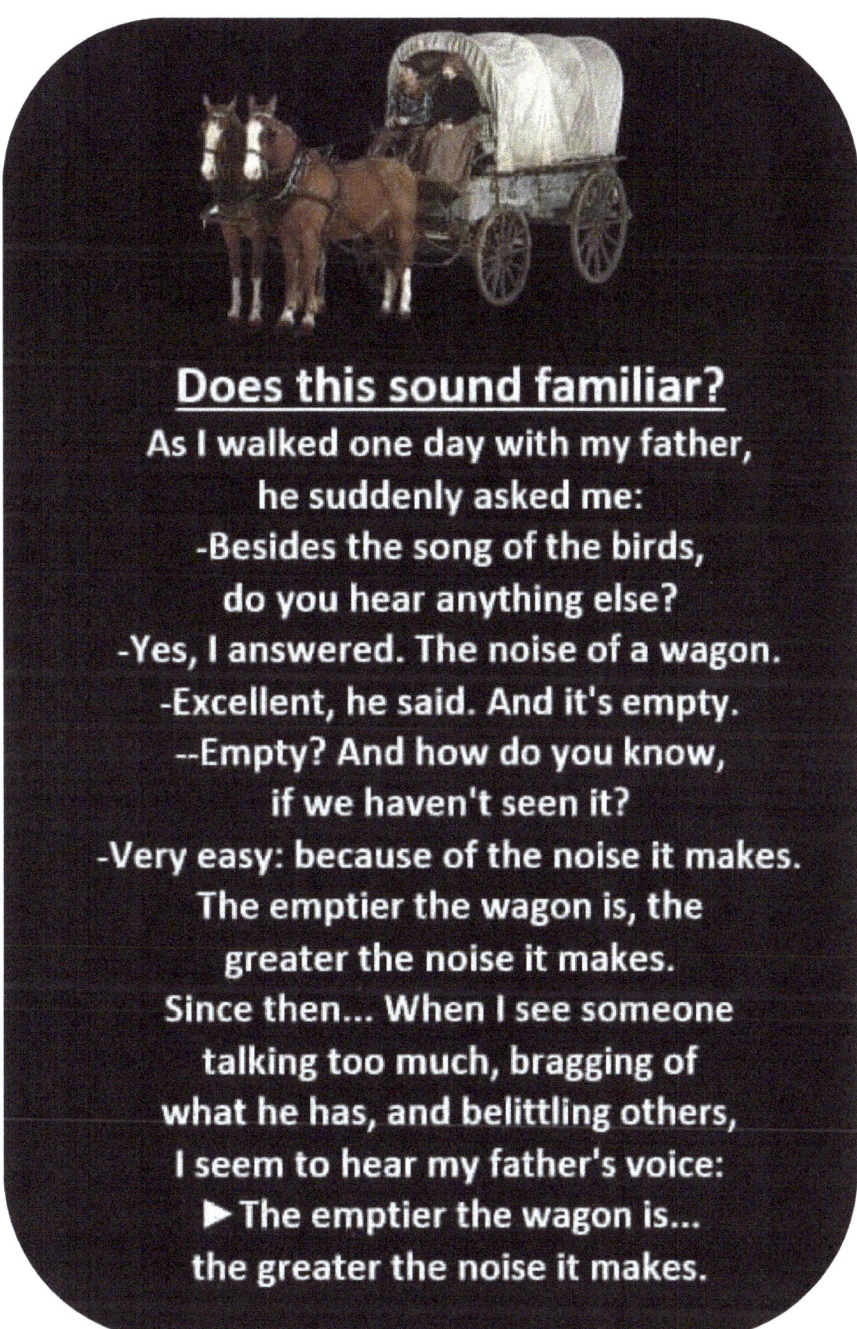

~ ~ ~

read read as read

Wednesday 10/23/2019 – Time for another journey into spelling/reading/pronunciation.

Are you laughing as hard as I am?

~ ~ ~

Clean the House?

Thursday 10/24/2019 – A number of years ago, I made the mistake of mentioning the Mary & Martha story to my sister. I was trying to make the point that too many people get caught up in an everyday hassle without taking time to read, to reflect, to ponder.

She took the opposite approach. "And who would have fed everybody if Martha hadn't been in the kitchen cooking? How would they have even gotten into the house if she hadn't kept it tidy and clean?"

She had a point, but she wasn't finished yet. "There's value in work done well."

Absolutely. I agree.

Still, given the choice—and it's ALWAYS a choice—between dusting and reading, guess what wins out in my house? That's why my sister's house is an open, airy, inviting space that people love to visit, and mine (my choice) is more like a peaceful hermit's den where I'm just as likely not to invite folks in. I don't live in squalor, but dusting is one of the least of my priorities.

So, if you've never seen inside my house, don't feel bad about it. Not many people have.

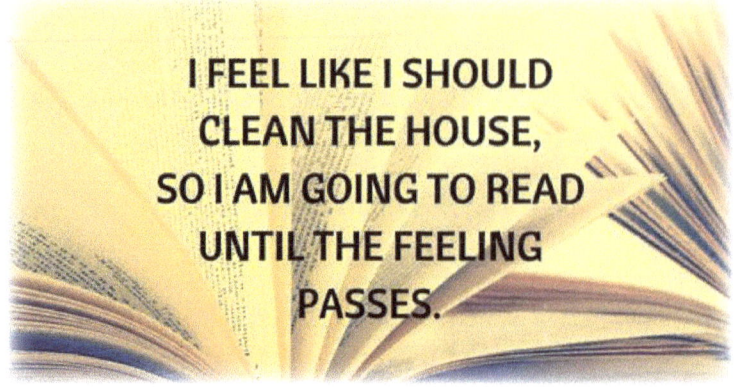

~ ~ ~

Musical Terms

Friday 10/25/2019 – Have you ever had a tempo tantrum? Ever been bothered by flute flies? Let's do some a patella singing in honor of these clever musical terms.

p.s. Why is this post so short? My sixth BeesKnees book will be released in e-book format on November 4th, so that's where I'm putting my energy this morning. Meanwhile, slap your knee and sing a little. Or a lot!

MUSICAL TERMS

ALLEREGRETTO: When you're 16 measures into the piece and suddenly realize you set a too-fast tempo

ANGUS DEI: To play, with a divinely beefy tone

A PATELLA: Accompanied by knee-slapping

APOLOGGIATURA: A composition that you regret playing

APPROXIMATURA: A series of notes not intended by the composer, yet played with an "I meant to do that" attitude

APPROXIMENTO: A musical entrance that is somewhere in the vicinity of the correct pitch

DILL PICCOLINI: An exceedingly small wind instrument that plays only sour notes

FERMANTRA: A note held over and over and over and over and...

FIDDLER CRABS: Grumpy string players

FLUTE FLIES: Those tiny insects that bother musicians in outdoor gigs

FRUGALHORN: A sensible and inexpensive brass instrument

GAUL BLATTER: A French horn player

GREGORIAN CHAMP: The title bestowed upon the monk who can hold a note the longest

PLACEBO DOMINGO: A faux tenor

SPRITZICATO: An indication to string instruments to produce a bright and bubbly sound

TEMPO TANTRUM: What an elementary school orchestra is having when it's not following the conductor

Fran Stewart

~ ~ ~

matter of a pinion

Saturday 10/26/2019 – Why did I mess up this joke photo that's been circulating around the Internet for an unconscionably long time? Ravens have been on my mind a lot recently. There was the time in Vermont when we rescued a raven who'd gotten his legs tangled up in fishing line. There was the book *Bellman & Black* by Diane Setterfield that my book club read for our meeting last week. Another book I recently finished reading is *Ravenmaster* by the man who leads the team that cares for the ravens at the Tower of London. And then along comes this joke about the "difference between crows and ravens."

The only trouble is that it's completely totally absolutely wrong!

Crows and ravens both have 10 pinions. And if you don't believe me, check out CorvidResearch dot blog/2018/12/21/a-matter-of-a-pinion/

Now, why would I want to ruin a good joke by quoting facts?

Come on! I'll always vote for the truth over the cheap laugh.

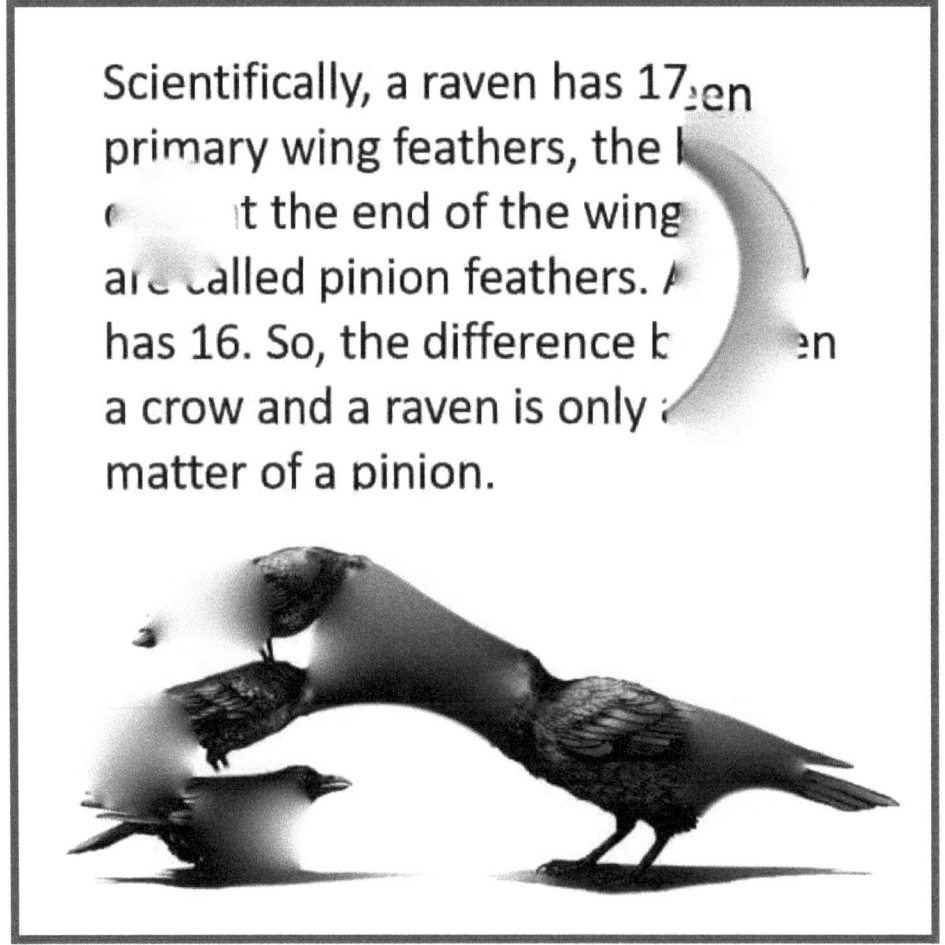

~ ~ ~

Raven at the Tower

Monday 10/28/2019 – Good morning! Yesterday I went from treachery and lots of blood (*Julius Caesar* at Atlanta's Shakespeare Tavern) to a virtual visit from the ravens at the Tower of London. I've saved a lot of raven photos from the Ravenmaster FB page, since I just happen to love these bright eyes and quizzical head tilts.

I wish you well in the coming week. I hope we remain alive to our curiosity. I hope we appreciate every breath. I hope we open our ears to the music of Mother Earth that surrounds us every moment.

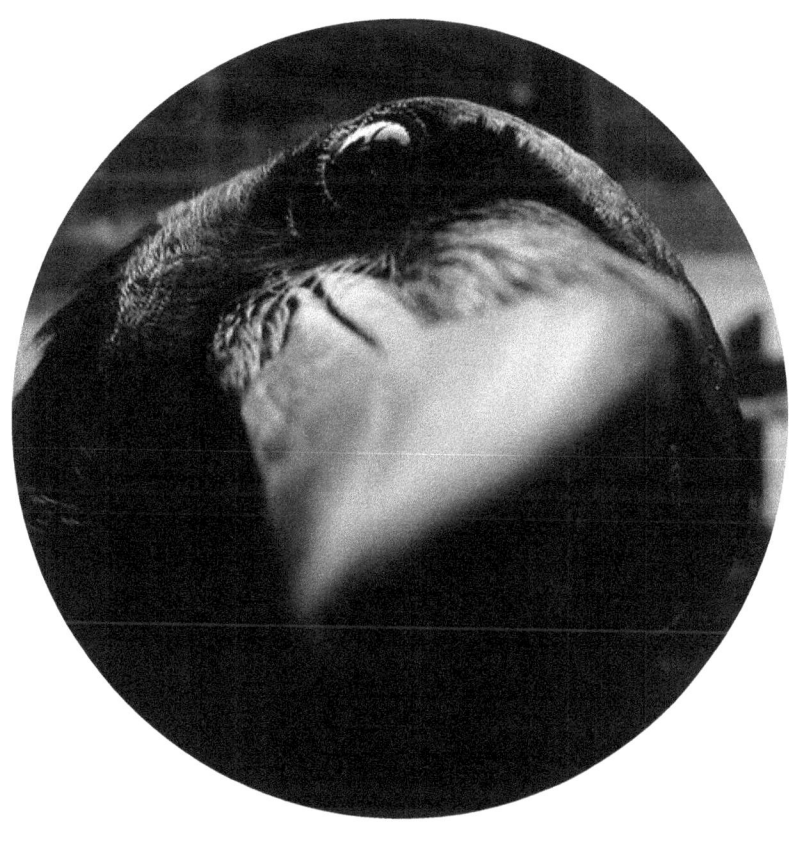

~ ~ ~

Who else loves it

Tuesday 10/29/2019 – My sister in Colorado is dealing with snow. My friend in Texas is dealing with floods. But here I sit in Georgia wishing for more rain—enough to end the drought and save the trees.

There's just something special about that smell of newly wet soil that can make me stop in my tracks. At that point, I don't care if I get soaked. I just want to breathe it in and relish the aroma. It's almost a taste.

Fran Stewart

And I can hear the trees saying, "Thank you, thank you, thank you."

There's a local hummingbird who tends to sit on the top of the birdfeeder pole and bathe in a downpour whenever it comes. I know just how she feels.

~ ~ ~

Coordinated Colors

Wednesday 10/30/2019 – Yesterday I showed off print copies of *BeesKnees #1* and *BeesKnees #2* to my memoirs class at Brenau. One of the women noticed that the covers were green (#1) and purple (#2)—and I was wearing a green turtleneck with a purple scarf. Honestly, I hadn't planned it that way. I hadn't even thought about it.

She took a picture and emailed it to me, but I can't figure out how to get it moved out of my computer and into this post. <<<sigh>>> So, today I'll be invisible. Maybe that will give me a chance to look at the world from a new perspective…

Meanwhile, I can show you the two covers. You'll just have to imagine the turtleneck and the scarf.

LATER THAT DAY: I finally figured it out! Here's the picture I meant to post this morning.

~ ~ ~

Halloween 2019

Thursday 10/31/2019 —I know what I want to be the next time I go trick-or-treating.

Only trouble is—I need some fur to start with.

And great big ears would help, too.

Guess I'll have to think of a different disguise—I mean costume.

Fran Stewart

November 2019

Cooperate like the trees

Friday 11/1/2019 – Wouldn't it be lovely if we all cooperated the way trees do?

That's all I have to say for today – except to wish you a November filled with gratitude.

~ ~ ~

Anty Bodies

Saturday 11/2/2019 – I sure am grateful for every healthy thing about my life. I must have good little anty bodies myself, just like the teeny critters who have invaded my house. They do it every fall and every spring. After 20-plus years in this state, I should get used to them.

When I took that Bugs 101 course from the University of Alberta, I had great fun learning about all the lessons we can learn from insects. Yes, some of them are annoying to have around, but if you have them, you might as well learn from them. Right?

My ants, for instance, teach me that Fuzzy Britches and Wooly Bear tend to drop little bits of cat food here and there. Ants to the rescue. They're the cleanup crew, showing me exactly where I missed with the mop. They also show me where I splashed a few soup dribbles and didn't even realize it.

Thank you, little anty folks. I appreciate you.

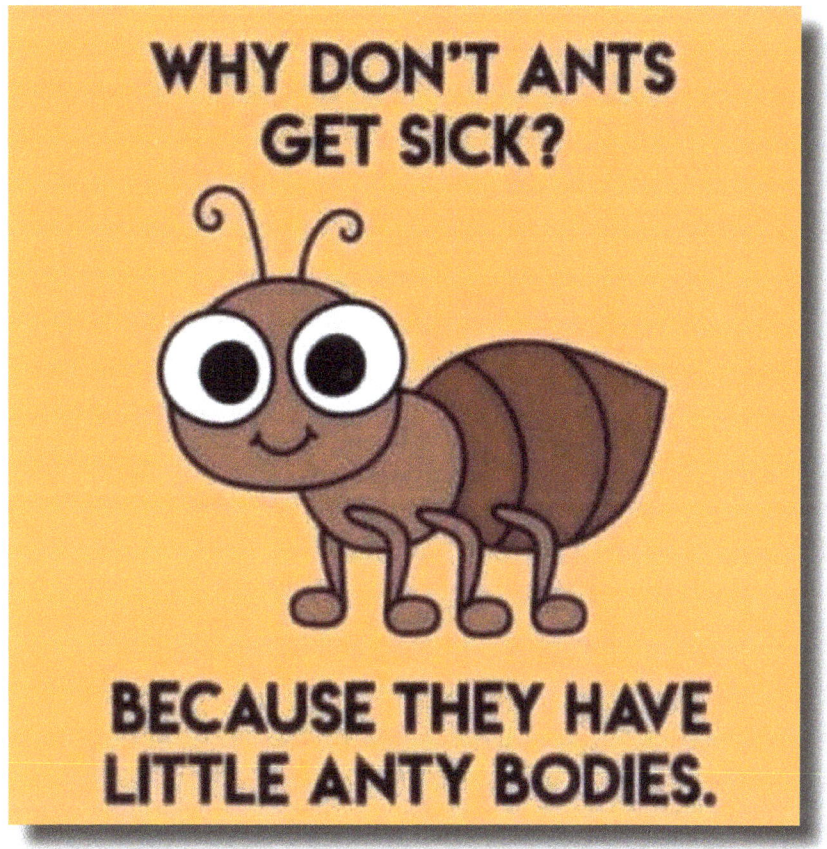

~ ~ ~

Two Postcards

Monday 11/4/2019 – Although I usually write novels or memoirs or how-to books (or this daily FB post), at one time I explored the genre of flash fiction.

While I was looking for something else altogether, I found the following email that I sent out exactly four years ago. It was too good not to share with you. If you've seen it before, I hope you'll enjoy it again. By the way – this story is exactly 100 words long, including the two sub-titles.

= = = = = = = = =

>Dear Friends and Family,
>
>The Pen Women organization I belong to has been posting a series of Flash Fiction stories (100 words or less). Naturally, I decided to enter one of mine. Poison is such a fun topic for a mystery writer! It was posted today on the Pen Women website, and I wanted to share it with you.

Fran Stewart

I hope you enjoy my little story.

In the meantime, Happy November!

Fran

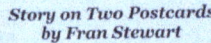

=========

Postcard #1

The second time the waiter spilled soup in Archibald's lap, he ended up with bouillabaisse stains on his pinstripes. The waiter—he'd better succeed next time—was positively abject with apologies. I plan to wear yellow to Archibald's funeral before I leave for Paris. See you soon, my dearest.

Postcard #2

Well, mum, you were right. Why didn't I see it as clearly as you did? Had to trip the blundering fool twice. If she could pay him, I can pay him more. Tonight, I think. Then I'll be home for a good long rest. After her funeral.

~ ~ ~

Aiden on the roof

Tuesday 11/5/2019 – Remember last year when I went up on my roof to clean off the accumulated leaves and then got stuck up there when the ladder shifted and I couldn't climb down safely? If you recall, you'll know that I—thank goodness!—had my cell phone in my pocket. After trying neighbors and daughter and a couple of friends (none of whom were either home or anywhere nearby, or simply weren't answering their phones), I called my granddaughter who came and rescued me. Before I came down, though, she took a picture of "Silly Grannie."

Well, yesterday, for the first time ever I allowed somebody else to sweep off my roof. My grandson Aiden came by and did the honors (safely, efficiently, and completely), so of course I had to take a photo before I held the ladder for him to descend.

Then we went inside to eat some fudge and had a grand talk about college plans and history and the glory of non-fiction books.

Thank you, Aiden! I love you bunches and bunches.

~ ~ ~

Do You Need It?

Wednesday 11/6/2019 – I've been thinking a lot about budgeting lately. Once the bare necessities are taken care of, it all boils down to choices.

Over the years I've made some bad ones, spending when I didn't need to, buying things that did not bring me joy. As I get older, though, I'm limiting my acquisitiveness. Not only choosing not to buy, but choosing to pare down. Why do I need all these mugs? Or all these wine glasses? Or all of these tee-shirts?

Fran Stewart

I've just about decided I could easily clear out half my house and not miss a bit of what's gone.

Now all I have to do is decide which half.

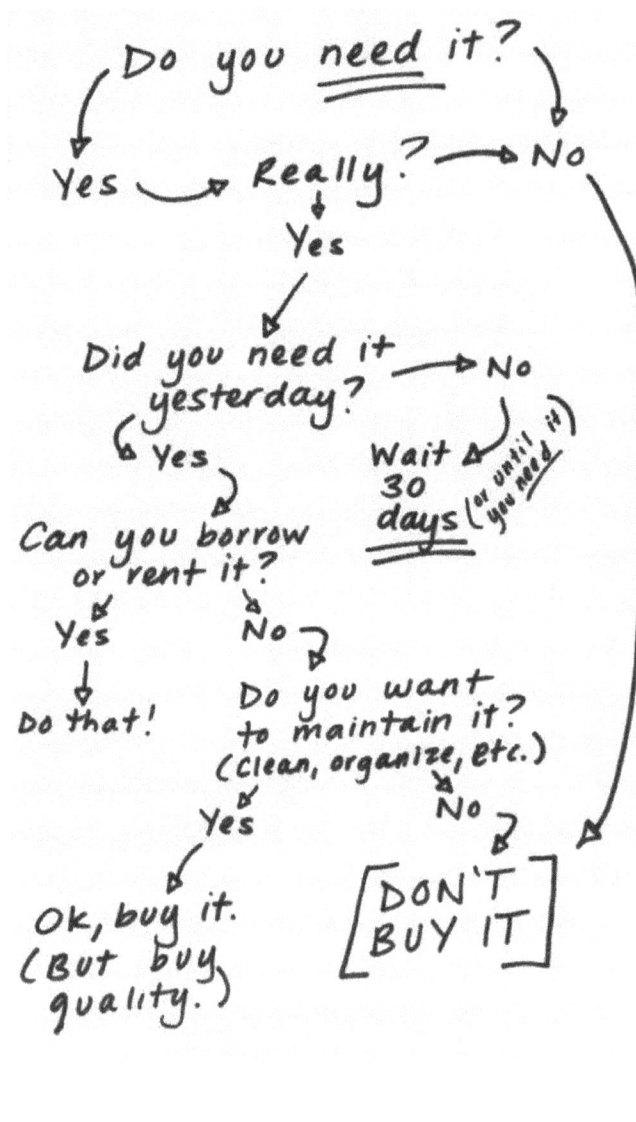

~ ~ ~

Proof that the earth is round

Thursday 11/7/2019 – I've spent a good deal of time over the last week doing some sewing. Some of it has been simple repair work, but I've also been making tunics from fabric I've had lying around in closets for – oh – maybe twenty years or thereabouts.

Wooly Bear helps me. She doesn't exactly push things off the table deliberately—at least I don't think it's deliberate—but she manages to lie on whatever fabric I'm working on. Then, when she stretches, anything nearby (pincushion, tape measure, scissors) just happen to connect with her back or legs or head. They end up on the floor. She ends up thoroughly satisfied.

What else can I do but pick her up for a big hug session?

~ ~ ~

Blue Horses

Friday 11/8/2019 – How could I possibly have gotten through all these years of my life without having discovered Mary Oliver until now? As I read her poems, I found myself time and again wanting to run to my desk to write her a thank-you note.

The only trouble is, she died last January.

You know what, though? I'm going to write her that thank-you note anyway. So what if I don't mail it? I can't help but feel that there is something sacred about the act of putting pen to paper—particularly if the words that flow out are words of gratitude. If I were an artist, I would inundate a canvas with my feelings. If I spoke mostly in music, I would write her a symphony—or try to devise an unforgettable melody.

But I write, so I'm headed to the stationery drawer in my desk right now.

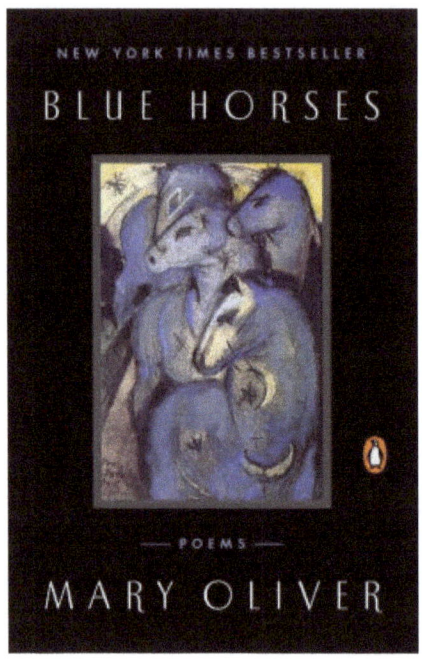

~ ~ ~

Got your back

Saturday 11/9/2019 – What is it about puns? If they're good ones, they can leave me doubled over, guffawing my insides out. Like this one. It's a shirt my massage therapist wore for Halloween last week. I'm still chuckling about it.

Here's another one – It's a murder of crows only it there's probable caws.

All right - you can quit groaning now. I'll go do something useful like filling the birdfeeders. See you on Monday.

~ ~ ~

W. E. Stewart 1915 – 2002

Monday 11/11/2019 – I'm remembering my dad this Veteran's Day. I've felt particularly close to him recently, mainly because in several of the memoirs classes I'm teaching, we've been talking about funerals—specifically about planning our own.

My dad was always pretty much in the background when I was growing up. In fact, I never truly appreciated him until he got closer to the end of his life.

I'm seeing more and more the ways I'm a lot like my dad. And the ways I'm different. It makes for some interesting—and very private—journal entries. This following story is one of the ones I'm willing to share:

When he died, my sister and I went to the funeral home to arrange things that hadn't been specified when Dad had pre-paid for his funeral years before. They asked us about the casket spray and began to show us photos of elaborate concoctions that looked more like something that should have been given a winning racehorse.

"That's not our dad," we both said. What we finally asked for was a "woodland scene" that looked like a fisherman had dropped his gear. We actually gave them our dad's orange tackle box. Afterwards, they told us that the designer had enjoyed this assignment more than any she had ever handled. She went out and gathered moss and pinecones, pine needles and fallen leaves, weeds, dried grasses, and a couple of dead branches. Then she created a masterpiece that summed up so much of what he was like. Besides lures and line, scaling knife and hand-tied flies, there was his folding ruler. Eighteen inches on one side, but flip it over and each "inch" was squeezed up near the next, so that a 12-inch fish would come out "measuring" at 36 inches.

When I wrote *Indigo as an Iris*, my 5th Biscuit McKee mystery, I included a casket decoration just like this one at the funeral of Wallace Masters, an old fisherman and military man who was patterned very much after my father.

My dad was buried with military honors in a plain blue cloth-covered coffin, like the one President Eisenhower was buried in. It was the same style of coffin that was used for most of the soldiers during World War II, which is why Ike had selected it. "If it's good enough for my soldiers," the president had said, "it's good enough for me."

"If it was good enough for my Commander in Chief," Dad told us when he chose that same model, "it's good enough for me."

When I die, I plan to be buried in Honey Creek Woodlands, the green cemetery in Conyers GA, in a plain pine box with no frills, no metal handles, no varnish—nothing to disturb Mother Earth. If it was good enough for my dad, it's good enough for me.

~ ~ ~

What to Pound

Tuesday 11/12/2019 – How to win a case in court:

> If the law is on your side, pound on the law.
> If the facts are on your side, pound on the facts.
> If neither is on your side, pound on the table.

This notion has been attributed to everybody from Supreme Court Justices to Carl Sandburg, but something very like it first appeared in print in 1911 (or so this particular source informs me). https://quoteinvestigator.com/2010/07/04/legal-adage/

This sort of reminds me of the "empty wagon" concept I talked about back on October 22nd: The emptier the wagon, the noisier the rattle. Nowadays, I guess you could say the noisier the tweets.

~ ~ ~

Fuzzy helps me knit

Wednesday 11/13/2019 – With the cold weather that's settled in, I find myself knitting a lot in the evenings. Of course, Fuzzy Britches has to curl up in my lap. She gives me a perfect surface for resting my work while I grab a sip of hot tea, and her orange coat is perfectly suited to making it easier for me to see the stitches if I'm working with dark yarn. To say nothing of the fact that she keeps my lap warm the whole time.

What am I knitting here?

I'm glad you asked.

Dancers need legwarmers. Writers have a different requirement. Because I do so much writing at my laptop, my wrists tend to get cold where they're up against the chilly metal surrounding the computer keyboard. So I've made a number of wrist-warmers. I got the idea years ago when I had a sock—a single sock, since the washer or dryer or sock-fairy had eaten the matching one. I was about to toss it out when I noticed how worn it was on the heel. For some unknown reason—the sock-fairy's inspiration, perhaps?—I grabbed my scissors and chopped off all but the ribbed cuff part.

Voilá! It felt warm. It felt comfy. I'd invented precisely what I needed to keep me comfortable as I labored away on my Biscuit McKee mysteries. Only trouble was—I needed a second one. Unwilling to sacrifice another sock, I took up a hank of leftover yarn and began experimenting with patterns and number of stitches.

These latest ones that Fuzzy Britches helped me with are double-layered for extra warmth. They're six or seven inches long, so they cover my arms from the heel of my hand halfway up to my elbow. Great idea.

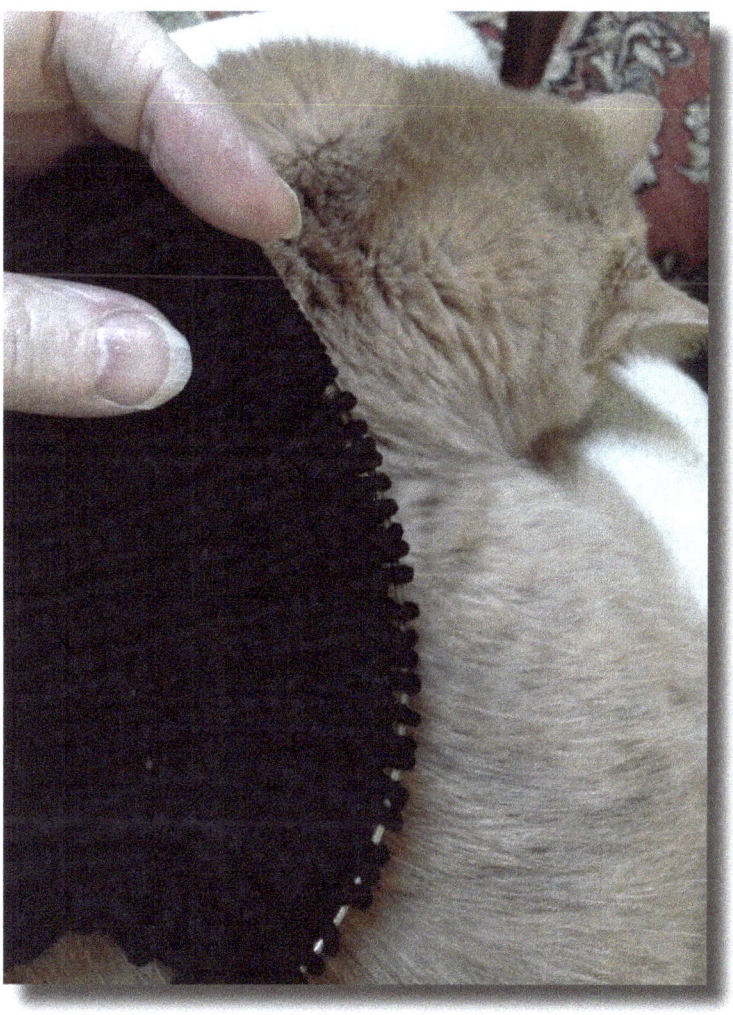

suggestions for gift-giving season

Thursday 11/14/2019 – As I've mentioned numerous times before, my friend Doug Dahlgren has a weekly Internet radio show. He's interviewed me a number of times about my various books. Well, two weeks ago, he did an entire show about gift-giving suggestions (and he just happened to mention my books.)

I've been doing a lot of thinking about gift-giving recently, what with the holiday season coming up. Instead of waiting till the last month of the year, I'd rather give gifts as they become appropriate (and certainly more affordable) throughout the year. I've always thought that the Thanksgiving season is a better time for giving gifts (in essence giving thanks) to those who have been of service throughout the years.

Giving books to my grandson, giving jigsaw puzzles to my daughter, giving soft hand-made handkerchiefs to my granddaughter – these are gifts from the heart that are not required by any season.

So, don't expect me to give any Christmas gifts. I never do. Nor do I expect any. But if you're into the gift-giving season, what could be better than books?

~ ~ ~

Someone Else's Ruler

Friday 11/15/2019 – Years ago I read that the source of all discontent is comparison. Since then I've read that we tend to compare our own perceived weaknesses to other people's perceived strengths. Great concept, eh?

Last week in one of the memoirs classes I teach, one of the women said she felt like a kindergartener compared to the "high school" writing of the other class members. "I don't use adjectives the way you do," she said. "I don't know how to describe scenes the way the rest of you do."

I was about to drag up this quote about weaknesses versus strengths when one of the women in the class said, "I remember just about every story you've shared in this class so far, and I've learned from every single one of them." Then she went on to list specific examples. Her response was so much more empowering to that first woman than mine would have been.

I'm grateful to the first woman for her courage in being able to talk about her insecurity. I'm even more grateful for the second woman's thoughtful, reasoned, and passionate defense of the importance of different points of view, different ways of expressing oneself. "You write the way you are," she'd said. "And that YOU is exactly what the rest of us need to hear."

Her powerful words showed so clearly that she had listened and learned. I could have quoted aphorisms all day and not made nearly the impact she did with her quiet summation of the value of the other woman.

~ ~ ~

real books

Saturday 11/16/2019 – Last week I told you about my grandson who swept the accumulated leaves off my roof for me. What I didn't tell you is that afterwards, while we were eating fudge and talking, he said, "Grannie, a bunch of years ago I told you I didn't like to read very much, and you told me that I just hadn't found the right books yet." He looked up at me with a gleam in his eyes. "Guess what? I've found the right books!"

That was the highpoint of my week. My month. My year. Not only the fact that he'd remembered my words for six or seven years but that he'd finally found a passion for reading about history (which happens to be a love of mine as well). My deepest gratitude to his history teacher who showed him the way.

Have you found the right books for your life?

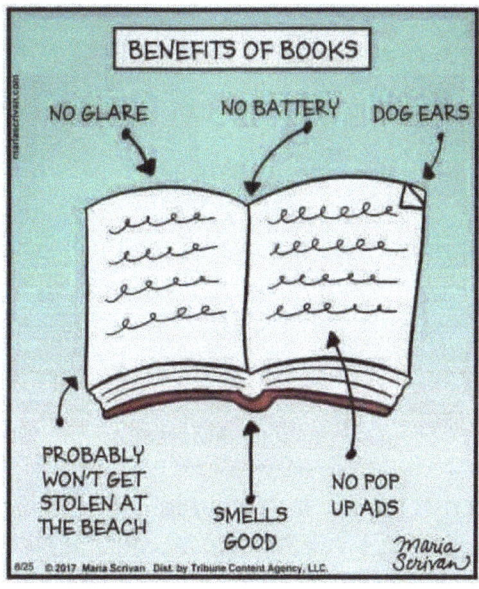

Fran Stewart

~ ~ ~

Squirrel baffle

Monday 11/18/2019 – Some time ago I shared a picture of the bottom of my peanut feeder that was being steadily chewed on by the squirrels. I wasn't too worried because there was still a lot of that recycled plastic protecting the wire mesh. Well, recently it began to get iffy—Mr. and Mrs. Squirrel had almost chewed through to the point where the metal tube at the bottom was about to give way. If that happened, the wire would drop down and they'd have instant access to all the peanuts (which at that point would have been on the ground).

What to do?

I'm glad you asked.

I took four great long nails and my handy Gorilla Glue. The end result may not look too fancy, but the woodpeckers and chickadees and all the other welcome guests don't seem to mind. And the squirrels (as far as I can tell) have given up!

I love success stories.

And, in case you're worried about those squirrels, the birds and I drop plenty of peanuts on the ground. They're not about to starve.

 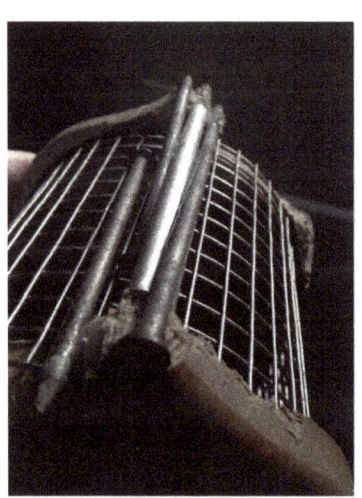

~ ~ ~

Timeless Address

Tuesday 11/19/2019 – For today's post, I'd like to share with you something I wrote in my beekeeping blog exactly eight years ago. As you know, I've collected all those blog entries and have published them (since they collectively represent my beekeeping memoirs). This entry, which I called "Deathless Address," is from volume 5, which is available in e-book form and will soon be out in print form:

= = = = = = = = =

> Yesterday was the 148th anniversary of the Gettysburg Address.
>
> Lord, what I wouldn't give to be able to write something even half that memorable. It seems apt to post the text—although I probably should have done it yesterday, but yesterday I was busy wondering about bugs.
>
> You probably had to memorize this speech when you were in high school. But do you ever pull it out and think about what it's saying? This is a lot like the Declaration of Independence, one of those documents we know about, approve of, but seldom consider at any depth. I read the Declaration of Independence every Fourth of July, as I've mentioned before in this blog. I think it would make sense for me to read Lincoln's words every November 19th from now on. I'm gonna do it. Will you join me, even if we're a day late this year?
>
> = = = = = = = = =
>
>> Four score and seven years ago our fathers brought forth on this continent a new nation, conceived in liberty, and dedicated to the proposition that all men are created equal.
>>
>> Now we are engaged in a great civil war, testing whether that nation, or any nation, so conceived and so dedicated, can long endure. We are met on a great battle-field of that war. We have come to dedicate a portion of that field, as a final resting place for those who here gave their lives that that nation might live. It is altogether fitting and proper that we should do this.
>>
>> But, in a larger sense, we can not dedicate, we can not consecrate, we can not hallow this ground. The brave men, living and dead, who struggled here, have consecrated it, far above our poor power to add or detract.
>>
>> The world will little note, nor long remember what we say here, but it can never forget what they did here. It is for us the living, rather, to be dedicated here to the unfinished work which they who fought here have thus far so nobly advanced. It is rather for us to be here dedicated to the great task remaining before us—that from these honored dead we take increased devotion to that cause for which they gave the last full measure of devotion—that we here highly resolve that these dead shall not have died in vain—that this nation, under God, shall have a new birth of freedom—and that government of the people, by the people, for the people, shall not perish from the earth.
>
> = = = = = = = = =

Now it's been seven score and sixteen years. Do we remember? Will we rededicate ourselves to government of, by, and for the people? Or will we degenerate into a nation that no longer cares?

5 bananas?

Wednesday 11/20/2019 – While we're still thinking about timeless prose—at least we were yesterday in these posts of mine—I have to wonder if we're in trouble nowadays.

I know as well as anyone that errors can creep into published works. Cancel that thought. They didn't creep in; they were there and were simply not dealt with. I'm sorry to say that I've discovered some mistakes in my last four Biscuit McKee books, which is one reason that I'll be republishing them in revised form over the coming year, but my mistakes weren't nearly so egregious as this one. Five bananas? Really?

~ ~ ~

Needles

Thursday 11/21/2019 – I'm reading a fabulous book called *Cat Sense* by John Bradshaw. Found it at the library a few days ago. His premise is that we humans make a big mistake when we expect cats to act and react like little furry humans or little fuzzy dogs. They've evolved with a completely different set of instincts. Even after having shared my home with numerous cats over the past thirty years, I'm learning a number of new things, such as the fact that you can get away with not cuddling a puppy until it's eight weeks old, and it will still be able to adapt to a trusting relationship with a human, but cats have to be introduced to holding and cuddling at three weeks. If not—they'll just never completely be content to relax around homo [called] sapiens.

Even though neither of my cats came to me as a kitten, I now can understand a great deal more about their past history. Fuzzy Britches is happy to curl up on my lap any time I sit. That means she was given plenty of cuddling when she was tiny. But Wooly Bear, although she's very loving and likes to nose-nuzzle, jumps off my lap after five or six seconds every single time. This indicates she was not held until she was at least six weeks old.

Feral cats who refuse any human contact may never have been picked up until they were eight weeks or older. Those cats will never be truly comfortable around us.

And only cats that have been raised with dogs from kittenhood will trust dogs.

It's not the cat's fault!

~ ~ ~

optimist

Friday 11/22/2019 – I've always loved the cha-cha. But I have a problem with the way it's usually taught. I realize that's a sweeping generalization. If I'm wrong about this and you learned my way, then bear with me. The how-to videos I've checked online stress **1**, 2, cha-cha-cha, **1**, 2, cha-cha-cha, 1, 2, cha-cha-cha, with the beat going 1, 2, 3, 4.

Way back when, I found I preferred to start on the second beat, so my pattern goes 2, 3, cha-cha-**cha**, 2, 3, cha-cha-**cha**—so the last cha occurs on the first beat of the measure.

Does this make sense at all?

Does anyone care?

And how, you ask, do I get my dance partner to agree to this? That's easy, I dance with Fuzzy Britches. She likes to go along for the ride in my arms.

Whichever way you dance it, the sign in this photo still applies. We cha-cha enthusiasts are optimists.

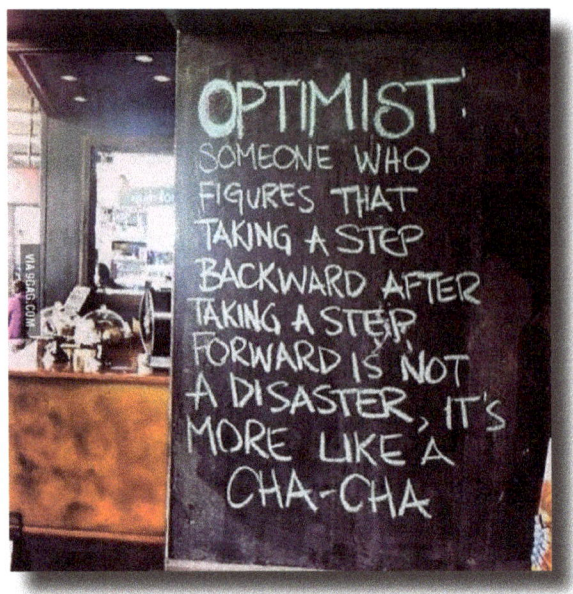

More than one way

Saturday 11/23/2019 – I'd like to end this week on a truly positive note. Sometimes it's easy to get caught up in thinking there's only one solution to a problem. If that solution seems impossible, then we may tend to give up before we even get started.

But let's start seeing those impossibilities as simply the world's way of asking us to see a wider picture, a different viewpoint.

Smooth and vibrant and full of the good stuff. Life is pretty special.

```
I once met a blind girl who told
  me I smelled of cherries and
 then asked me if I looked like
   they did. I laughed and said
   what, small and round? She
 laughed and said no, smooth skin
and vibrant and as if you're full
 of the good stuff? Without sight,
  she showed me there is always
      more than one way to see
              something.
                s.r.w
```

~ ~ ~

farming us

Monday 11/25/2019 — We are so content usually to believe that we humans rule the universe – or at least this particular sphere of it. What if, however, we are truly minor players in this dance called life? I should think trees would do a better job of taking care of things around here. They know how to cooperate; they always give back in balance; they add beauty to the world; they are patient.

Maybe we could shift our way of thinking?

Just an idea.

~ ~ ~

baa-baa-baa

Tuesday 11/26/2019 — If I used this toilet paper holder, I can just imagine what fun Wooly Bear would have shredding it to pieces. And look—there aren't any cat or dog hair dust bunnies on the floor (the way there always are on mine).

When my children were in elementary school, I was talking one day with Shirley Murray, who had taught both of them in kindergarten. Over the years she became a dear and well-respected friend. That day I bemoaned my toy-strewn, dog-hair and bunny-hair infested house. "Don't you worry about that, dear." She laid a comforting hand on my arm. "In all my years of teaching I've had only two students that I worried about—only two I was afraid to see grow up for fear of how they would act in the world."

Fran Stewart

I didn't see where she was going with that until she added, "I've been in the homes of a lot of my students, and those two were the only ones that consistently looked like something out of '*House Beautiful.*' Not a single mess anywhere. Not ever."

"Maybe they just cleaned up because you were coming," I said.

Shirley looked at me with a great deal of empathy. She knew a lot more about children than I did. That was when I remembered the times I'd cleaned up extra specially only to have both kids prancing along behind me dropping things and "rearranging" them.

What isn't there can tell a lot more about a person than what is here, wouldn't you say?

What ISN'T in your house?

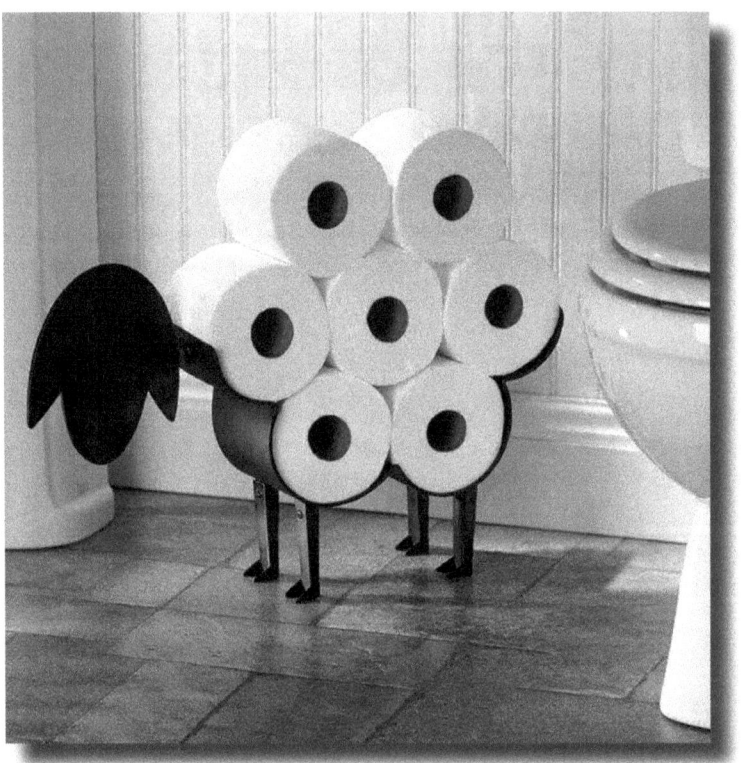

~ ~ ~

dandelion fractals

Wednesday 11/27/2019 – I'm constantly amazed at the wonders of natural art. These dandelion fractals, for instance. A few days ago I shared with you my respect for the beauty of the Gettysburg Address. Today I want to share the miracle of dandelion seed heads.

I could look at these all day and still never fully appreciate their intricacy. To say nothing of the expertise required to take these photos. Makes me feel humble on the one hand and proud on the other to be a (small) part of such a wonderful world.

~ ~ ~

hanging out with your adult children

Thursday 11/28/2019 – Thanksgiving Day. My children are adults. There is so much to be thankful for. I've never understood women who talk about their grown children as if they were still toddlers. "She's my baby!" "He'll always be my little boy!" and so on.

One of the deepest joys of my life is that both my children grew up to become happy productive individuals with whom I can have fabulous conversations without ever having to feel as if I'm in charge of anything anymore. If they ask for advice, I'm willing to give it, but there is such relaxation in knowing that they are steering a fine course.

They remind me of my motto: "I am no longer afraid of storms, for I have learned to sail my own ship." Louisa May Alcott wrote that more than 100 years ago, and it's still a fine recipe for achieving balance in life.

Have a joy-filled Thanksgiving, my precious and beautiful Eli Reiman and Veronica Lowe. You certainly bring a great deal of joy into my life.

leaves you in stitches

Friday 11/29/2019 – So, why am I late posting this morning? Thanks for asking. I woke this morning thinking it was Sunday, a day when I seldom open my laptop very early (since that's the one day a week I don't post to this page). I fed the cats and the birds, did my other normal morning chores, puttered around, worked on a delightfully devilish Kakuro, and finally got around to going to the end of the driveway to retrieve the paper. On Sundays I always cut out the huge crossword puzzle and mail it the next morning to my sister in Colorado.

Surprise! No Sunday paper. Instead, there was a Friday paper.

Gulp!

So here I am, late for sure. It still feels like a Sunday to me, but I can deal with that. After all, I have nowhere to go today. I always avoid getting into traffic on Black Friday. So, other than posting this, I'll probably treat the rest of the day like a Sunday as well.

Meanwhile, I think I'll knit—and laugh about my silly time sense (or lack thereof).

~ ~ ~

4-letter words

Saturday 11/30/2019 —. – Here's a thought not just for the end of this week, but for the end of this month.

'Bye for now. I'll see you [next month] on Monday.

Fran Stewart

December 2019

Composting in Tennessee

Monday 12/2/2019 — I've been a composter for more years than I can remember. It always made sense to me to return as much to the earth as I possibly could. The problem with a home compost pile, though, is that it's pretty much wasted (not really, since the worms love it) if one isn't a gardener. My gardening days are long since gone, so my compost pile just sits there.

Imagine how excited I was when I saw an article about the facility at Dollywood to compost and recycle EVERYTHING.

Only trouble is, I did some research—as I always do—and found out that the article in question had some serious errors in it. So, I went looking farther and found this one about Sevier County Tennessee's recycling and composting process. Yes, Dollywood does send all their trash there, but the whole process deals with a lot more than just Dollywood.

Yes, it's a long article, but well worth reading.

Now, how do we go about convincing county officials that THIS is the sort of business to put investment into?

https://www.yesmagazine.org/environment/2014/08/28/sevier-county-composting/

~ ~ ~

Quiet Spot

Tuesday 12/3/2019 — A (L O N G) while ago, I got tired of listening to the jingle jangle of collar tags, especially when my husband's dogs shook themselves in the middle of the night, so I designed little fabric pouches to enclose the tags and eliminate the noise. The dogs seemed as relieved as I was. Not knowing anything about the patenting process, it never occurred to me to try to protect my invention. It was a great idea at the time, and all my friends were amazed at the ingenuity of it.

Look what's available now. I have no idea whether this is patented or not, but the idea is pretty much the same as the one I came up with.

How many other items get invented every day by people who see a need and quietly fill it—until someone else comes along and mass-markets the idea?

When I was a teenager, I wrote the Kotex Company and told them how uncomfortable those horrible sanitary napkin belts were. "I just use doubled-over scotch tape," I wrote, "to secure the pad to my underwear."

I'm not saying they used my idea specifically—somebody else must have had the same thought as I—but it wasn't too many years before belts were a thing of the past.

~ ~ ~

oxymoron museum

Wednesday 12/4/2019 — I spent some time thinking about virtual reality this morning. I tend to send people virtual hugs in emails—I call them telehugs. While I thought about it, I remembered seeing this oxymoron museum diagram by John Atkinson. Thank goodness I found it so I could share it with you.

What, after all, is current about current history? Or what is historic about it when we haven't lived through it yet and don't know how far the repercussions of today will expand? And then there are permanent loans. Shouldn't they be called gifts? What is ever civil about a war? What is real about virtual reality?

Of course, when a virtual hug is the only kind possible because my niece is 1,000 miles away or my friend from 11th grade is equally far, then I suppose a telehug is not only permissible but—I hope—welcome.

If you feel you need one . . . here's a telehug just for you.

Fran Stewart

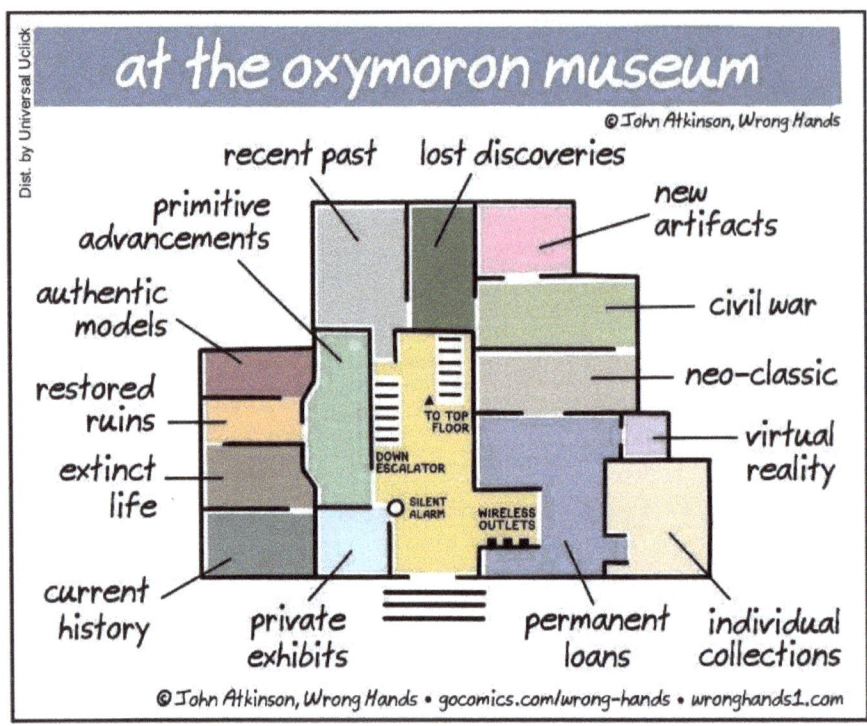

~ ~ ~

book from Ikea

Thursday 12/5/2019 — "I have a great idea for a book!" That's something authors hear a lot from people who attend our book signings.

"Great," I always say. "How much of it have you written?"

Then the excuses start.

The major difference between a published author and a wannabe author is that the first person sits down and writes. And writes. And writes. The wannabe doesn't.

I dreamed of writing a mystery for years and years. And I had a jillion excuses. Until the Universe clopped me upside the head (it was called a hysterectomy) and said, "We're giving you a whole lot of time. What are you going to do with it?"

If I hadn't followed that dream of mine, I'm fairly sure the next head-clop would have been a lot more serious. When I started writing, I started healing. And it was funny how all my excuses—not enough time, not enough energy, don't know how to start—simply faded away as I made the time, developed the energy, and watched the words flow.

Twenty-plus books later, I'm still going strong.

Did you buy a book from Ikea? Have you begun to put it together?

Just bought a book from IKEA

~ ~ ~

Table Decoration

Friday 12/6/2019 — Last night I attended a simply lovely dinner with some of the members of my book club. It was put on by the women of one of the local churches, so it was very Christmas-themed. Each table hostess decorated her 8-person table—and the results were stunning.

Do you like to decorate for Christmas?

I'm always fairly stupefied by elaborate decorations. Why on earth would anyone ever want to go to all that trouble? Of course, I understand that this attitude is a reflection of my own unwillingness to expend so much effort, especially for just one evening.

Not that I can't appreciate the beauty of such elaborate offerings. I walked around the room before the festivities got under way so I could see the myriad ways in which these women expressed themselves. But I kept thinking, "My gosh, they had to haul all this stuff up here, set it up, and then afterwards, while I'm headed home, they'll have to dismantle it, load it, haul it, unload it, and then figure out what to do with it."

It reminded me of the time back in Vermont when my first husband asked me, in the presence of our children, why I didn't spend more time in the kitchen. His mother had been one of those women who made a production of every meal, and I realized soon into the marriage that he expected me to be just like his mother. My answer to his question was, "It's such a lot of bother, when all you do is just eat it."

After a (stunned) silence, he broke into peals of laughter. "Isn't that the idea?" he asked.

So, if I don't spend my time in decorating, and I still don't spend much time in cooking, what am I willing to pour my heart into?

Fran Stewart

Well, words. Writing. Re-writing. Self-editing. The crafting of my books is worth every bit of effort I expend. Writing these daily FB posts is a ritual without which my day wouldn't feel complete. It's not a meal for the tummy. It's not a temporary delight for the eyes. Instead, it's something that will hopefully last for a century or more—especially when I get around to publishing the last three or four years of these posts. They are my memoirs. I'll leave them for my children and grandchildren and great-grandchildren (and maybe you, too) to digest for a very long time.

Enjoy the feast.

~ ~ ~

bee stockings

Saturday 12/7/2019 — If I still had my beehives, I think I'd want to decorate them with lots of little fuzzy red stockings, although there wouldn't be a way to fit enough on the hive for every worker bee to have her own. Maybe they could share? And what would I put in there? I'm no good at gathering pollen or nectar, and that's about all they'd want.

What would you like to see in your stocking this year?

I'd like a bicycle—an old-fashioned bike without any gears or fancy doodads. Eli said that when he comes for a visit next spring, he'll help me mount it on a stand in my upstairs room so I can use it each morning as a leg exerciser.

The only trouble is—I have to find a bicycle first. Where are the garage sales when I need them?

Clearly Me

~ ~ ~

Wooly Bear's paper

Monday 12/9/2019 — Why on earth does anybody ever spend money on cat toys? When I ordered a bunch of the new 2nd edition of my sister's book *Depression Visible: The Ragged Edge,* they came packed with long sheets of paper as packing material. Ditto with the copies of my BeesKnees books.

Wooly Bear dives in and out of those paper labyrinths with great abandon. She takes her catnip toys (pieces of fabric I've sewn together with catnip inside) and drops them inside the paper jungle. Then she pounces.

Sometimes she simply dives in there and hides. Occasionally all I see is a tail. This time it was one golden eye.

Fuzzy Britches doesn't like paper. She'd rather pounce on the homemade fabric lizards I stuff with sewing odds and ends. If I remember, I'll take a picture of one of them and show you. Wish I could get a video of her throwing them up in the air, but as soon as I get out the camera, she slinks beneath the loveseat.

My point—and there truly IS a point to this—is that we don't need to invest in expensive toys when our cats are happy with the simplest solutions. I think the same thing is (or ought to be) true of people. A little creativity (like the bicycle I mentioned yesterday) can result in just as much exercise as the expensive electric machines.

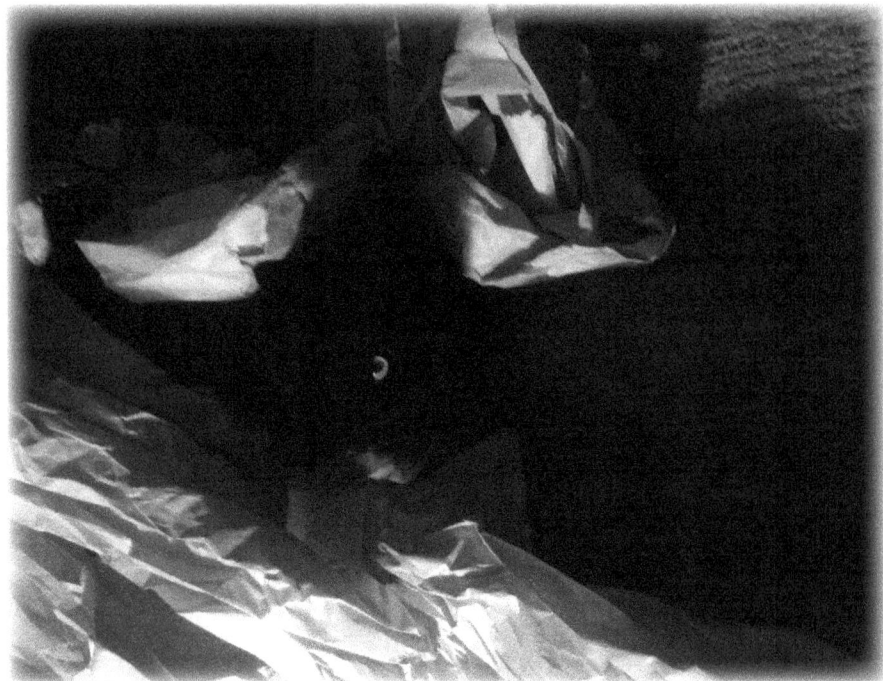

~ ~ ~

grandpa with vitiligo

Tuesday 12/10/2019 — Having had vitiligo for the last 45 years—I contracted it when I was pregnant with my first child—I can attest to how discomforting it can be to the one who has it and how disconcerting to people who don't know what it was. I was delighted to learn about this granddad who crocheted a doll for his granddaughter—a doll that looked like him, to help her understand that patchy-looking skin was okay. And then he decided he could make other dolls – dolls with vitiligo for children with vitiligo, crocheted dolls in crocheted wheelchairs. If you want to read the article about it, Google "grandpa with vitiligo knits dolls."

Yeah, the headline says "knits," even though it's very clear these are crocheted.

Anyway, the point of all this is that way back when, before the vitiligo crept across my whole body and wiped out all my melanin, my face and hands and arms used to look like this guy's face only worse. Time and again I had people offer condolences for the horrific burns I must have received.

Sometimes when I didn't feel like explaining, I'd tell people it wasn't a fire. I'd been attacked by a bear (or a mountain lion) or I'd gotten splashed while touring a steel factory, whatever my fertile mind came up with.

Vitiligo is what Michael Jackson had, but instead of using the God-given chance to educate people, he chose to wear a fancy glove, and then eventually to have himself bleached all over. I like this grandpa's solution better.

~ ~ ~

the last time

Wednesday 12/11/2019 — This poem is about all the moments of childhood that slip away before we realize that THAT moment was the last time it would ever happen. It's a lovely poem, and so appropriate for thoughts of the fleeting nature of childhood.

But it works at all ages. A couple of weeks ago I went to the Shakespeare Tavern to see King Lear. I brought my program home with me and was glancing idly through the listings at the back of all the various donors. One of the gifts listed was "In Memory of Phyllis Schiwal."

Phyllis? I didn't believe it. I went online and—sure enough—found her obituary. How did I know Phyl? Well, I kept running into her at Sunday performances at the Shakespeare Tavern. She and her husband Jim loved to attend, and Phyl always brought her knitting along to keep her hands busy during the intermission. I frequently did the same thing, so we began to compare knitting projects. She was always such fun, and her knitting was exquisite. I hadn't seen her in quite a while, but then again, I'd begun going to Saturday performances instead of Sunday ones. The last time I saw her, I had no idea it would be the last time.

And then, yesterday, I opened my mail—a Christmas card from Jeff Watkins and his family. Jeff is the Artistic Director at the Shakespeare Tavern, and he mentioned in the accompanying note that he had been so saddened at the loss of Kristin Dunstan.

Kristin? Again, I could hardly believe it. Kristin was only 49. I've known her for 20 years, ever since she first started working at the Tavern. Then she moved away to pursue other work and educational opportunities. When she came back to the Atlanta area, I kept thinking, "I ought to get together with Kristin for lunch sometime so we can catch up."

But our last lunch together (seven or eight years ago) was our last time together. Only I didn't know it.

I'm feeling rather sad right now. How many other last times have I already had that I'm not even aware of?

The Last Time

From the moment you hold your baby in your arms,
you will never be the same.
You might long for the person you were before,
When you had freedom and time,
And nothing in particular to worry about.
You will know tiredness like you never knew it before,
And days will run into days that are exactly the same,
Full of feedings and burping,
Nappy changes and crying,
Whining and fighting,
Naps or a lack of naps,
It might seem like a never-ending cycle.

But don't forget...
There is a last time for everything.
There will come a time when you will feed
your baby for the very last time.
They will fall asleep on you after a long day
And it will be the last time you ever hold your sleeping child.
One day you will carry them on your hip then set them down,
And never pick them up that way again.
You will scrub their hair in the bath one night
And from that day on they will want to bathe alone.
They will hold your hand to cross the road,
Then never reach for it again.
They will creep into your room at midnight for cuddles,
And it will be the last night you ever wake to this.
One afternoon you will sing "the wheels on the bus"
and do all the actions,
Then never sing them that song again.
They will kiss you goodbye at the school gate,
The next day they will ask to walk to the gate alone.
You will read a final bedtime story and wipe your last dirty face.
They will run to you with arms raised for the very last time.

The thing is, you won't even know it's the last time
Until there are no more times.
And even then, it will take you a while to realize.

So while you are living in these times,
remember there are only so many of them
and when they are gone, you will yearn for just one more day of them.
For one last time.
                —Author Unknown

EmbracingHomemaking.net

Clearly Me

~ ~ ~

snow joy

Thursday 12/12/2019 — It's not cold enough here in Georgia for mattress sledding like this, but I couldn't resist the joyfulness of the picture. These kids are all in high school and college now, but the memories of these joyful days will live on in my heart for a very long time.

~ ~ ~

she needs a cat

Friday 12/13/2019 — My friend Linda in Florida sent me a hooded sweatshirt with this slogan on it. I love it! My idea of a great day is to pull on sweats first thing in the morning and then live in them all day long, so her hoodie gets a great workout on days when I don't have anything to dress up for.

Of course, if I'm headed to the library, the bookstore, the pet food store, the birdseed store—all the places where they know me and don't care what I look like—I wear my sweatshirt in winter, a flannel shirt in the fall or spring, and a loose tunic in the summer.

Life is good. Especially when I'm comfy.

~ ~ ~

what is love

Saturday 12/14/2019 — Do you remember losing teeth when you were a kid? I'm not sure whether the tooth fairy came to our house. She probably did, but it was never very special. But I DO remember the excruciating moments when my father used a pair of pliers to pull out my loose teeth—an experience I'd never want to inflict on anyone. I'm not sure what the reasoning was—maybe that long ago it wasn't considered healthy to hang onto loose teeth for too long. Or maybe I complained about them so much my dad got fed up with listening to me.

At any rate, I wish I'd had this sort of attitude about missing teeth. Emma K sounds like a very well-loved and well-adjusted person.

Till Monday . . . fill your days with Joy.

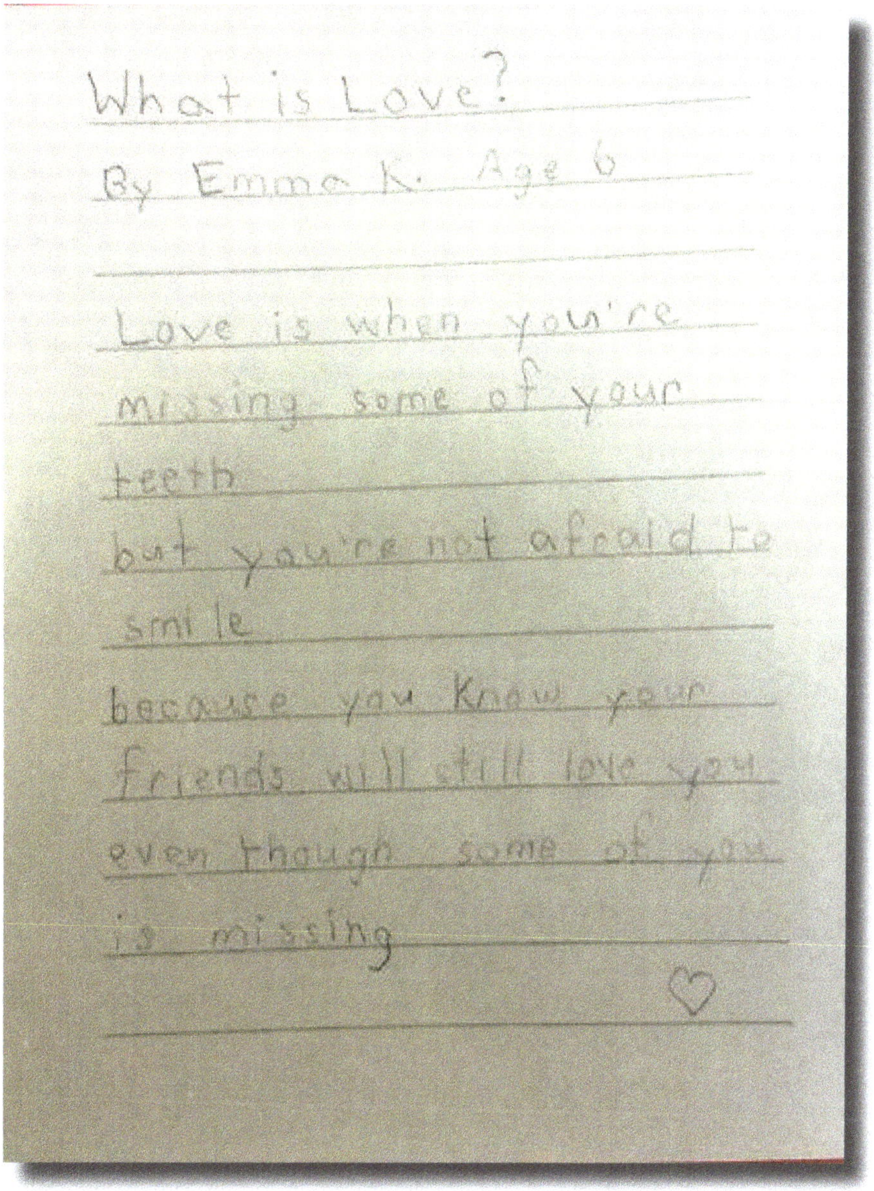

> What is Love?
> By Emma K. Age 6
>
> Love is when you're missing some of your teeth
> but you're not afraid to smile
> because you know your friends will still love you even though some of you is missing ♡

~~~

Herbivore

Monday 12/16/2019 — I'm still remembering the Dino 101 course I took from the University of Alberta a few months ago, so this week—at least the first five days of it—I'm going to feature dinosaur cartoons.

This first one is for my vegan son, who managed to go through Marine boot camp umpty years ago without sacrificing his vegetarian principles. "I ate lots of potatoes, Mom," he told me once. "And carrots. And beans with rice, so I'd get a complete protein." Apparently there were always enough veggie choices for him to fill his nutritional needs."

So, let's hear it for herbivores!

Fran Stewart

~ ~ ~

short arms

Tuesday 12/17/2019 — I was going to save this Off the Mark rendition until next February, but realized that giving gifts is appropriate year round. So is loving someone. So is meeting the unexpressed needs in both ourselves and others.

Short arms, too short for hugging, may have been a problem for the T-Rex, but sometimes our arms (not too short) remain folded in distrust when they could just as easily be opened to encompass the people around us.

Sometimes the people nearby don't seem very loveable or huggable—but that may be just the reason we need to start a conversation, to learn more about their hopes and challenges, to proffer a smile instead of a frown.

So, what about today? Could you benefit from some arm extensions?

I'm open to hugs if you need some practice.

~ ~ ~

advent calendar

Wednesday 12/18/2019 — Gone are the days when I created an individualized advent calendar for each of my children. The calendars (with their names embroidered in bright colors) featured two-inch-square numbered doors that hid little pockets I filled with tiny treasures.

Part of the reason those days are gone is that my kids eventually got to where they didn't want tiny treasures anymore. They wanted big treasures. But I couldn't figure out how to fit a pound of candy behind a little fabric door that was big enough for only a single piece.

I probably could have come up with a solution if I'd thought long enough and hard enough.

The first year they (both) turned up their noses at the lone M&M they each received on December 2nd, was the last year I went to the bother of filling what I'd thought of as masterpieces—ones that would be treasured for years and passed down through generations.

Instead, I threw out the calendars along with the leftover boxes and torn wrapping paper.

Do I wish I'd saved them? Well, no. I think the memories are enough. At least I remember them, especially the delight of the first three years we used them. I have no idea whether or not anyone else ever thinks about them.

baby brontosaurs

Thursday 12/19/2019 — This picture took me by surprise as well. They DO look like baby b'saurs. I love the creativity that allows someone to look at an ordinary scene in an extraordinary way.

What have you looked at from a different angle recently?

~~~

gingerbread dinosaur

Friday 12/20/2019 — Years ago, we used to host gingerbread house-building parties. We had a HUGE dining room table. I'd line it with aluminum foil and pile stacks of fake gingerbread (also known as graham crackers) here and there across the wide surface. Everyone who came to the party was encouraged to bring a bag of g'house-appropriate candies. You wouldn't believe what folks brought.

Or maybe you would.

M&Ms of course (or as my friends Mikki and Wendell Dillon call them—Ms&Ws), licorice strips, gum drops, and Neccos (they made great shingles and steppingstones) were the standards. But then there were the extra spectaculars, like the Hershey Kisses, entire Almond Joys (from which someone built a barn), and so on.

We'd end up with a whole village spread across the table. There were numerous houses, farms with the various outbuildings (including an outhouse), a church, a synagogue built by one of our Reformed Jewish friends who never missed a Christmas party. Somebody one year even built a brothel, complete with little gumdrop "ladies" leaning over a stick-pretzel balcony railing.

Afterwards, people could take their creations home or gift them to others, or leave them for us to eat at our leisure.

We had some collapses occasionally. I wish I'd seen this dinosaur idea way back then. It would have added a certain flair to the proceedings, wouldn't you agree?

~ ~ ~

Beautiful Day

Saturday 12/21/2019 — Enough about dinosaurs for now. I went to see the movie "A Beautiful Day in the Neighborhood" a couple of weeks ago, and thoroughly enjoyed it. Wouldn't mind seeing it again, as a matter of fact. In this final frantic spate before Christmas, Mister Rogers could bring some sanity. And here's something good to know about today's kids. It's an article from *The Washington Post.* Do a search for "what happened when i showed vintage mister rogers to my 21st century kids"

Couldn't we all use a dose of Mister Rogers right about now?

Have a peaceful rest of your weekend, and I'll see you again on Monday.

~ ~ ~

Banish some of the darkness

Monday 12/23/2019 — Today as we begin this week that for many will involve work and for others a vacation, let's each light our own flame. No need to blow out anyone else's.

I used to enjoy the candlelight ceremony that happened in a number of churches I attended here and there. One candle would start the process. One candle would light the candle held by the person at the end of each row. That person would share their flame with the person next to them, and so on down each row until the entire room was awash with glorious light.

And it all started with just one tiny flame.

Let's all light a candle today and share it with someone else. Sound like a good idea?

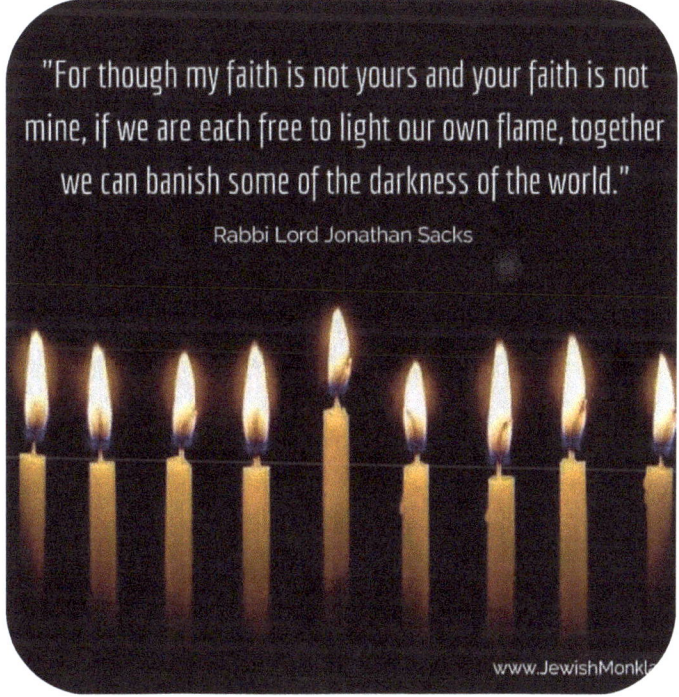

~ ~ ~

whole box of crayons

Tuesday 12/24/2019 — It's Christmas Eve, and that, despite one's personal leanings, tends to feel a bit special. I'm not a Christian, so I don't celebrate in a Christmasy way – but I do like to pay a little extra attention around this time of year.

- o   Attention to the birds that brighten my world—and eat a whole lot of bugs.

- Attention to the possum family that brings me laughter when the mama shows up with her babies on her back.

- Attention to the deer who browse my hostas periodically and curl up for a nap in a swirl of weeds at the edge of the forest behind my house.

- Attention to the trees that shade my house in the summer and let the sun through their bare branches in the winter

- Attention to the people who are so very dear to me—both longstanding friends and family members as well as the new-found friends who bring such light to my life. And the people I meet along the way for a moment or two with whom I share a smile

- Attention to the books—and the people who make them available to me—that stretch my mind and feed my spirit.

- Attention, in short, to all the many blessings that surround and uplift me every day.

You are one of those blessings, and I wish you joy.

~ ~ ~

Merry everything

Wednesday 12/25/2019 — What more need I say, other than "Merry Everything and a Happy Always."

~ ~ ~

Eli's perfect timing

Thursday 12/26/2019 — A few days ago, my son was paddle-boarding on Florida's Ochlockonee River and captured this moment as an eagle caught its meal. What a joy (except, perhaps, for the fish) that Eli was in exactly the right place at exactly the right moment, and had his camera at the ready. A few feet farther on, or a few seconds later, and he wouldn't have been able to share this "Moment of Nature."

I always have to laugh when I think of that phrase. Years ago, my sister and her daughter and I were riding along a back road somewhere or other when a red fox began dumping a load of poop in the middle of the road a few hundred feet ahead of us. My sister braked the car and we sat in quiet, simply watching. "This moment of nature," my niece finally intoned in a broadcaster's voice, "was brought to you through the auspices of Mama Fox."

Mesa Verde at Xmas

Friday 12/27/2019 — One of the best vacations of my life was when I was a kid and we went to Mesa Verde. I loved walking through those cliff dwellings where the Anasazi had lived and worked and loved, laughed and argued, talked and sang.

This photo was captured a number of years ago when the park rangers and employees placed candles in and around the dwellings. To me, this picture captures such a feeling of peace. I'd like to see waves of it reverberate throughout the world—beginning with my heart and yours.

empty bag

Saturday 12/28/2019 — Years ago, when my daughter was tiny, we gave her a gift-wrapped present of some sort. The toy inside was largely ignored, but the big red bow on the package received her special attention. It was the perfect gift.

Then, when my son was eight or nine, he made a necklace for me from a piece of sturdy cord on which he'd strung a series of metal nuts, interspersed with metal washers for spacers. He tied a knot at each end, to keep the (heavy) creation from shifting around or falling off the cord. He wrapped it in a bright piece of scrap fabric and gave it to me with a note that said, "I'm Nuts about you, Mom."

Clearly Me

Let's give someone a (perfect for them) empty bag today. Then let's do the same thing tomorrow for someone else. And keep on doing it. A little something each day. Think of the joy that will bring us as we see eyes light up.

p.s. All these years later, I still have the photo of Veronica balancing her bow on top of her head, and I still wear the nuts-necklace with my green turtleneck.

New Year's at home

Monday 12/30/2019 — I always spend New Year's Eve at home. I can think of few things less appetizing than driving somewhere to watch fireworks, and then having to sit for hours in the parking lot while all the other thousands of people try to squeeze out of the place to get home.

If you're a fireworks aficionado, that's fine with me. I hope you enjoy them tomorrow night.

I plan to go to bed early, wake up when all the firecrackers in the neighborhood explode between ten and twelve-thirty, and then tuck back in for a good night's sleep. No cars. No hassle. Warm and cozy. What could be better?

First page of a blank book

Tuesday 12/31/2019 — I've always thought it was funny that we make such a big deal of New Year's Eve and the next day. After all, Rosh Hashanah (the Jewish New Year) occurs in the autumn (September 18th-19th this coming year); Buddhists have four different New Year's days (most frequently in the spring I think—but don't quote me on that); Muslims celebrate Hijri, their New Year based on a lunar schedule—

this year it was in September.

> Then there's the Chinese New Year – January 25, 2020
> Aluth Avurudda (Sri Lanka) – April 12 & 13, 2020
> Diwali (northern India) – November 14, 2020
> Nowruz (Iran) – March 21 every year, the Spring Equinox
> Nyepie (Bali) – March 25, 2020 (celebrated with silence rather than with parties!)
> Seollal (Korea) – January 25, 2020

And let's never forget October 30th, which was the New Year of the now-extinct Aboriginal Murador people of Australia. We know about it only through artifacts and text. It marked a time of friendship, reconciliation, and giving thanks to the year gone by.

Not a bad idea. Thank you, 2019.

~ ~ ~

And so ends *Clearly Me*. The next volume of my FB memoirs will cover the year 2020. The title? *Crystal Clear*. I hope to see you there.

Sending virtual hugs,
    Fran / Mom / Grannie …

Doodles, Notes, Musings, and Miscellany